DATA MODEL PATTERNS
Conventions of Thought

DATA MODEL PATTERNS
Conventions of Thought

DAVID C. HAY

Foreword by Richard Barker

Dorset House Publishing
353 West 12th Street
New York, New York 10014

Library of Congress Cataloging-in-Publication Data

```
Hay, David C., 1947-
    Data model patterns : conventions of thought / David C. Hay.
        p.    cm.
    Includes bibliographical references and index.
    ISBN 0-932633-29-3
    1. Database design.  2. Data structures (Computer science)
 I. Title.
    QA76.9.D26H39   1995
    658.4'038'011--dc20
```

                                                                95-24983
                                                                   CIP

Trademark credits: Microsoft® is a registered trademark of Microsoft Corporation; CASE*Method™ is a trademark of Oracle Corporation; IBM® and ThinkPad® are registered trademarks of International Business Machines Corporation. Other trade or product names are either trademarks or registered trademarks of their respective companies, and are the property of their respective holders and should be treated as such.

Passages reprinted in Chapter 7 from *Accounting* appear courtesy of Richard D. Irwin, Inc. Reprinted by permission. Portions of some models have been previously presented in *Oracle User RESOURCE,* published by the East Coast Oracle Users' Group.

Cover Illustration: Amy McTear
Cover Author Photograph: Richard Chin
Cover Design: Jeff Faville, Faville Design

Copyright © 1996 by David C. Hay. Published by Dorset House Publishing, 353 West 12th Street, New York, NY 10014.

Distributed in the English language in Singapore, the Philippines, and Southeast Asia by Toppan Co., Ltd., Singapore; in the English language in India, Bangladesh, Sri Lanka, Nepal, and Mauritius by Prism Books Pvt., Ltd., Bangalore, India; and in the English language in Japan by Toppan Co., Ltd., Tokyo, Japan.

Printed in the United States of America

Library of Congress Catalog Number: 95-24983

ISBN: 0-932633-29-3   12 11 10 9 8 7 6 5 4

DEDICATION

To Perry Carmichael,
my high school debate coach,
for teaching me how to ask questions
and how to make sense of the answers

ACKNOWLEDGMENTS

*I*f a man is known by the company he keeps, your author has certainly achieved great fortune. The long list of people I must thank for the ability to write this book begins with my wife, Jola, and my children, Pamela and Bob. (Bob thought the title should be *Fun with Pictures*.) They put up with a lot, and I love them dearly.

The book would not have been possible without Richard Barker, who pioneered the philosophy toward data modeling reflected here. He and my good friend Mike Lynott spent many hours teaching me the approach, and together they inspired me to put it to use enthusiastically. Mike also gets my special appreciation for his encouragement and help with this book.

It has been my privilege to have others to stimulate my imagination and my thinking, and with whom to discuss ideas. This list begins with Ulka Rodgers, who convinced me that I could, indeed, write a book, and who has been of great help with some of the book's thornier chapters. I also thank Chris Bird, Roger Gough, Dave Guthrie, Cliff Longman, Dale Lowery, and Eric Rosenfeld for their many ideas and thought-provoking conversations over the years.

The models presented here are not mine alone. Mike, Cliff, Ulka, and Eric, along with many others, contributed many of the ideas expressed here. Eric was particularly helpful in showing me how to add the quality movement to the contracts, laboratory, and process manufacturing chapters.

My thanks also go to the many people who reviewed parts of the book, including Kathi Bean, Howard Benbrook, John Butler, Howard Eisenstein, Mike Frankel, Mark Gokman, Terry Halpin, John King, Chris Lowde, Sue Peterson, and Becky Winant. And I particularly appreciate Wendy Eakin and David McClintock of Dorset House for their patience and help as I worked my way through this project.

I must of course thank all my employers and clients, each of whom has had something important to teach me in the course of my career. In particular, I would like to single out the Associated Press, which gave me my first opportunity to do a strategic data model for a large, heterogeneous organization. I also thank Texaco, which gave me the biggest organization I've modeled, and the U.S. Forest Service, which provided me with insights about land management and the workings of large Federal agencies.

Tony Ziemba and Adirondak Systems helped me greatly by giving me the *Oracle User RESOURCE* as a forum for the series of articles that provided the seed for this book.

And of course, I thank Oracle Corporation, both for sponsoring the CASE*Method and for giving me the opportunity to learn and promulgate it.

Thanks as well to Continental Airlines, which provided me with "office space" during my weekly three-hour jaunts from Houston to New York and back. Let's hear it for laptop computers and portable disc players!

Finally, I would like to thank the man who, one morning in the summer of 1969, had just cracked up his expensive car in the streets of New York City and was drowning his sorrow in coffee and bagels, when he struck up a conversation with an equally unhappy young man.

As that young man, I was just out of college with my newly minted degree in philosophy. I had come to the Big Apple to seek fame and fortune, but after two very unhappy days, I hadn't found either. Indeed, even the prospect of getting a job was looking pretty dodgy.

After a short conversation, however, the man with the broken car took a chance on me and signed me up to sell a strange new computer service called *time-sharing*. Imagine! As he described it, a customer could attach a teletypewriter to the telephone and call up a computer. Type in a message and it types something back! In 1969, this was clearly black magic, but who was I to argue?

Homer Cates, you got me started in the computer business—way out in left field. It has worked out well for me, and for this I will always be grateful.

CONTENTS

12 LOWER-LEVEL CONVENTIONS   235

FIGURES AND TABLES

FOREWORD

*S*ntity modelling, or data modelling as it is sometimes called, may be used as a passive way of modelling exactly what exists—providing little interpretation or insight as to its meaning. There is a more active form of modelling, however, commonly found in mathematics and science, which has a model predict something that was not previously known or provide for some circumstance that does not yet exist. Such models are invariably much simpler, easier to understand, and yet deal with more situations than mirror-image models.

For example, the Ptolemy model of planetary motion was complex but accurately described the observable motion of the planets, the moon, and the sun around the earth. The model from Copernicus was simpler but even more accurate, however, giving us the notion of a solar system with planets in motion around the sun. This idea later helped astronomers predict the existence of the previously undiscovered planets Neptune and, years later, Pluto.

If we can model in this sense, using simpler and more generic models, we will find they stand the test of time better, are cheaper to implement and maintain, and often cater to changes in the business not known about initially. For example, rather than just model the exact organisation structure in our business, we could use a generic organisation model that can accommodate executive change (often just whim!). The generic model should even be able to handle the acquisition of another company or a merger with another department—without changing the implementation design. It should be possible simply to declare the new structure to the system.

If used effectively, entity modelling enables a good analyst to talk to users and systems people in their own language and about the issues with which they are concerned. On one hand, a model can be used precisely to articulate the information needs of a business. Used correctly, in discussions with executives and other users, such a model can be used to tease out exceptions that must be dealt with and can then be used to quickly correct misunderstandings, without the analyst having to lapse into technical jargon. On the other hand, the same model can be used in discussions with systems designers to provide them with rich and rigorous definitions of the data. Such models can show much of the processing logic that is implied, not described, by the users. These definitions may be mapped onto relational database designs, with stored procedures and other techniques enforcing the implied processing logic—such as advanced referential integrity constraints. The generic patterns may also be mapped onto object-oriented designs. This flexibility makes the technique very useful when applied by enlightened practitioners.

Part of the benefit of the approach comes from the layout or positional notation. The notation, described in this book and in my *Entity Relationship Modelling* book, was derived many years ago by Harry Ellis and myself when working on a particularly complex project. We were striving for even greater accuracy in systems analysis, whilst minimising redundant interactions with the users. How could we converge even faster on the desired level of completeness, quality, and simplicity? As a lateral thought, we tried drawing the diagrams in different ways and eventually found the one described herein—often called the "dead crow" notation!

An interesting side effect was that where entities tended to group themselves together on the picture, we often found that they had identical or very similar attributes and relationships. This raised the question, Are they really the same object with different names? This focused question enables the modeller to create a simpler model that caters to *all* the previous concepts already discovered and suggests new ideas that had not been thought of. (It really surprises users when you ask them about things they had forgotten to tell you. You can get responses like, "How did *you* know about that? We only started to think about that last week!") Later, the resulting implementation is usually much quicker and cheaper.

Finally, as you read this book, you may realise that the term "analyst" becomes less and less relevant. It is the concept of "synthesis" that provides the greatest added value to your business—that is, the creation of a model and subsequent system that actively delivers what the business needs for its future success.

In *Data Model Patterns*, David Hay has pulled together many such useful models from his experience and that of the friends and experts that he mentions. If analysts use the well-proven modelling approach described in this book, and then implement the results on relational or object database management systems, they should be able to develop highly business-oriented systems quickly.

May 1995   Richard Barker
Near-Maidenhead   Senior Vice President
Berkshire   Product Division
England   OpenVision
                                                         Pleasanton, California

PREFACE

*L*earning the basics of a modeling technique is not the same as learning how to use and apply it. Data modeling is particularly complex to learn, because it requires the modeler to gain insights into an organization's nature that do not come easily. For example, an analyst may be expected to come into an organization and immediately understand subtleties about its structure that may have evaded people who have worked there for years.

This book is intended to help those analysts who have learned the basics of data modeling, but who are looking for help in discovering subtleties and in obtaining the insights required to prepare a good model of a real business. Moreover, the book is intended to help analysts produce models that are easier to read, by virtue of standards of diagram structure and organization.

The book is based on the assumption that the underlying structures of enterprises are similar, or at least that they have similar components. Understanding those similarities gives an analyst a starting model, which can then be massaged and adjusted as necessary to match the specific circumstances of a particular company. This is not to say that all companies' models will look the same. Quite the opposite is true. In your author's experience, no two organizations' models have been identical. On the other hand, widely differing organizations, from government health protection agencies to oil refineries, have many similar components.

An analyst who has these components in his intellectual tool kit is in a good position to grasp quickly what is unique about an enterprise and to draw a data model that both embodies universal truths and specifically represents the business at hand.

This book has a second audience as well: As a child of the Sixties, I got into the business world only reluctantly. Among the problems I faced was understanding just how business works. Even in business school, I was never able to find an introductory-level course that described how it works as a whole. Each course analyzed a specific area in detail, but none really provided the overview I sought. It was only as I saw the patterns expressed in the structure of business information that a business uses, that I began to come to grips with the issues involved. Perhaps this book can be useful to a similarly disadvantaged student trying to understand the nature of the business world.

April 1995   D.C.H.
Houston, Texas   Davehay@essentialstrategies.com

1

INTRODUCTION

A data model is a representation of the things of significance to an enterprise and the relationships among those things. It portrays the underlying structure of the enterprise's data, so this can then be reflected in the structure of databases built to support it.

This book takes the position that the underlying structures of many businesses and government agencies are very similar, and that it should therefore be possible to model these similar structures in similar ways. Using common shapes for common situations makes the models easier to read, and it guides the modeler closer to identifying truly fundamental things.

DATA MODELING'S PROMISE—AND FAILURE

Data modeling* serves two purposes in the systems analysis process: First, as a graphic technique, it aids in communication between analysts and the ultimate users of the systems they will specify, and between analysts and those who will design and build systems for those users. Second, as a rigorous technique, it imposes discipline on the specification of problems, ensuring due consideration of logical implications.

Creation of a data model is supposed to focus the user's, the analyst's, and the designer's attention on things that are most fundamental to the nature of the business. The technique promises to lead to the development of stable, robust, and reliable information systems, so that normal changes in the busi-

---

* There is some controversy these days about the terms "data model" and "entity/relationship model." Some would have it that the abstract model of business structures (the topic of this book) should be called the "entity/relationship model," and the term "data model" should be reserved for a drawing of a database schema. Conventional usage, however, has blurred this distinction in the language, and while it is important for analysts and designers to understand the difference between these things, it is also important to get models of business structure before the public. It is easier to suggest to a business manager that you would like to discuss the company's data than it is to propose discussing entities and relationships. For this reason, this book calls the logical models it discusses "data models."

1

ness will not affect them. Moreover, data models promise to be useful as the basis for discussions among all three sets of players (users, analysts, and designers) about the future of information systems development in the organization. A data model can show, for example, the effect that a change to the organization will have on its information systems.

Alas, data modeling has not always kept these promises. If it is not used effectively, the technique neither improves communication nor imposes discipline.

Data modeling as currently practiced suffers from two problems:

- Diagrams are often difficult to read.
- Diagrams do not represent the fundamental nature of the organizations they are supposed to describe.

Herein lies the purpose of this book. It describes an approach to data modeling that can restore those promises by producing models that are both clearer than those produced without using this approach, and more likely to address fundamental issues.

Clarity

As typically produced, data model diagrams can be less than inviting. While the use of graphics is supposed to make the ideas presented more accessible, the use of graphics without regard to aesthetic principles has the opposite effect. A mass of boxes and lines with no identifiable shape or organization aids in neither the understanding of an organization nor the planning of its future systems development efforts. A common reaction to the typical data model is: There are so many symbols! Where do I start? What is really going on here? How can I use this?

Defining a set of symbols to represent data structures is not enough. It is necessary to add a method for *organizing* those symbols, so that the reader of the model can deal with the drawing as a whole. It is also necessary to apply some aesthetic standards, in order to ensure that meaning encoded in the symbols can be accessible to the viewer.

Fundamentals of the Business

If you choose to build a new system, you want it to reflect the true requirements of your business—not simply to reproduce the techniques and technology now in use. The reason for making the investment in the first place is that you want to change *the way things are done*, without necessarily changing the *nature* of your enterprise.

A data model can help change the way things are done without affecting the nature of your business if it presents what is unchanging in an organization. It is intended to portray the things of significance, about which the company wishes to hold information. If the model succeeds, the things represented are unlikely to change significantly, either with the application of new technology (computer or other) or with the making of routine changes to the business of the organization. Technology whose architecture is based on what is fundamental will improve the operational aspects of an organization while remaining robust, stable, and flexible.

Unfortunately, what most people see in the course of their work (and consequently tell systems analysts about) is not this unchanging nature at all, but merely examples of it. They see only today's problems, and the particular technology they must use to do their jobs—to the point that the technology becomes their job. Since the information an analyst gathers, therefore, is usually expressed in terms of current practices, distinguishing between what is essential to a business and what is merely an accident of current technology is not always easy. The essential facts are the things that "go without saying"—so they don't get said. These facts don't get described or explained—or reflected in new systems. Instead, new systems are often built on superficial views of today's problems.

A plant that makes carbon black for printing ink and tires spent many weeks discussing the best ways to determine production rates and yields. The discussions concerned the best ways of predicting yield from the grade of natural gas that was used, but clearly something was not getting across. Finally, the manager let slip the fact that yield is also a function of the production unit used. The yield varies from unit to unit. This was obvious to him, so he didn't mention it. Because it was not so obvious to the analyst, the original database design had not taken this into account and had to be substantially redone.

The elements of a business that are typically portrayed in data models reflect this difficulty. Instead of these essential facts about a business, model diagrams are often dominated by references to the objects that represent the particular way things are done now. A careless analyst may interpret transient things to be things of importance. The resulting model will reflect only those things that are important to *current* business practices.

A purchasing agent, for example, might describe the company's purchasing system, giving special emphasis to its shortcomings (such as the fact that there may not be enough room on a purchase order for notes), while neglecting to describe the essential facts about a purchase order (such as the fact that "terms of sale" must appear). To build a new system based solely on the structure (and failings) of an existing system is to fail to take advantage of technological opportunities. Suppose, for example, purchasing were to do away with paper forms altogether and dial directly into vendors' computers. What would remain essential to the transaction?

How Standards Can Help

Both communications and discipline can be improved. Moreover, we can make better use of each other's work. What is needed is standardization of our approach to the modeling process. This does not mean simply using a common system of notation, although that would certainly help. What it means, rather, is using a common approach to *the way we think about* business situations, and to the way we organize our presentations of them. This book is about these "conventions of thought." It identifies common situations that are present in a variety of businesses and government agencies, and which can be modeled in a standardized way. This standardization can make models both easier to read and more descriptive of what is fundamental to an enterprise.

The modeling conventions presented here are an attempt to establish that common approach to modeling. They do not represent the final models of any real company or agency. Rather, they are starting points, showing ways of looking at a business situation that should allow an analyst quickly to come to terms with the most important aspects of it. Having done so, the analyst is expected to apply creativity and imagination to adapt technology to those aspects.

Each chapter of the book presents concepts fundamental to a topic. It describes a typical business situation, provides basic models for portraying the situation, and enumerates variations that can be expected across different organizations.

ABOUT MODELING CONVENTIONS

Using standard approaches—"conventions"—in the way we approach our work greatly improves communication among analysts, and it makes the analytical work easier. Because conventions establish a framework, entire categories of decisions do not have to be made. Until now, the data modeling field has not yet been mature enough to have established a complete set of standard practices. While much has been written about the syntax and grammar of data modeling, precious little has been written about the other elements that make up good modeling standards. In fact, three levels of convention apply to data modeling:

- *Syntactic conventions* are at the most basic level of defining models. These conventions dictate the symbols to be used. The symbols portray the things of significance to the enterprise (*entities*), and the relationships among them. Relationship symbols include those for *cardinality* (the "one" and "many" in a "one-to-many" relationship) and *optionality* (whether or not an occurrence of one entity must be related to an occurrence of the other entity). Many notation schemes also include symbols for describing how occurrences of entities are identified, even to the point of specifying the primary keys that would be used in relational database implementations of the models. Syntactic conventions may also include rules for the structure of phrases used to name relationships and entities. Syntactic conventions are the subject of most data modeling books.*

- *Positional conventions* define the way symbols are organized on a page. That is, they concern the relative positions of elements, and they address the overall organization of a drawing.

- *Semantic conventions* have to do with the grouping of entities according to their meaning. These are the primary subject of this book. These conventions pertain to the way we think about common business situations.

The three levels of conventions in data modeling are discussed more fully in Chapter Two. Here, it is important only to point out that it is through establishing conventions at all three levels that the full power of data modeling can be realized. It is the third level, the "conventions of thought," that has been given the least attention, and which is the focus of this book.

Taking this pattern-based approach to data modeling has several advantages:

1. It makes the task of building a new model easier and faster (and therefore cheaper, which after all, is what makes us popular with our bosses), since the modeler has only to modify and blend existing structures, rather than create new ones from scratch.

2. It makes the models easier to read, since the same kinds of things will tend to take the same shape in all diagrams.

3. This in turn makes it possible to highlight those things that are genuinely unique about a particular enterprise.

4. It helps reduce or eliminate gross modeling errors, since the basic elements of a model are already defined.

5. It will result in a system with fewer tables to maintain, simplifying it and making it more reliable, since relatively few entities can describe many specific aspects of a situation.

---

* See the Bibliography for books describing different modeling conventions. Note in particular the works of James Martin, Tom Bruce, David Embley *et al.*, James Rumbaugh *et al.*, and Sally Shlaer and Stephen Mellor.

THESE MODELS AND YOUR ORGANIZATION

It is important to recognize that this book does not claim to present a single definitive model that will apply to all businesses and government agencies. All company models should not be identical. Rather, these are patterns and structures that can provide a basis for examining a wide variety of situations.

Companies differ from each other. They provide different products and services, and they operate on different scales. They also differ significantly from one another in their operating procedures and organizational structures. Companies differ also in the emphasis placed on various aspects of the business. Where the model of one area of interest may be greatly detailed and sophisticated for one type of business, it may be simple for another. (Even in these cases, however, while the complexity of the models is not the same, the overall data organizations should be similar.)

While these variations dramatically color the appearance and experience of the company, they can be made to reside in the *contents* of data, rather than in the *structure* of those data and the systems built to manage them. For example, a data structure that explicitly records the relationships in terms of "divisions," "companies," "departments," and so on would require *database* maintenance to change that structure. On the other hand, a data structure concerned only with "organizations" and "organization types" could be changed through maintenance of the *data*. (This example is described in more detail in Chapter Two.)

In any real organization, there will be numerous entities other than those described here. Moreover, a company's entities may well have different names than those used in this book, and there will certainly be changes to the relationships. It will be the modeler's job to translate the models here into his or her own organization's terms. To help the modeler, however, this book will include references to possible variations on many of the models.

Models and Systems: A Word About Implementation

Data models are only of value if they can be used as the basis for designing real systems that will provide value to an organization. Data models are typically converted into relational databases by mapping each entity to a table, and each attribute to a column. Many-to-one relationships in the data model become foreign keys in the "many" table, pointing to rows in the "one" table. Supertypes, subtypes, and arcs (described in the next chapter) require some decisions to be made before they may be implemented. For the most part, however, conversion of a data model to a database design is a mechanical process, and most CASE tools will do it at the press of a button.

The models presented in this book, however, are more abstract than those typically used to develop *real* systems. This causes some developers to be uneasy about developing databases from them. Because of the peculiar nature of the models created using the approach described in this book, two assertions about the implications of these models on the systems that result from them are in order:

First, if these models are implemented as shown, the resulting systems will be much more robust and flexible than if they are not. The tables will be organized according to aspects of the enterprise that are unlikely to change soon. As mentioned above, the *content* of the tables will define much of what traditionally has been part of program code and table *structure*. The *user* will now specify the configuration of the business, rather than the *programmer*. This is not what we are used to, but it is not a bad thing.

Second, these models are expected to be produced during the strategic planning and requirements analysis phases of system development. They are not intended to represent the physical structure of databases that are finally implemented. In response to problems of processing time, system capacity, or other constraints, the designer may have to construct database structures that differ from these, in order to reflect the circumstances of the particular system being built.

Remember, however, that the technology and its limitations will change. An accommodation made today to relieve a particular bottleneck may be completely inappropriate three or five years from now.*

It is important for those who follow to be able to distinguish between the aspects of a design that were responses to implementation considerations and those aspects that represent the underlying problem. If the conceptual data model remains available for reference (ideally, along with documentation of the rationale behind each design decision), a subsequent designer will be able to make this distinction.

WHO SHOULD READ THIS BOOK?

This book is intended to help the person who has learned the mechanics of data modeling and is now trying to learn the art. "O.K.," a student says, "I understand how to read diagrams, but how do I go into my company and make sense out of the morass that I find there?" This book gives you a method for doing that. Instead of having to create models from scratch, you can pull a model or two out of this "tool kit," and modify it to make it look like your company or agency.

This book can also help analysts who have been commissioned to analyze a particular application area, but who haven't the benefit of a prior strategy study to put that area in context. In the absence of a strategy study, these mod-

---

* A noisy controversy in the 1970s was whether or not a company should adopt COBOL as a programming language—it wasn't nearly as efficient as assembler, and caused serious performance problems in large systems!

els can provide a context within which to place models specific to your application. For example, you may be working in sales and know that, although there is an interaction with manufacturing, no one is looking at the plant to determine what that interaction will be. In this case, you can look at the manufacturing models described in this book, and at least see the dimensions and elements of manufacturing to consider.

Had a strategy study been done, you may assume that its general shape would be similar to the models presented here. The models in this book are based on models from many strategy studies in many industries.

Most of the business situations described in this book will be familiar to most readers, but some of the more specialized chapters cover territory unfamiliar to many. Modelers who use this book to broaden their understanding of how different aspects of business work will gain an additional benefit.

The remaining chapters in the book develop models of an organization, piece by piece. Each chapter describes a specific business situation, and presents a candidate data model, depicting the core elements of that business situation. In the course of the descriptions, possible variations are pointed out, along with the organizational issues that might call for one variation or another. The models generally build chapter by chapter throughout the book. Specific circumstances may require names to be changed as we go along, as the entity names encompass progressively more general concepts. This means that while in early chapters entity names are reasonably concrete, they will become progressively more abstract as we go along.

Again, the premise here is that each data model presented is a reasonable starting point for describing a typical situation. Think of this book as a model-building kit.

Chapter Two describes the three levels of conventions in more detail, setting the stage for what follows. In that chapter are presented the syntactic and positional conventions used in the book, followed by a more extensive discussion of what exactly is meant by semantic conventions.

The next five chapters treat general topics that apply to most companies and agencies. People and organizations are modeled in Chapter Three, the things the enterprise deals with are examined in Chapter Four, its activities and procedures are the subject of Chapter Five, its dealings with the outside world are covered in Chapter Six, and accounting is dealt with in Chapter Seven.

Chapters Eight, Nine, and Ten address more specialized topics. Chapter Eight describes a laboratory, Chapter Nine discusses the planning of material requirements and supply in manufacturing, and Chapter Ten deals with the special problems of process manufacturing. While these topics are more specialized, they are included because their structures are not well understood even in the industries to which they apply, and because they introduce some very interesting modeling problems. Because they are specialized, each chapter begins with an introductory description of the situation the models will portray.

The final two chapters return to topics of more general interest: Chapter Eleven discusses the management of documents—a particularly knotty problem, as the chapter explains. Chapter Twelve identifies model elements that were components of the models that appeared in the previous chapters. This introduces the idea that even our data model patterns contain patterns within them. This final chapter concludes the book with a single model that takes the book's premises to extremes, presenting a model that, with seven entities, appears to model everything.

2

DATA MODELING CONVENTIONS

*C*onventions in an industry are the actions followed by practitioners to insure effective communication and adherence to "good"
practices. Even at forty-something years old, the information processing industry is relatively young, and conventions that are
well-understood and widely followed have been slow in coming. In the area of
systems analysis in particular, there have been a succession of methods that
have introduced conventions and standard practices, but as the methods have
been found to be less than perfect, the conventions as quickly have fallen out of
fashion.

It has so far been the easiest to at least talk about conventions in the symbols we use to represent things. Whether it was standards for flow charts, data
flow diagrams, or, now, data models, most of the books published have focused
on explaining the notation, with fewer notable works describing how to use the
notation and apply it.

In this book, conventions will be shown from three points of view. First,
the *syntax* of a drawing is the set of symbols and labels used to construct it.
Each of the data modeling techniques in use today can be described in terms of
its syntax for representing entities, relationships, attributes, and so forth.

Second, rules can be applied to the way these symbols are arranged on the
page. These come from the need to make drawings attractive and easy to follow. These *positional* conventions are typically less commonly used and less
well articulated than are the syntactic conventions.

Finally, and this is the subject of this book, we can apply conventions to the
way we think about business problems and apply these symbols to represent
them. These *semantic* conventions build upon the syntactic and positional conventions. They recognize that all businesses (and many government agencies
as well) share common characteristics, and when we identify these, we can
model them in the same way.

This chapter describes these three kinds of conventions in more detail.

SYNTACTIC CONVENTIONS

At least conventions exist for the symbols used in data models. Unfortunately,
many conventions exist. Different methodologies use different sets of crows'
feet, arrows, lines, circles, and so on, to represent various aspects of a data
model. Arguments about the advantages of one set over the others sometimes
take on a religious fervor.

Logically, all the notations for conceptual data modeling are nearly equivalent. Some define special symbols for elements that others leave described with the basic symbols. Some are more oriented toward database design than the inherent structure of business data that concerns us in this book. Some notations are weak in particular areas, but all of them can represent most situations. The models presented here can be readily translated into any of them.

This book uses the CASE*Method™ notation, devised by Richard Barker, Ian Palmer, Harry Ellis, and others at the British Consulting firm CACI [1]. The CASE*Method is used extensively by the Oracle Corporation. Figure 2.1 is a sample model diagram that uses this syntax. It portrays a purchase order, its vendors, and the products or services being bought. This particular model will be described in more detail in Chapter Six.

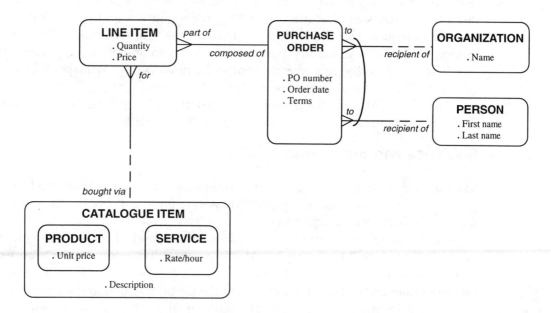

Figure 2.1: A Data Model.

The following sections present a brief description of the CASE*Method's syntax for *entities, subtypes and supertypes, attributes,* and *relationships*:

Entities

An *entity* is a thing of significance about which the organization wishes to hold (which is to say, collect, maintain, and use) information. This may be a tangible thing like a product or a customer, or it may be an intangible thing like a transaction or a role. An *entity type* is the definition of a set of entities. That is, an entity gets its attributes from the definition of its entity types. Entity types are represented by round-cornered rectangles. In Figure 2.1, ORGANIZATION, CATALOGUE ITEM, and PRODUCT, for example, are all entity types.

In recent years, the language of data modeling has evolved from its original definitions. In common usage, the distinction between "entity" and "entity type" has been lost. This book is concerned more with entity types than with specific occurrences of entities. In the interest of brevity, however, and because this usage has become common, references to "entity" will mean "entity type." That is, we will be discussing the definitions of entities as kinds of things, and the word "occurrence" will be used to describe the individual examples. Calling them "entities" and "occurrences of entities" is not meant to imply that there will be any lapse in the discipline required to tell the difference, simply an acknowledgment of the evolution of the language.*

Each entity name is written in the singular on the diagrams, to show that, in fact, references to an entity are to the object that constitutes a representative occurrence of that entity. When relationship sentences are constructed to describe occurrences of entities, however, both singular and plural forms will be used as required for the sentence to make sense. For example, in our sample model, to speak of the entity PURCHASE ORDER is to speak of a representative purchase order. In the relationship sentences, however, we will speak of a party's being the source of one or more PURCHASE ORDERS.

This book will show the names of entities in small capital letters, as was just done with PURCHASE ORDER.

Subtypes and Supertypes

Most data modeling techniques use round-cornered or square-cornered rectangles to represent entities. The CASE*Method is unique, however, in the way it represents *subtypes* and *supertypes.*

A subtype of an entity is the definition of a subset of its occurrences. For example, in Figure 2.1, CATALOGUE ITEM is a supertype, while PRODUCT and SERVICE are subtypes. That is, each occurrence of CATALOGUE ITEM is also an occurrence of either a PRODUCT or a SERVICE. In the CASE*Method, the subtypes must be mutually exclusive and completely describe all occurrences of the supertype. For example, each CATALOGUE ITEM must be *either* a PRODUCT *or* a SERVICE, but it cannot be both. Moreover, there is no CATALOGUE ITEM that is not either a PRODUCT or a SERVICE. Conversely, each PRODUCT must also be a CATALOGUE ITEM and each SERVICE must also be a CATALOGUE ITEM.†

---

* Your author asserts his right to be old-fashioned in one regard, however: Throughout the book, data are plural.

† Some modeling techniques relax one or both of these rules. Indeed, even the CASE*Method in practice relaxes the "all occurrences" rule, by allowing the OTHER ... subtype. OTHER CATALOGUE ITEM, for example, gets us off the hook if it turns out that there are other CATALOGUE ITEMS besides PRODUCTS and SERVICES. This is probably cheating, but it works.

The CASE*Method shows subtypes as rectangles within the rectangles of their supertypes. Most other notations show them as separated rectangles, with relationship lines connecting them.

Attributes

One or more *attributes* describe an entity, and the *values* of those attributes describe occurrences of the entity. If an entity is a thing of significance about which an enterprise wishes to hold information, then an attribute defines one of the pieces of information held.

For example, if an entity is PRODUCT, its attributes might be "description," "price," "size," and so forth. For a particular PRODUCT, say a Model 78-g widget, the value of the attribute "name" is "Model 78-g widget," and the value of "price" is "$7.98," and so forth.

A data model diagram may or may not show the attributes, but the supporting data dictionary must always document them. The CASE*Method allows representation of the attributes as text on the entity box, but does not require this, and does not use separate symbols for them as is done in other methods [2].

Attributes are of two kinds: *descriptor* and *identifier*. Descriptor attributes describe each occurrence of the entity. These could be things like "color," "amount," "category," and so forth. Identifier attributes label the object. These could be "name," "id," "label," and so forth. In Figure 2.1, for example, PURCHASE ORDER would have the identifier attribute "PO number," and the descriptor attributes "order date" and "terms." LINE ITEM has the descriptor attributes "quantity," "price," and so forth.

An attribute of or a relationship to a supertype is also an attribute of or relationship to every subtype within it, but an attribute or relationship specified for a subtype is not known to any other subtype. The subtype is said to *inherit* the attribute or relationship from the supertype.

In the example, "description" (an attribute of CATALOGUE ITEM) is an attribute of both PRODUCT and SERVICE. "Unit price" (an attribute of PRODUCT), however, is not an attribute of SERVICE.

It is possible for what appears initially to be an attribute to turn out ultimately to be an entity in its own right. For example, an attribute of an entity called BOOK might seem to be "author." But this is an attribute that itself has attributes ("first name," "last name," "nationality," and so forth). The second draft of the model, then, should show a new entity by that name, and establish a relationship between the original entity and the new one.

In the text of this book, attribute names and attribute values will always be shown enclosed in quotation marks, as in "order date"; in the figures, they are shown preceded by a small solid circle and begin with a capital letter.

Relationships

The model in Figure 2.1 shows *relationships* between the entities as combinations of solid and dashed lines.

The CASE*Method differs from others, both in the particular symbols used for relationships, and in its specification of strict rules for formulating and reading relationship names. In the CASE*Method, each relationship can be read as two sentences, each with a specific structure. Specifically, each relationship sentence is always of the form:

Each

<first entity>

must be	<solid half line>
(or)	
may be	<dashed half line>

<relationship name>

one and only one	<no end mark>
(or)	
one or more	<crow's foot>

<second entity>

When naming relationships, the two entities being related will occupy the spaces shown by "<first entity>" and "<second entity>," above. It is important, then, to select words that can fit "<relationship name>" so that the resulting sentence is reasonable.

For example, in Figure 2.1, one of the relationships says that "each LINE ITEM must be *for* one and only one CATALOGUE ITEM," and, reading it from the other direction, "each CATALOGUE ITEM may be *bought via* one or more LINE ITEMS."

This book will show relationship names in sans serif italic typeface, as seen above with *bought via*.

Note that the CASE*Method forms a prepositional phrase (*composed of* one or more LINE ITEMS) or gerund phrase (*concerning* one and only one BOOK) from the names of a relationship and its following entity. It does not use verb phrases for relationship names. This is because the verbs in all relationship names are implicitly "to be" (in the form of "must be" or "may be"), and it is the prepositions and gerunds that are the grammatical parts of speech that describe relationships themselves. Relationships are contained in words like "in" or "above," not in words like "has" or "orders." Verbs denote action—which is to say functions—not relationships.

This makes it possible to translate a relationship into sentences that not only sound natural but which precisely describe its nature, its cardinality, and its optionality.

Among other things, this naming convention for relationships has permitted the bulk of the text of this book to be taken directly from the data models, even as that text appears to describe business situations in ordinary English. That is, you will be able to see that the relationships shown in the diagrams exactly correspond to the language in the text. This could not be done with techniques that are less disciplined in their use of language. Compare the two sentences above with "a LINE ITEM *buys* 1 CATALOGUE ITEM" and "a CATALOGUE ITEM *has* 0, 1, or many LINE ITEMS."

The fact that it is important to use language effectively in naming relationships does not make it easy. The CASE*Method is very demanding in requiring the analyst to think about what things are called, and to use the right words to describe things.*

In Figure 2.1, the curved line (called an *arc*) connecting the relationship between PURCHASE ORDER and PERSON and the relationship between PURCHASE ORDER and ORGANIZATION denotes mutual exclusivity. That is, "each PURCHASE ORDER must be *either to* one and only one ORGANIZATION, *or to* one and only one PERSON." An arc represents the case in which an occurrence of an entity may (or must) be related to an occurrence of *either* one entity *or* another.

If the entities that are the object of the two relationships could be viewed as belonging to a higher-level category, a supertype may be defined to encompass the two. Then, a single relationship could be extended to the supertype. This would have the same meaning as the arc. In Figure 2.1, for example, you could create the supertype PARTY to encompass both PERSON and ORGANIZATION, and then say that "each PURCHASE ORDER must be to one and only one PARTY, where a PARTY must be either a PERSON or an ORGANIZATION." This would have exactly the same meaning as the arc shown.

It is often more economical use of the real estate on a page to apply supertype/subtype notation rather than arcs, but this only makes sense if a meaningful supertype can be defined.

The CASE*Method notation includes additional symbols that will not be used in this book, since they describe subtleties that are not necessary to describe the important features of the patterns:

---

* As an indication of how important it can be to use the right relationship name, the editors of *The Hitchhiker's Guide to the Galaxy* were once "sued by the families of those who had died as a result of taking the entry on the planet Traal literally (it said 'Ravenous Bugblatter Beasts often make a very good meal for visiting tourists' instead of 'Ravenous Bugblatter Beasts often make a very good meal *of* visiting tourists')."
—Douglas Adams, *The Restaurant at the End of the Universe* (New York: Pocket Books, 1980), p. 38.

- In this book, attributes are shown on entities in many of the diagrams—in all cases preceded by a period. In fact, the correct CASE*Method notation is to precede the attribute with a small circle (o) if the attribute is optional, a solid dot (•) if it is mandatory, or a number sign (#) if it is part of the entity's unique identifier.

- In the CASE*Method, a short line across a relationship line near one of the entities may be added to show that the relationship is part of that entity's unique identifier. In this book, this is not done.

In this book, however, we are mostly concerned with whether we have identified the right entities and whether they are properly linked. Issues of unique identifiers and the mandatoriness of attributes come up later in the analysis process, and do not have to be taken into account as the data model is first being drawn. This is not to suggest that this information should not be gathered, but success in analysis depends on collecting information in the right order. In order to maintain perspective, it is important to begin by capturing general concepts and then filling in details as you go along. A common failing among analysts is to become so bogged down with details as to lose sight of what is to be accomplished.

POSITIONAL CONVENTIONS

The next level of convention concerns how the symbols of a model (as defined in syntactic conventions) are organized. Many analysts show no organization at all, placing entities randomly on a page. Perhaps some effort is made to minimize the crossing of lines, but otherwise there is often no pattern to the arrangement of the model elements. Figure 2.2 shows an example of a randomly arranged data model.

As an alternative, the CASE*Method technique orients entities so that the "toes" of a relationship's crows' feet (>-) always point to the left and the top of the diagram. This has the effect of putting entities representing tangible objects in the lower right area of the diagram, and putting those representing the less tangible roles, interactions, and transactions in the upper left. Figure 2.3 shows the same model as that shown in Figure 2.2 arranged according to this positional rule.

The approach in Figure 2.3 has several benefits: First, by knowing that different kinds of entities are in different parts of the model, someone who has never seen the model, but who knows the conventions, will still be able to get some idea of what it is about. From the model's overall organization, even the most casual observer can get a sense of its topic and contents. In Figure 2.3, the basic reference data describe VARIABLES, TEST TYPES, PEOPLE, and SAMPLES, while the transactions are TESTS, EXPECTED MEASUREMENTS, and MEASUREMENTS. This placement of entities makes it clear that the diagram is about the tests conducted on samples, and the results of those tests. This is not immediately obvious in Figure 2.2. Note that the ordered drawing in Figure 2.3 also suggests a parallel structure between the two kinds of measurements—EXPECTED MEASUREMENT and (actual) MEASUREMENT.

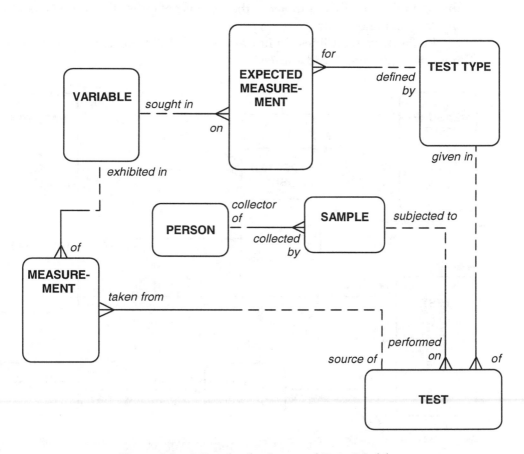

Figure 2.2: A Randomly Arranged Data Model.

A second benefit of following a positional convention is that doing so makes patterns easier to see. These patterns become candidates for consolidation of entities, as we shall see in subsequent chapters. The laboratory example shown in Figure 2.3 is an example of a recurring pattern—one that Chapter Eight discusses more fully, and that recurs in Chapters Ten and Eleven.

Other positional conventions followed by the CASE*Method affect the aesthetics of the drawing. The most important of these says: Keep your lines straight! It is usually possible to stretch entity boxes and position them so that it is not necessary to add elbows by bending the relationship lines. In the worst case, you may have to use a diagonal line, but this can actually add interest to the drawing.

A bend in the line looks like another symbol on the drawing, even though it has no inherent meaning. The bend is "something," which draws the eye to it, suggesting a meaning. Having too many symbols, especially if some are meaningless elbows, clutters the diagram and makes it confusing to the viewer.

It sometimes may become necessary to cross relationship lines. To be sure, this should be avoided, but *not* at the expense of either the "crow's foot" rule or the "no bent lines" rule.

In short, crossed lines do not affect readability nearly as much as do bent lines or randomly placed entities.

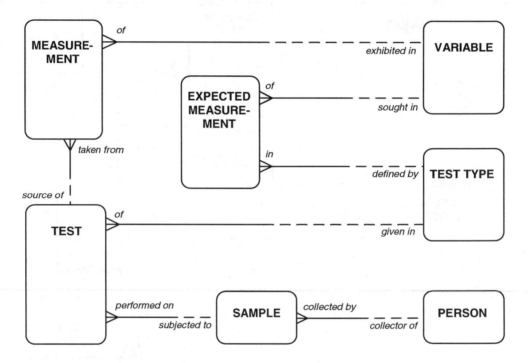

Figure 2.3: An Orderly Data Model.

Conventions about the position of entities on a page are less well articulated in the industry (and certainly less frequently followed) than are conventions about syntax. Among those who do follow positional conventions are some who argue that the crows' feet should point down and to the right. While this policy is clearly heresy to your author, it does at least impose the required consistency, and he will grudgingly admit that it does no harm if everyone within the same organization follows it. What is important is that a single convention is used within the organization.

SEMANTIC CONVENTIONS

Now that we have defined the symbols and, in general, organized them on the page, the third level of convention—the subject of this book—consists of modeling similar business situations in similar ways.

Chapter One described two problems with data modeling as it is practiced today: Models are often difficult to read, and they often do not describe that which is truly fundamental to a business. The use of common model layouts to depict common phenomena can address both of these problems: Familiar shapes make models easier to read (at least by fellow analysts who know the conventions); and similar shapes used by many enterprises are more likely to describe things that are fundamental to all of them.

Semantic conventions can be defined at two levels:

- In terms of the organization as a whole, similar business situations can be modeled the same way. For example, the models for purchasing raw materials, management of a laboratory, or management of large projects are similar, no matter what kind of company has need for them. This is analogous to saying that all automobiles are similar in structure to each other, as are all boats and all airplanes.

- Within these models, certain configurations are common. For example, in many different business situations, you will find things classified into "thing types." As another example, you will see many models that describe various kinds of activities and the roles people and organizations play in those activities. The "activity" and "role" parts of each model are the same in all of them. This is analogous to saying that all gasoline engines have similar structure, whether they are used in automobiles, boats, or airplanes.

At the level of the business as a whole, pharmaceutical clinical research, nuclear power generation, chemical manufacturing, news gathering, and government regulation all exhibit similar patterns in their data models. While each model is different, it is the contention of this book that they are all constructed from a common set of "conventions of thought." The fundamental aspects of creating an organization, buying raw materials and supplies, manufacturing products, and testing materials in a laboratory are not as different from company to company as one might imagine. Indeed, even government agencies have more in common with private corporations than you would expect.

For example, a COMPANY may be *composed of* DIVISIONS, each of which may be *composed of* DEPARTMENTS, each of which may be *composed of* GROUPS. Figure 2.4 shows this. COMPANY, DIVISION, DEPARTMENT, and GROUP are but specific examples, however, of the more general ORGANIZATION, as shown in Figure 2.5, where each ORGANIZATION may be *composed of* one or more other ORGANIZATIONS. Each ORGANIZATION, in turn, must be *an example of* one and only one ORGANIZATION TYPE, that defines (in data) if it is a "division," "group," or whatever.

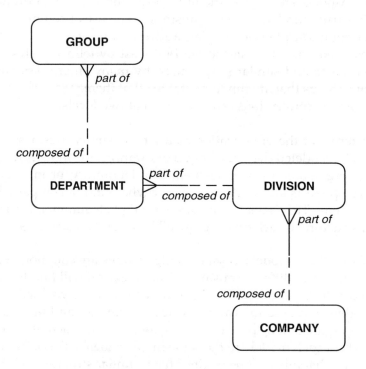

Figure 2.4: One Model of Organizations.

The model in Figure 2.5 encompasses nearly all the meaning of Figure 2.4, but it has fewer components, and it leaves room for the company to define new groupings sometime in the future and encompass other organizations not considered before.*

This generality is not without cost, however. Figure 2.4 showed business rules that cannot be represented directly in Figure 2.5. In Figure 2.4, a GROUP, DEPARTMENT, DIVISION, or COMPANY may not be *part of* itself. Moreover, a DIVISION may not be part of a DEPARTMENT, and so forth. In Figure 2.5, these business rules cannot be expressed. Nothing in the model prevents an ORGANIZATION from being *part of* itself or *part of* any other kind of ORGANIZATION.

---

* In Figure 2.5, the relationship of ORGANIZATION to itself (often called a "pig's ear") says that each ORGANIZATION may be *composed of* one or more other ORGANIZATIONS, and that each ORGANIZATION may be *part of* one and only one other ORGANIZATION. The pig's ear symbol appears again in Chapter 3.

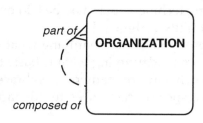

Figure 2.5: A More General Model of Organizations.

The second constraint (DIVISIONS can't be *part of* DEPARTMENTS) can be partially addressed by adding the entity ORGANIZATION TYPE, as shown in Figure 2.6.

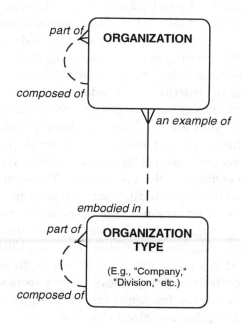

Figure 2.6: An Attempt to Impose Constraints.

Figure 2.6 shows that each ORGANIZATION must be an example of exactly one ORGANIZATION TYPE, and that ORGANIZATION TYPE also has a structure ("each ORGANIZATION TYPE may be composed of one or more ORGANIZATION TYPES"). This allows you to specify that a GROUP is part of a DEPARTMENT, and a DEPARTMENT is part of a DIVISION. Even that, however, does not show (and this modeling approach does not have the syntax to show) that the *part of* relationship in ORGANIZATION must be *consistent with* the *part of* relationship in ORGANIZATION TYPE.

This limitation of the more general model can be addressed by explicitly documenting such business rules outside the model. Indeed, Ron Ross has developed a modeling technique that may be laid over a data model to describe such rules and constraints as these [3].

Note that the closer you get to identifying what is basic to a particular business, the closer you are to identifying what is basic to businesses in general. In the example here, nearly any company may embrace the notion of an organization, while the more specific references to "department" or "group" do not apply as widely.

Note that semantic conventions may be applied at more than one level. As mentioned in Chapter One, Chapters Three through Eleven of this book describe and model "large" business situations—purchasing, manufacturing, and so forth. Chapter Twelve, on the other hand, addresses the patterns within the patterns—the common model elements that recur in the patterns describing the larger parts of an enterprise.

The organization of product structure information, for example, is the same, no matter who needs it. Whether a manufacturer is describing what it puts into a product, a maintenance department is describing what is necessary to fix a piece of equipment, or a regulatory agency is describing what should *not* be in a food or medicine, the data structure for *composition* is the same. Moreover, the idea of structure can be adapted to situations not involving products at all—project critical paths, reporting relationships, and so forth. (Chapter Three discusses this pattern of organizational structure in more detail.)

This means that, at several levels, we can develop a vocabulary of common business situations and natural structures, with a data model pattern corresponding to each element in the vocabulary. These models constitute semantic conventions to guide us in building our company models. These conventions of thought can help us understand *what the models mean*.

The following chapters describe some common semantic conventions in detail, and identify common model elements. In addition, the chapters present the issues involved in adapting the models to specific situations. The book provides guidance both in making models easier to read, and in making them more representative of the fundamental nature of an enterprise, and leads the analyst to better discipline and clearer models.

REFERENCES

1   R. Barker. *CASE*Method™: Entity Relationship Modelling* (Wokingham, England: Addison-Wesley Publishing Co., 1990).

2   See P. Chen, for example: "The Entity-Relationship Model—Toward a Unified View of Data," *ACM Transactions on Database Systems*, Vol. 1, No. 1 (1976). Chen's notation shows attributes in circles connected to, but separated from, entities.

3   R.G. Ross. *The Business Rule Book* (Boston: Database Research Group, 1994).

3
THE ENTERPRISE AND ITS WORLD

e'll start the modeling exercise with some entities that can be specified without interviewing anyone. You know that they will be required, no matter what the business.

An enterprise cannot exist without people. Whether an employee, a vendor agent, or the president of a company, a PERSON can be assumed to be a "thing of significance" to most companies. It should be no surprise, therefore, that the PERSON entity will appear on virtually all data models for all companies. Oh, there may be pressure to name it something different, like EMPLOYEE, CUSTOMER, AGENT, or whatever. But ultimately, the thing of significance is a PERSON, and as a modeler, you will save a lot of time by simply putting that entity on the diagram before you start interviewing.

A few of the things to be known about a person, such as "name" or "birth date," are attributes of the PERSON entity. Others (more than you might suppose) are not actually attributes, but are relationships to other entities, as we shall see. A person may enroll in one or more courses, for example, or may play a role in one or more activities. (More examples of these roles will be shown throughout the book.)

If an enterprise is concerned with people, it must surely also be concerned with aggregations of people. An ORGANIZATION, then, must also be a thing of significance to nearly any enterprise. An ORGANIZATION may be a department, a committee, a vendor, a labor union, or any other collection of people or other organizations. It is described by such attributes as "purpose," "Federal tax ID," and so forth.

Again, save yourself some time. Put ORGANIZATION on your model even before you start to interview.

PARTIES

People and organizations share many attributes and many relationships to other entities. A corporation is, after all, a "legal person." Both people and organizations have "names" and "addresses" as attributes, and both may be parties to contracts. For this reason, while PERSON and ORGANIZATION are things of significance, so too is the super-set of the two, which we shall here call PARTY. This is shown in Figure 3.1.

So, we now have three entities—among the most important entities on our model—and we haven't spoken to anyone yet!

To get attributes, however, we will have to interview someone. Enterprises differ greatly in the kinds of information they want to hold about people and organizations. Even here, though, we can make some educated guesses. For example, PARTY probably has the common attributes "name" and "address," while PERSON has the attribute "birth date," and ORGANIZATION may have an attribute such as "purpose." Now while both PERSON and ORGANIZATION have "names," however, PERSON actually has two names (plus a middle name or initial, if you want to get thorough*). This could be handled by moving "name" to ORGANIZATION and giving PERSON "first name" and "last name." An alternative is shown here, with the principal "name" being equivalent to a person's surname, and with only the given name specific to PERSON. How this should be handled in your model depends on the requirements of the organization.

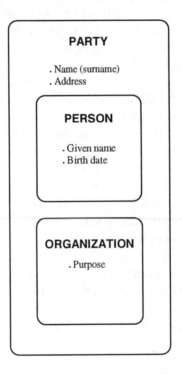

Figure 3.1: Parties.

<hr />

* In the United States, that is . . . most of the time . . . but not counting George Herbert Walker Bush. Many other cultures use multiple middle names, plus "de," "von," "van," "la," and the like. If the model describes an organization operating entirely within the United States, assumptions can be made about names. If the organization is multinational, these attributes have to be made more general.

One premise that must be established when generalizing models is the context in which this is to happen.

While virtually all companies and government agencies have need for the PERSON and ORGANIZATION entities, how these entities are divided into subtypes will vary from company to company. (At this point, you really do have to speak to someone.)

Beginning with the PERSON entity, a common practice is to assert that a PERSON may be either an EMPLOYEE or an OTHER PERSON. (See Figure 3.2.) An EMPLOYEE is usually thought of as a thing of significance to an employer.

From a practical point of view, this can work, especially since employees often have an extensive set of attributes that don't apply to other people. It turns out, for example, that "birth date" is probably an attribute of interest only for an employee, and there are others, such as "social security number," "number of exemptions," and so forth.*

There are problems with defining EMPLOYEE as an entity, however: First, a person may fall into more than one of these categories. That person may have worked for a customer as an agent and is now an employee—or vice versa—but the "agentness" of the person is to be kept. Consultants and other contractual workers are also problematic, since a lot of employee-type information may be held, even though such people are not, strictly speaking, employees. If these are significant issues in your organization, then the EMPLOYEE/OTHER PERSON distinction is *not* appropriate.

This is one example, by the way, of a common trap for the unwary. (We will encounter others.) What you have in the word "employee" is a common name for something including in its meaning not just the thing itself, but also its *relationship* to something else. A PERSON is a human being with specific characteristics, whether employed by anyone or not. An EMPLOYEE, on the other hand, is a PERSON who has established a relationship of employment with an ORGANIZATION. Figure 3.3 shows this relationship: Each PERSON may be *currently employed by* one and only one ORGANIZATION, and each ORGANIZATION may be *the employer of* one or more PEOPLE.

---

* Note to readers outside the United States: Federal income taxes are adjusted according to the number of people in the family. An "exemption" from a certain amount of tax is granted to each member, and additional exemptions are granted to people in special circumstances. The number of exemptions an employee declares affects the amount of money withheld from each paycheck for taxes.

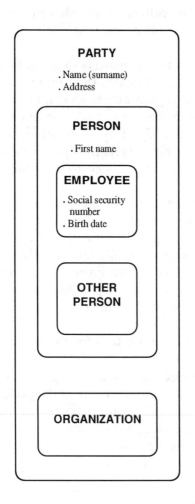

Figure 3.2: Employees.

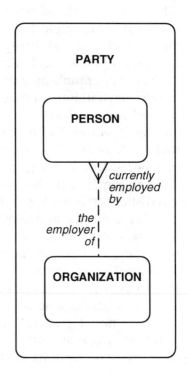

Figure 3.3: The Employment Relationship.

Showing it this way, however, raises the question of what to do with the employment-specific attributes. It is also probably true that over time, a PERSON may be employed by more than one ORGANIZATION. For these reasons, an additional entity probably will be required to describe the relationship fully. Figure 3.4 shows the addition of the entity EMPLOYMENT, to solve both problems. Note that each EMPLOYMENT must be *of* a PERSON *with* an ORGANIZATION. Each PERSON may be *in* one or more EMPLOYMENTS, and each ORGANIZATION may be *the source of* one or more EMPLOYMENTS.

Employment attributes such as "number of exemptions" go in this entity. EMPLOYMENT may also have the attribute "type," to distinguish between full-time employees, part-time employees, and contractors. It may be argued that "birth date" or "social security number" should go there, since they are of interest only in the context of employment. In fact, however, these are attributes of PERSON, and should be placed in that entity. If your client can claim *never* to want to know the birth date of a nonemployee, you might get away with making them attributes of EMPLOYMENT—but when the time comes that you *do* want to know the birthday of a nonemployee ("I know what I said, but that was then . . ."), you will appreciate that you did the more philosophically correct thing and made it an attribute of PERSON.*

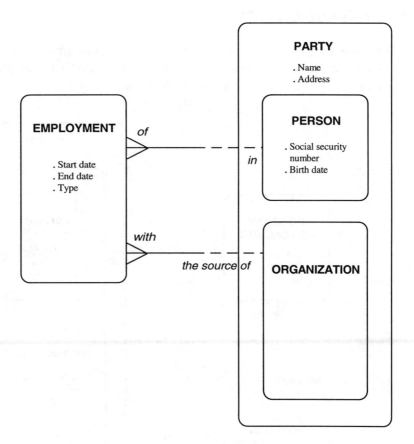

Figure 3.4: The Employment Entity.

* Of course, by making "social security number" an attribute of PERSON, you promote the insidiously infectious practice common in the United States of collecting social security numbers for everyone, in all kinds of inappropriate situations. Here, political views on privacy may conflict with those of a modeling purist.

Note that there is some ambiguity in this model. The model does not and cannot make explicit an assumption probably made by viewers—that a PERSON will be *in* only one EMPLOYMENT at a time. One could assume that the "more than one" EMPLOYMENTS are a succession of jobs *of* the PERSON. The model does not prevent, however, the PERSON from having multiple EMPLOYMENTS at once, possibly even with different ORGANIZATIONS. Constraints to prevent such a situation are business rules, which would have to be specified outside the model.

EMPLOYEE ASSIGNMENTS

Figure 3.4 shows that each PERSON may be *in* one or more EMPLOYMENTS *with* an ORGANIZATION. A PERSON's complete relationship to an ORGANIZATION, however, can be more complex. Figure 3.5 shows this.

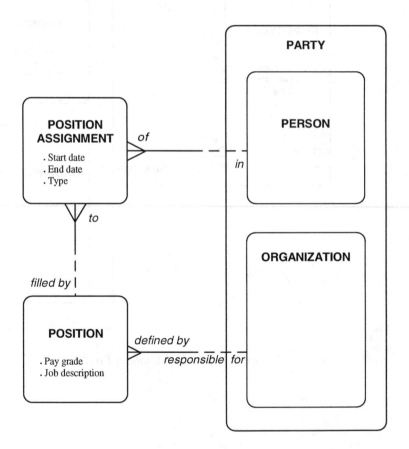

Figure 3.5: Positions.

First, the POSITION held by a person is itself something of significance, with attributes such as "pay grade" and "job description." Typically *defined by* one

ORGANIZATION, the POSITION is likely to be held by more than one PERSON, at least over time, and a PERSON may also reasonably be expected to hold more than one POSITION over time. Indeed, the PERSON may hold multiple POSITIONS at the same time. For example, a scholar might progress through the titles of Teaching Assistant, Assistant Professor, and Professor. While holding the last title, the Professor might become a Department Chairman as well.

All this argues for specification of POSITION ASSIGNMENT (the fact that a PERSON holds the POSITION, for a period of time, beginning with the "start date" and lasting until the "end date"). That is, each POSITION ASSIGNMENT must be *of* a PERSON *to* a POSITION. Each PERSON, then, may be *in* one or more POSITION ASSIGNMENTS, each of which must be *to* a POSITION *defined by* an ORGANIZATION.

There are many variations on this model. If, for example, POSITIONS are defined company-wide, and departments use them with different TITLES, the situation is as shown in Figure 3.6. Each POSITION ASSIGNMENT must be *to* a TITLE, not a POSITION. This TITLE, in turn, must be *for* a POSITION, and the TITLE, not the POSITION, is *defined by* an ORGANIZATION, which in this context is a department.

Most uses of TITLE and POSITION might be expected to be concerned only with INTERNAL ORGANIZATIONS. The relationship is shown connected to ORGANIZATION, however, because it may be important to keep track of titles and organizational structures in other companies as well.

The POSITION ASSIGNMENT, TITLE, and POSITION entities need not be limited to formal employment. In companies that use "matrix management" techniques, where a person plays a role for many different departments, a PERSON may have a permanent assignment to one department while being *seconded* to another.* A second POSITION ASSIGNMENT (of "type" "secondment") for the same person would then be specified.

---

* "Seconded" is a British term for "temporarily assigned."

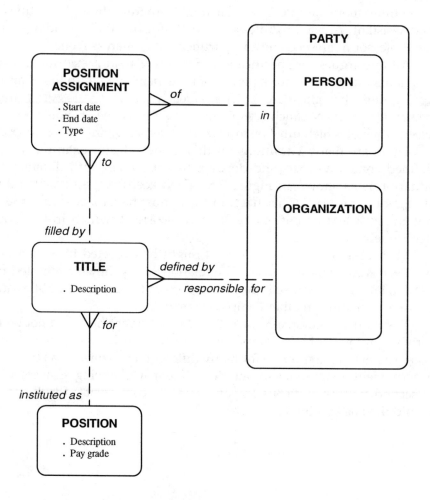

Figure 3.6: Titles.

If your organizational situation calls for a more elaborate model, PARTY and POSITION ASSIGNMENT entities could be related to the EMPLOYMENT entity introduced in Figure 3.4, thereby producing the diagram shown in Figure 3.7. POSITION ASSIGNMENT is now *based on* the EMPLOYMENT *of* the PERSON *with* an ORGANIZATION. Note that this new model allows EMPLOYMENT to be *with* one organization (such as a company), while a POSITION may be *defined by* a different ORGANIZATION (such as a department). This representation would allow a PERSON to have EMPLOYMENT *with* one company and to have a POSITION *defined by* an unrelated ORGANIZATION. This includes, for example, the seconding example cited above, exhibited in government agencies where employment might be defined for one agency but the person is temporarily assigned to another.

This also describes a consultant who is employed by a consulting company but assigned to a POSITION in a client company.

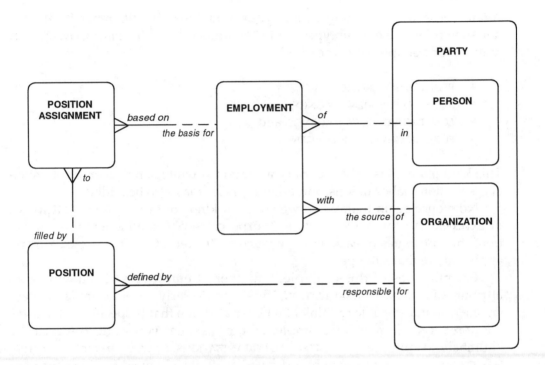

Figure 3.7: Employment (Revisited).

ORGANIZATIONS

As with PERSON, the specific nature of the organization being modeled dictates the way the entity ORGANIZATION is divided into subtypes. To resolve this, again, we actually have to interview someone.

A common approach to ORGANIZATION is to divide it into INTERNAL ORGANI-ZATION and EXTERNAL ORGANIZATION.

An INTERNAL ORGANIZATION could be, for example,

- a DEPARTMENT,
- a DIVISION, or
- some OTHER INTERNAL ORGANIZATION.

Figure 3.8 shows this, as well as the world of the EXTERNAL ORGANIZATION, which could be

- a CORPORATION,
- a GOVERNMENT AGENCY, or
- some OTHER EXTERNAL ORGANIZATION.

Again, these are just examples, and your model may be different. While it is not shown here, these subtypes could be broken down further. GOVERNMENT AGENCY, for example, could be divided into

- FEDERAL GOVERNMENT AGENCY,
- STATE GOVERNMENT AGENCY,
- LOCAL GOVERNMENT AGENCY, and
- FOREIGN GOVERNMENT AGENCY.

This kind of detail is only necessary in certain situations, however. Professional associations, labor unions, and other agencies may also be added.

Note once again that, when we split out kinds of organizations, attributes of EXTERNAL ORGANIZATION, such as "purpose," apply to all external organizations, but attributes of each subtype (such as "Federal tax ID" in CORPORATION) apply only to that subtype.

For purposes of this example, "number of employees" is shown as an attribute of INTERNAL ORGANIZATION. It is a particularly weak example, however, and you may be able to think of a better attribute that is specific to INTERNAL ORGANIZATION. It may, for example, be the case that you want to record the "number of employees" for EXTERNAL ORGANIZATIONS, as well. In fact, for INTERNAL ORGANIZATIONS, this may be a derived attribute, obtained for an occurrence by simply counting the number of occurrences of EMPLOYMENT that are *with* that occurrence.

Note also that this view of INTERNAL and EXTERNAL ORGANIZATIONS, like the inclination to define EMPLOYEE as a subtype of PERSON, implies a strong orientation toward a world divided between "us" and "them." A subtype FOREIGN GOVERNMENT AGENCY, for example, suggests that all governments except the one in our home country is foreign. This is the view taken by many companies, but the modeler should be aware of its bias. For an international company, governments are governments and each division may have its own definition of what is "foreign." This would make FOREIGN GOVERNMENT AGENCY a meaningless entity.

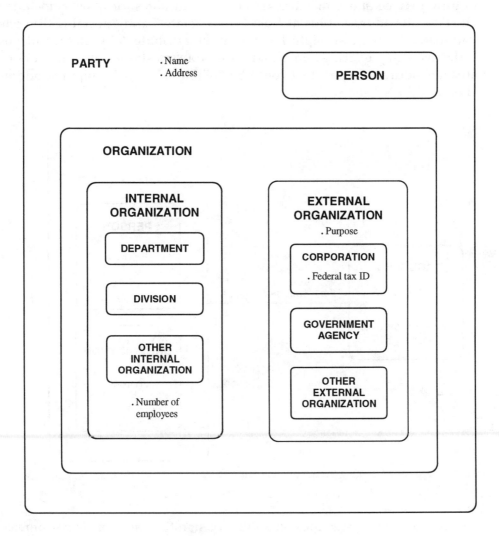

Figure 3.8: Organizations.

ADDRESSES

PARTIES are usually located somewhere. In its simplest form, the model could simply include "address" as an attribute of PARTY, as shown in Figure 3.1. (This would be inherited by both PERSON and ORGANIZATION.) The problem with this is that organizations at least, and many people too, have more than one address, such as "shipping address," "billing address," "home address," and so forth.

This argues for adding a second entity ADDRESS, as shown in Figure 3.9. Here, each ADDRESS must be *the location of* one and only one PARTY. Each PARTY, in turn, may be *at* one or more ADDRESSES. Attributes for ADDRESS include the "text" of the address, plus at least "city," "state," and "postal (ZIP) code."* Alternatively, ADDRESS might have only the attribute "city, state, and postal code" as a single string. In either case, ADDRESS should also include as an attribute address "type," that could be "billing address," "shipping address," "home address," and so forth.

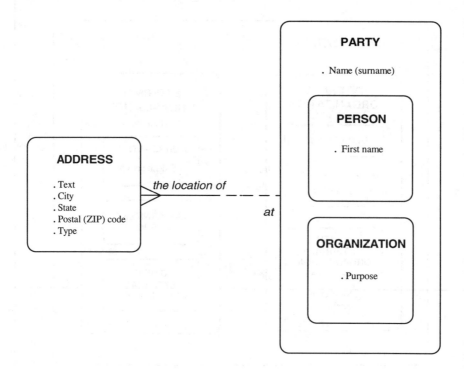

Figure 3.9: Addresses—First Try.

So, we have now made ADDRESS a thing of significance. This is not unreasonable, if you think of an office, a home, or a work center. Making ADDRESS a thing of significance, however, leads to a problem: We have asserted that each ADDRESS must be *the location of* one and only one PARTY, but when you think about it, more than one PERSON or ORGANIZATION can be at the same ADDRESS.

---

* The context of the model will determine whether this attribute is "ZIP code" or "postal code." If the client organization will operate entirely within the United States for the foreseeable future, the assumption of a nine-digit, two-part numeric "ZIP code" can be made. If not, "ZIP code" must become "postal code" and no formatting assumptions are possible.

Indeed, the word "address" is ambiguous: In ordinary conversation, an address may be associated with a single party ("What's Steve's address?"), but in other contexts, it can also be associated with multiple parties. ("The Grand Junction, Colorado, office at 2476 Galley Lane employs twenty people.") We have not expressed the concept of address as an identified place.

To clarify this, we will rename the ADDRESS entity as SITE. A SITE (such as the Grand Junction office) is a place with a designated purpose. It is not a geographic location (like the city of Grand Junction, itself); that is simply a location on a map. A SITE may be an office, a work center in a factory, a warehouse location, or an archaeological dig. The key word in the definition is "purpose."

In this example, we can distinguish between the attribute "purpose"—that might be "administration," "manufacturing," "storage," and the like—and "type," which describes the kind of site it is, such as "office," "work center," or "warehouse location." This distinction represents a purist approach: In some circumstances, one attribute might cover both the type and the purpose of the SITE.

Because more than one PERSON or ORGANIZATION may be located *at* a SITE, we now need an entity to represent each fact that a PARTY is located *at* a SITE. We could call this ADDRESS, and in many companies' models, it is. Because of the ambiguity described above in the way we use the word "address," however, perhaps it would be better to invent a new word. In Figure 3.10, it is shown as PLACEMENT. Each PLACEMENT must be *of* a PARTY *at* a SITE.

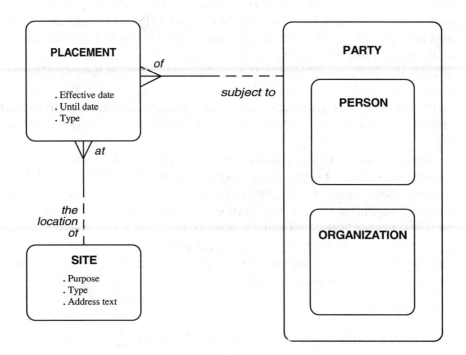

Figure 3.10: Site (Another Way to Show Addresses).

Attributes of PLACEMENT include the date it happens ("effective date") and the date it is discontinued ("until date"). PLACEMENTS may also be categorized via the attribute "type."

To summarize, then, each PARTY may be *subject to* one or more PLACEMENTS *at* a SITE. That SITE determines the PARTY's "address." That is, a PARTY will have one "address" for each SITE where it is located.

GEOGRAPHIC LOCATIONS

Such a solution may be adequate for many applications, but often it is of interest to collect addresses by city, county, postal code, or other GEOGRAPHIC LOCATION where the address is located. Each SITE, then, must be *in* one GEOGRAPHIC LOCATION—which means that each GEOGRAPHIC LOCATION may be *the location of* one or more SITES. (See Figure 3.11.)

The attributes of GEOGRAPHIC LOCATION would of course include its "name," and possibly a "geographic location type," such as "state," "country," "province," and so forth.

With all this, though, what about our original problem of modeling a mailing address? Unfortunately, the answer is, "It depends."

If GEOGRAPHIC LOCATION simply located the SITE in general terms, the "address text" and "city, state, and postal code" attributes could remain in SITE. GEOGRAPHIC LOCATION is itself hierarchical, however, where each GEOGRAPHIC LOCATION may be *part of* one and only one other GEOGRAPHIC LOCATION.* Thus, you may include all the countries, states, provinces, cities, postal codes, neighborhoods, major statistical metropolitan areas (MSMA's), and streets as examples of GEOGRAPHIC LOCATION and then link them together as a hierarchy. Correctly populating the GEOGRAPHIC LOCATION entity would then make redundant at least the "city, state, and ZIP code" in SITE. A building at "544 East 11th Street, New York, New York 10009," for example, could have as the "address text" of its SITE "544 East 11th Street," and then be shown as being *in* ZIP code "10009," which is *part of* "New York" (the city), which is *part of* "New York" (the state).

Indeed, carried to extremes, even "East 11th Street" could be a GEOGRAPHIC LOCATION, as could "building 544," which is *part of* "East 11th Street." The only "address text" required in SITE, then, would be the apartment number that uniquely identifies the PARTY's location. (In this case, the PARTY is probably an ORGANIZATION of "type" "family.")

The purest answer, then, in terms of the logic of the model, would be to put most of the address in successive GEOGRAPHIC LOCATIONS as shown, with only the most detailed element defined in SITE.

---

* This kind of relationship is called "recursive." In *Hay's First New Dictionary,* the entry for this word is, "recursive—*see recursive.*"

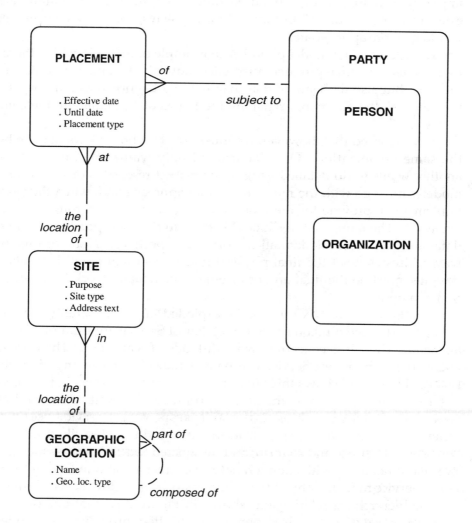

Figure 3.11: Geographic Location.

If all we ever will want are mailing addresses for invoices and labels, however, this latter approach is clearly overdoing it. For mailing labels, an address is a single piece of information. This puts us back to the original model with three text attributes in ADDRESS or PARTY. ADDRESS could still point to the appropriate GEOGRAPHIC LOCATION for classification purposes, although it should be understood how this introduces redundancy in the data. (This is not necessarily bad, as long as the business understands it and takes responsibility for it.)

Note that this deference to practicality is not an example of concern for more efficient computer processing. It is recognition of the fact that the data *mean* different things to different people. If, to a user community, "address" is a single attribute, the model should reflect that—as long as that community is made aware of the possibility that this view could change in the future, and the implications of that change. If, on the other hand, the user community is interested in using "address" in many different ways, the more complex model would be more appropriate.

The address data model provides an example of a case in which there is no *right* model. The final product must reflect not only the underlying structure of the data, but also the view of that data held by the organization. Specifically, we must ask the question, "What are the things of *significance* to the company or agency?"

Having asked that, however, we must note that both views may be held in the same organization: One department only wants mailing labels, while another wants to do detailed geographic market research. In such a case, the modeler must go with the more conceptual approach and, when the system is implemented, provide for the more mundane user needs through application "views."* The more complex model is truer to the conceptual structure of the data, and can accommodate all the other perspectives. None of this, by the way, addresses what the final physical database structure will look like. The designer must be the final arbiter of what will actually work in the organization's computers.

GEOGRAPHIC LOCATION can also be exploded into considerably more detail. A large part of the mission of the USDA Forest Service, for example, is to manage land. Thus, it is concerned with all kinds of real estate. The GEOGRAPHIC LOCATION for the Forest Service can be generalized to mean any kind of LAND PARCEL. Figure 3.12 shows this. In this view, a LAND PARCEL includes: GEOPOLITICAL LAND PARCELS, such as the STATES, CITIES, and COUNTIES discussed above; MANAGEMENT AREAS, such as NATIONAL FORESTS, FOREST SERVICE REGIONS, and other ADMINISTRATIVE AREAS; SURVEYED LAND PARCELS, described in terms of TOWNSHIPS, SECTIONS, and so forth; and designated NATURAL AREAS, such as HABITATS and other areas with common natural characteristics. In fact, in the actual Forest Service model, many of the subtypes are broken down even further.

The hierarchical relationship shown in Figure 3.11, that one GEOGRAPHIC LOCATION is *part of* another, has common application throughout the model. We first saw this pig's ear symbol in Chapter Two, and we will encounter it again frequently. Note that the hierarchical relationship must be all optional, since if you said, for example, that "each GEOGRAPHIC LOCATION *must be part of* one and

---

* That is, program logic could be *implemented* so that a particular user is shown a "view" of a PARTY (or PERSON or ORGANIZATION, as appropriate) table (entity), with the column (attribute) "address," as though it were derived from the models in either Figure 3.5 or Figure 3.1. In fact, however, when asked for "address," the program traverses other tables to retrieve it.

only one other GEOGRAPHIC LOCATION," there would be no way to deal with the GEOGRAPHIC LOCATION at the top. Similarly, to say that each GEOGRAPHIC LOCA-TION must be *composed of* one or more GEOGRAPHIC LOCATIONS is to fail to deal with the bottom of the tree.

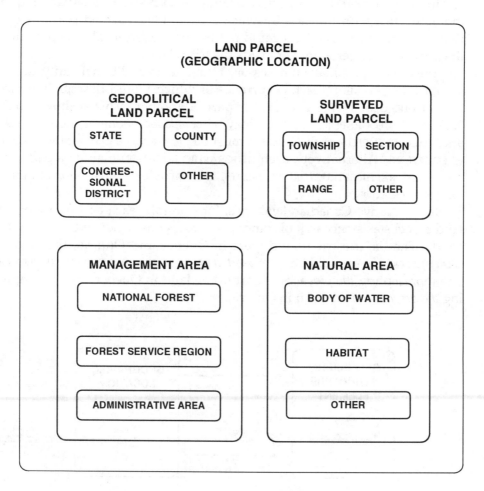

Figure 3.12: Land Parcels.

Note also that this relationship contains a business rule assumption that must be documented somewhere else: There is nothing in the model to prevent a GEOGRAPHIC LOCATION from being specified as part of itself, either directly or through a chain (that is, A is part of B, which is part of C, which is part of A). This is the case when any hierarchy is represented like this.

The idea of GEOGRAPHIC LOCATION itself can get trickier than this, and again, how it is modeled depends entirely on how sophisticated the company wishes to be in dealing with geography.

Life is more complicated, for example, in those cases in which geography is not strictly hierarchical. Cities are usually inside counties, except for New York

City, for example, which has five counties inside it. Also, in the United States, a ZIP code is normally entirely within a city, but not always: In Oregon, ZIP code 97401 encompasses both Coburg and part of Eugene. Eugene also has several other ZIP codes within it.

In another example, a project dealing with Native Canadians required a model to deal with the case in which a tribal land covered portions of more than one province. The land could not be considered inside the province, and the province was certainly not inside the tribal land.

These examples make it necessary to define an additional entity, GEOGRAPHIC STRUCTURE ELEMENT, each occurrence of which would describe the fact that part of one GEOGRAPHIC LOCATION is part of another. This is shown in Figure 3.13. Each GEOGRAPHIC LOCATION may be *composed of* one or more GEOGRAPHIC STRUCTURE ELEMENTS, each of which must be *the presence of* one other GEOGRAPHIC LOCATION. Alternatively, each GEOGRAPHIC LOCATION may be *a part in* one or more GEOGRAPHIC STRUCTURE ELEMENTS, each of which must be *in* another GEOGRAPHIC LOCATION.

In the Native-Canadian land case, for example, each occurrence of a tribal land parcel's existence in a province constitutes one GEOGRAPHIC STRUCTURE ELEMENT. That is, if a tribal land were in Quebec and Ontario, the land's GEOGRAPHIC LOCATION would be *composed of* two GEOGRAPHIC STRUCTURE ELEMENTS— one representing *the presence of* part of the land in Quebec, and one representing *the presence of* part of it in Ontario.

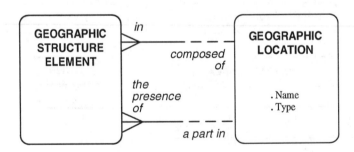

Figure 3.13: Geographic Structure Elements.

REPORTING RELATIONSHIPS

EMPLOYMENT and POSITION ASSIGNMENTS are examples of relationships that may exist between PEOPLE and ORGANIZATIONS. There are in fact many others—too many to be modeled as specifically as this. Consequently, we need a more general approach to relating PEOPLE and ORGANIZATIONS to each other. Such an approach is presented in this section.

Figures 2.5 and 2.6 of Chapter Two showed the derivation of the ORGANIZATION and its hierarchical structure. Part of Figure 2.6 is reproduced here as Figure 3.14, showing that each ORGANIZATION may be *composed of* one or more other ORGANIZATIONS.

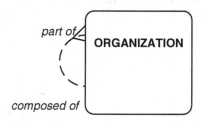

Figure 3.14: Organizational Structure.

In Chapter One, we ended the discussion of ORGANIZATION when we established that all organizations are fundamentally the same. It is important, however, that we also know how to draw a hierarchy when the top (or bottom) element (in this case, ORGANIZATION) is significantly different from the others.

For example, we might wish to assert that a CORPORATION is fundamentally different from an OTHER ORGANIZATION. This distinction may be expressed in either of two ways: The first is shown in Figure 3.15. In this, each OTHER ORGANIZATION must be *part of* one and only one OTHER ORGANIZATION or it must be *part of* a CORPORATION. Note that we can now say each ORGANIZATION must be *part of* another ORGANIZATION, since at the top of the hierarchy the other side of the arc takes effect. For that last step, each ORGANIZATION must be *part of* a CORPORATION. We still must say "may be" going *down* the hierarchy ("each OTHER ORGANIZATION may be *composed of* one or more OTHER ORGANIZATIONS"), since there is no defined bottom to it.

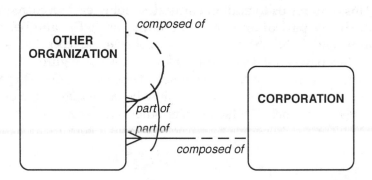

Figure 3.15: Top-Heavy Hierarchy—Version 1.

The second way a distinction may be drawn between the top element in a hierarchy and all the others (which is either more elegant or more arcane, depend-

ing on your taste) is shown in Figure 3.16. In this diagram, each OTHER ORGANI-
ZATION must be *part of* an ORGANIZATION (which in turn must be either a CORPO-
RATION or an OTHER ORGANIZATION). Going the other way, each ORGANIZATION
(whether it is a CORPORATION or an OTHER ORGANIZATION) may be *composed of*
only one or more OTHER ORGANIZATIONS.

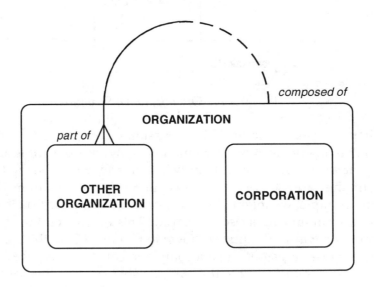

Figure 3.16: Top-Heavy Hierarchy—Version 2.

All of this is well and good, until you start dealing with a government agency
that, over time, has been part of several different departments and other agencies. It turns out *not* to be the case that an ORGANIZATION may be *part of* only *one*
ORGANIZATION. The pig's ear turns out to represent a many-to-many relationship. This requires us to add an entity describing each occurrence of an ORGA-
NIZATION being part of another. The entity added is another example of a
"structure" entity, like the GEOGRAPHIC STRUCTURE ELEMENT discussed above. In
this case, we have added REPORTING RELATIONSHIP in Figure 3.17. Each REPORT-
ING RELATIONSHIP must be the occurrence *of* one ORGANIZATION *in* another ORGA-
NIZATION. That is, each ORGANIZATION may be *composed of* one or more REPORT-
ING RELATIONSHIPS, each of which is *of* another ORGANIZATION.*

---

* As with the hierarchy, we will stipulate outside the model that an ORGANIZA-
TION may not be related to itself. That is, an occurrence of a REPORTING RELA-
TIONSHIP may not be both *in* and *of* the same ORGANIZATION.

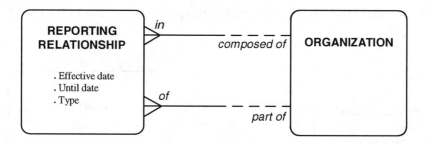

Figure 3.17: Reporting Relationships.

Having established REPORTING RELATIONSHIPS between ORGANIZATIONS, we face another issue. It is possible and often necessary to describe relationships between PEOPLE as well, and relationships between PEOPLE and ORGANIZATIONS.

We've already seen EMPLOYMENT as one relationship between PEOPLE and ORGANIZATIONS. Because this relationship is often referred to directly, and requires special treatment, it was modeled explicitly. This is only one example, however, of a relationship that can exist between two parties. People are married to each other; people belong to unions and clubs; departments are contained in divisions; and companies band together into industrial associations, buying groups, and so forth.

For this reason, we have generalized REPORTING RELATIONSHIP in Figure 3.18 to cover *any* relationship between two PEOPLE or ORGANIZATIONS. We also generalized the relationship names, to say that each REPORTING RELATIONSHIP must be *from* one PARTY *to* another. Conversely, a PARTY may be *on one side of* one or more REPORTING RELATIONSHIPS, and a PARTY may also be *on the other side of* one or more REPORTING RELATIONSHIPS.

This does not negate the value of also showing EMPLOYMENT as we did before, but it does allow us to represent any other relationship between two parties. The most important attributes of this entity are the "effective date" of a relationship, its "until date," and its reporting relationship "type," such as "organizational structure," "club membership," "family relationship," and the like. REPORTING RELATIONSHIP, then, is the fact that one PARTY is related to another at a particular time.

The power of this concept may be seen in many areas. For example, hospitals commonly band together into buying groups to obtain quantity discounts on purchases of pharmaceuticals and other hospital supplies. A buying group's blanket purchase order specifies a group discount, and allows each member hospital to issue a purchase order for items at that group price. To handle this arrangement, it is a simple matter to define the buying group as an ORGANIZATION, and identify a blanket purchase order for it, specifying the

prices. When a participating hospital's purchase order is received, it is necessary only to look up any buying group with which the hospital has established
a REPORTING RELATIONSHIP. Once the contract price negotiated for that group has
been found, it may then be applied to the purchase by the individual hospital.

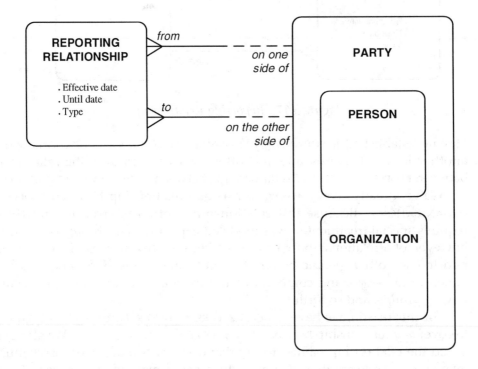

Figure 3.18: Reporting Relationships Between Parties.

REPORTING RELATIONSHIP allows *any* relationships among people and organizations to be defined. As mentioned above, the special case of people's relationships with their employers is elaborated in the entities POSITION ASSIGNMENT,
TITLE, and POSITION. These entities will appear in many data models.

ABOUT TYPES

Note, that we have specified reporting relationship "type" as an attribute. Previously, EMPLOYMENT, SITE, GEOGRAPHIC LOCATION, and POSITION ASSIGNMENT also
had "type" attributes. PARTY didn't show a "type" attribute, but it could have.
In each case, presumably there is a finite list of possible values for the attribute.
The "... type" attribute may be handled in one of three ways: If this list is relatively stable, it may be contained in a domain for the type. That is, the list of
values for the attribute is documented in the data dictionary as a relatively

fixed list. Alternatively, if the list is also comparatively short, each of the "... types" could be shown as a subtype of REPORTING RELATIONSHIP.

If the list is more dynamic and variable, however, or if there is a reason to display the fact that such a list exists, it can be shown in the model as a new entity. This entity can be named REPORTING RELATIONSHIP TYPE, where each REPORTING RELATIONSHIP must be *an example of* one and only one REPORTING RELATIONSHIP TYPE, and each REPORTING RELATIONSHIP TYPE may be *embodied in* one or more REPORTING RELATIONSHIPS.

In short, it is possible to deal with REPORTING RELATIONSHIP TYPE (or any other ... TYPE) either as an attribute with a defined domain, as a set of subtypes, or as a relationship to a ... TYPE entity.

ABOUT POINTS OF VIEW

You will find in this book a bias toward creating the purest models possible, with an emphasis on describing things in terms abstract enough to encompass a wide range of circumstances. In the course of this chapter, however, we have discovered the purest model to be often in conflict with practical issues of addressing the perspectives of future systems users. (The case of ADDRESS and mailing lists is a good example.)

In real projects, however, you rarely are called upon to encompass a wide range of circumstances. Your client or user will have a particular problem to be addressed quickly and in terms that he or she understands. It may be unavoidable that you have to draw a model in those terms. So be it. The rent must be paid. Even when this happens, however, it is to your advantage at least to *understand* the more abstract model. You may even want to sketch it out on paper and file it, so you will have an answer if (when?) the client has a change of mind and a widening of perspective—immediately followed by the demand for you to deal with it ("I know that's what I said then, but this is *now*!").

IN SUMMARY

The first anchor for any data model is the entity PARTY, which encompasses the PEOPLE and ORGANIZATIONS of interest to the enterprise. By convention, we will put it along the right side of the model, along with such entities as PLACEMENT *at* a SITE, which is *in* a GEOGRAPHIC LOCATION, as well as EMPLOYMENT, which is *the basis for* a POSITION ASSIGNMENT *to* a POSITION. REPORTING RELATIONSHIP will lie alongside PARTY as well.

The second anchor for any data model is the stuff that the company uses, makes, and otherwise manipulates. That is the subject of the next chapter.

4
THINGS OF THE ENTERPRISE

*W*hereas the previous chapter described the enterprise and its people, this chapter is concerned with what that enterprise manipulates. This includes the products it makes, the raw materials it uses, and its physical assets. Since all companies deal with something, the structure of this portion of the model can be similar for all. The differences, however, are at the heart of what makes each company's model unique.

Previously we spoke of entities as being "things of significance," and included in that category transactions and other intangible things as potential entities. Here we will speak only of the tangible things that a company uses, makes, and sells.

Organizations deal with "things" in different ways—and they describe these dealings in many different ways. Some organizations are most concerned with the products that they make. Others may only perform services, but require tools to do their work. As an example of this, the people in a power plant ostensibly manufacture electricity, but in fact they only maintain the machinery that makes the electricity. In this case, the things that concern them are the compressors, valves, and fuel that are doing the job.

Accountants, on the other hand, look at the physical world in terms of the value of the company's assets. The relationship between physical assets and financial ones can be subtle and complex, but the idea of physical resources remains the same. We will introduce these financial ideas here and explore them further in Chapter Seven.

In all these cases, it will be your job as a modeler first to recognize the products an organization uses and produces, and then to see how they are related to each other, to other aspects of the enterprise, and to its mission.

PRODUCTS AND PRODUCT TYPES

Understanding this part of the model requires a mental grouping of things frequently thought of as distinct, and, conversely, the drawing of a distinction between two things often treated together.

First the distinction: For a model to make sense, it is essential to distinguish between the specification of things and the physical things themselves. A

PRODUCT TYPE describes the nature of a product—the Platonic "idea."* A PROD-UCT, on the other hand, is the physical thing itself. Both PRODUCT TYPES and the PRODUCTS themselves are things of significance to the organization. A PRODUCT TYPE is usually identified by a "model number" or its equivalent, and its other attributes describe characteristics of the model, regardless of the number of physical copies that may exist.

An occurrence of PRODUCT TYPE, for example, might be SuperStar Comput-ers' Model S4/33 computer. Another could be the Discus Model 106 hard disk drive, and so on. Attributes that might appear in a catalogue entry *defining* the object (such as "name," or "clock speed," in the case of the computer, or "capacity," in the case of the disk drive) are attributes of the PRODUCT TYPE.

Similarly, Microsoft® Word, Version 2.0, is an example of a PRODUCT TYPE.

Your author's desk, on the other hand, might be the site of a *particular* SuperStar 33 MHz computer (serial number 98987789) that happens to contain an equally particular Discus Model 106 hard disk drive (serial number unknown). These represent two occurrences of PRODUCTS—which are *examples of* PRODUCT TYPES "SuperStar Computers' Model S4/33" and "Discus Model 106" respectively.

The set of Microsoft Word disks with serial number 00-059-0200-56713945 is also an example of a PRODUCT.

Figure 4.1 shows this distinction. It shows that each PRODUCT must be *an example of* one and only one PRODUCT TYPE, and each PRODUCT TYPE may be *embodied in* one or more PRODUCTS. Note that a PRODUCT TYPE is usually defined before any physical copies—PRODUCTS—are actually made.

This discussion is a continuation of that concerning "type" domains in the previous chapter. We are speaking here of a type just like the GEOGRAPHIC LOCA-TION "type," POSITION ASSIGNMENT "type," REPORTING RELATIONSHIP "type," and so forth. In this case, however, we make the domain into an entity, for several rea-sons:

First of all, PRODUCT TYPE is clearly something of significance to the compa-ny. The list of PRODUCT TYPES is a list of the kinds of products with which the company deals, and this must be explicit in the model.

Second, the list of PRODUCT TYPES is probably dynamic. Occurrences are being added and deleted all the time. This means that the list should be main-tained as a table, not encoded into a program as a domain.

---

* "But take the case of the other, who . . . is able to distinguish the idea from the objects which participate in the idea, neither putting the objects in the place of the idea nor the idea in the place of the objects. . . ."

     —Plato, *The Republic*, trans. B. Jowett (New York: The Modern Library), p. 207.

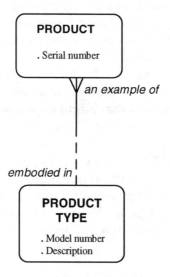

Figure 4.1: Products and Product Types.

Figure 4.2 shows that it may be useful to group both PRODUCTS and PRODUCT TYPES into PRODUCT CATEGORIES.

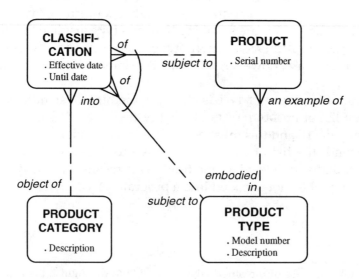

Figure 4.2: Product Categories.

While a PRODUCT is *an example of only one* PRODUCT TYPE, a PRODUCT or PRODUCT TYPE may be classified into *more than one* PRODUCT CATEGORY. This requires us to define CLASSIFICATION, where each CLASSIFICATION is *of* either a PRODUCT or a PRODUCT TYPE *into* a PRODUCT CATEGORY. Your author's Model S4/33 computer could be a beige computer, as well as an Intel™-based computer. One occurrence of CLASSIFICATION, then, would be *of* the Model S4/33 computer *into* "beige computer," and another would be *of* the Model S4/33 *into* "Intel computer." The primary attribute of PRODUCT CATEGORY is "description," while the main attributes of CLASSIFICATION are the effectivity dates ("effective date" and "until date").

So much for the distinction. Now for the grouping: Sometimes, in addition to discrete pieces of hardware, it is important to deal with powders and goo (that is, chemicals). The model just presented applies to them as well, since with them, we also must distinguish between the definition of a material (a MATERIAL TYPE) and examples of it (typically in INVENTORY somewhere). It is not a stretch to expand our definition of PRODUCT TYPE, then, to include products that are not discrete items. For example, you may be in need of five gallons of robin's egg blue house paint (a MATERIAL TYPE). A nearby hardware store could obtain five actual gallons for you (or, more likely, 4.98 gallons or 5.05 gallons) of a paint (the MATERIAL) that is approximately robin's egg blue in color.

While the examples above dealt with personal possessions, the entities PRODUCT and PRODUCT TYPE are in fact introduced here to describe the items a company makes, or those that any organization uses to carry out its work.

Indeed, the International Standards Organization (ISO), in its discussions of quality standards, defines PRODUCT as any "result of activities or processes . . . [including] hardware, processed materials, software, or a combination thereof. . . . A product can be tangible (e.g., assemblies or processed materials) or intangible (e.g., knowledge or concepts*), or a combination thereof . . . [and] can be either intended (e.g., offering to customers) or unintended (e.g., pollutants or unwanted effects)." [1]

In addition to expanding PRODUCT and PRODUCT TYPE to include chemicals, we can also expand these terms to accommodate the physical equipment that constitutes the manufacturing facility itself. Like the products or materials made there, all the valves, boilers, instruments, and pipes that make up a plant must be defined and specified. In addition, the concept of MATERIAL TYPE can also neatly cover supplies, such as lubricants, catalysts, and cleaning agents.

Once we have expanded the list of things that concern us beyond the realm of the products that we make, we require a more general set of terms. In fact,

---

* Indeed, your author had experience with one market research firm for which the entity occupying the place in the model usually taken by PRODUCT or ASSET was indeed CONCEPT. It seems that concepts are the things that a market research company measures, describes, and trades in.

what concerns us are all the physical ASSETS of the company. This more general term can ultimately encompass all physical things of interest—buildings, roads, and bridges; the hardware that constitutes the plant; inventories of the company's products; and so forth. Because of the wide range of situations to be described in this book, this general term ASSET will help prevent confusion later on.

In a real modeling situation, of course, the analyst will be called upon to give this and all entities names that preserve their generality but which are as meaningful as possible to the organization involved. In a model for a manufacturer, for example, the entity almost surely must be named PRODUCT. Because we are concerned with more than manufacturing in this book, however, we will use the term ASSET (and ASSET TYPE, ASSET CATEGORY, and so forth).

Feel free to use a different term in your models.

Figure 4.3, then, shows PRODUCT TYPE generalized to ASSET TYPE. The diagram shows how an ASSET TYPE may be a PRODUCT TYPE (in the original sense of a piece of hardware sold by the company), a MATERIAL TYPE, a PART/EQUIPMENT TYPE, or an OTHER ASSET TYPE. The particular combination of products, parts, and materials in your plant may affect the particular way you divide up and name this entity, but Figure 4.3 is representative.

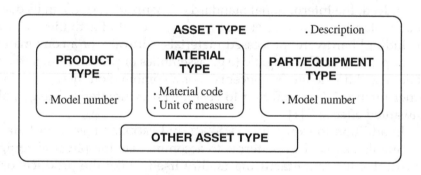

Figure 4.3: Equipment and Materials.

Note that here we are treating the definition of a PRODUCT, MATERIAL, ASSET, and so forth, as though each occurrence were well defined. That is, for a given item in our company's catalogue, we assume that we know its attributes and characteristics, how to make it, and so forth. For purposes of this chapter so far, that has been a reasonable assumption to make. Be aware, however, that with the advent of the Total Quality Management (TQM) movement, companies (especially chemical companies) are moving increasingly toward products whose characteristics are defined by customers when ordered. This more complex situation requires an extensive elaboration on the model we've built so far, and is described in Chapters Six and Eight.

INVENTORY

If Figure 4.3 expanded ASSET TYPE to include PRODUCT TYPE, MATERIAL TYPE, and PART/EQUIPMENT TYPE, what does this expansion mean for the physical ASSET? Dealing with ASSETS gets a little more complicated, since physical products, parts, and materials are kept track of in several different ways. Physical items show up as individual pieces, inventory, buildings, and so forth. The model must capture what is unique about each kind of physical example of an ASSET, even as it captures those characteristics that are common to all of them.

If an asset is identified by individual pieces (that is, by serial number or company tag number), it is a DISCRETE ITEM. Each DISCRETE ITEM constitutes a uniquely identifiable occurrence of ASSET, as previously described. This could be the case with pieces of equipment the enterprise uses, large or expensive items that it manufactures, and such things as buildings and roads. If, on the other hand, the ASSET is only kept track of in bulk quantity (like screws or toilet paper), each physical occurrence of an ASSET exists in the form of INVENTORY of that ASSET.

For this reason, in Figure 4.4, two kinds of ASSET are shown—DISCRETE ITEM and INVENTORY. The primary attribute of DISCRETE ITEM is typically "serial number" (or its commonly used synonym "item number"), while the most important attribute of INVENTORY is "quantity" on hand. It should be noted that this distinction is not always clear cut, and may differ, depending on the enterprise's perspective. Software vendors, for example, may keep track of the serial numbers of their products. Their customers, on the other hand, may not. Even vendors may only use serial numbers for control, without actually using them as the basis for inventory accounting.

Because of its physical existence, an ASSET (either an INVENTORY or a DISCRETE ITEM) must be *(currently) at* a particular SITE, such as a warehouse location or a manufacturing work center. That is, one definition of ASSET is that it is the physical occurrence of an ASSET TYPE at a SITE.

But what about companies that don't make parts? They make chemicals or foodstuffs or pharmaceuticals. How do we represent the materials they manipulate?

Like physical ASSETS, physical MATERIALS can simply be another kind of INVENTORY, where the "quantity" is in gallons or liters, instead of units. Although fluids and powders can be accommodated by this model and treated like other INVENTORIES, however, some industries, such as pharmaceuticals or food processing, require more: While quantities of material are kept track of, each quantity produced by a LOT (a PRODUCTION ORDER—see Chapters Five and Ten) must itself be kept track of discretely. As Figure 4.5 shows, a LOT may be *the source of* one or more LOT INVENTORIES—each another kind of INVENTORY. As with all other INVENTORY, the lot would have "quantity" as an attribute (in this case, usually called lot size). Lots are also counted discretely, however, just like pieces of equipment, so in the manner of a DISCRETE ITEM each also has a "lot number." LOT INVENTORY, then, combines the ideas of DISCRETE ITEM and INVENTORY.

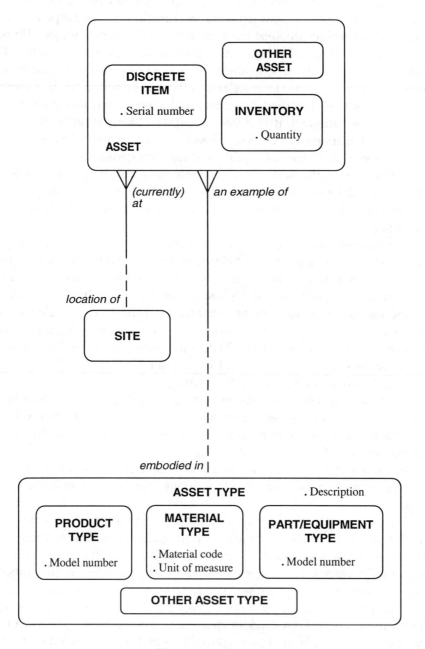

Figure 4.4: Inventory.

While a plant that produces MATERIALS does not necessarily make DISCRETE ITEMS, it (like all plants) *is* concerned with the PIECES OF EQUIPMENT that consti-

tute the facilities of the plant. PIECES OF EQUIPMENT, in turn, are either PRODUC-
TION FACILITIES, directly involved in the manufacturing activities of the plant, or
INSTRUMENTS of various kinds that measure the production process and product
quality, either on the shop floor or in the laboratory.

INVENTORY also may be further broken down. For example, the PART INVEN-
TORY of parts and equipment used in a plant might be explicitly distinguished
from the PRODUCT INVENTORY of products made. There are other possibilities,
but the one shown in Figure 4.5 is typical.

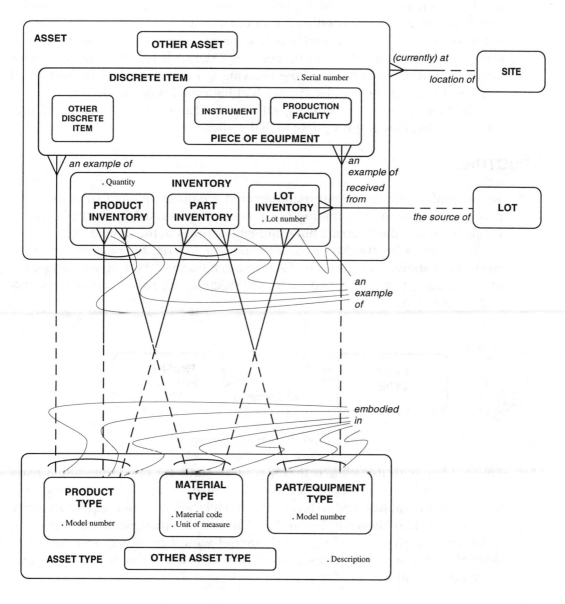

Figure 4.5: Parts Inventory.

Here we see the PRODUCT TYPE made and sold by discrete manufacturers being *embodied in* one or more DISCRETE ITEMS, PRODUCT INVENTORIES, or PART INVENTORIES; and the MATERIAL TYPE made and sold by process manufacturers being *embodied in* one or more PRODUCT INVENTORIES or LOT INVENTORIES. The PART/EQUIPMENT TYPE used in the manufacturing process is either *embodied in* one or more PART INVENTORIES or *embodied in* one or more PIECES OF EQUIPMENT.

Figure 4.5 illustrates something else as well. Figure 4.4 simply asserted that each ASSET must be *an example of* an ASSET TYPE. No attempt was made to identify which subtypes of ASSET were related to which subtypes of ASSET TYPE. Figure 4.5 tries to remedy this by explicitly saying, for example, that a PART INVENTORY must be *an example of* either a PRODUCT TYPE or a PART/EQUIPMENT TYPE but not a MATERIAL TYPE. This is certainly being conscientious, and in some circumstances, this kind of detail can be very important. It is at the cost of clarity, however, and if the purpose of the drawing is to win converts to the overall concepts involved, the simpler approach of Figure 4.4 is more effective.

The first rule of data modeling, after all, is: Know your audience and present a drawing that is appropriate to that audience.

STRUCTURE

To a manufacturer, the things manufactured are quite different from the parts that constitute them. Continuing our process of generalizing ASSETS, however, we shall see that these too are but different examples of the same thing.

Two entities for PART TYPE and FINISHED PRODUCT TYPE, for example, might be modeled as shown in Figure 4.6. Each FINISHED PRODUCT TYPE may be *composed of* one or more PART TYPES, and each PART TYPE may be *part of* one or more FINISHED PRODUCT TYPES.

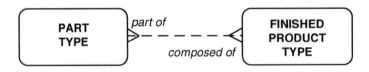

Figure 4.6: Manufacturing.

The problem with this view is that it only accounts for one level. Often parts are assembled into subassemblies, which in turn are assembled into the next level of subassemblies, and so forth. The model shown would require an entity for every level, as shown in Figure 4.7. For complex manufacturing processes, a database created according to this model would be nearly impossible to maintain. This model also doesn't work in any company that sells parts or subassemblies as finished products.

In short, such a model would only be appropriate in a company for which all products can permanently and irrevocably be classified as either a part or a finished product, and which makes finished products in a defined number of steps from parts. Such companies are rare.

For these reasons, it is better simply to extend ASSET TYPE yet again—this time to consider parts, subassemblies, and finished products (or, for chemical manufacturers: raw materials, intermediates, and finished products) in the same entity. In this case, ASSET TYPE refers to the specification of any physical item in the plant, regardless of what level it is in the product's structure. An ASSET TYPE, then, defines anything used or produced by the company.

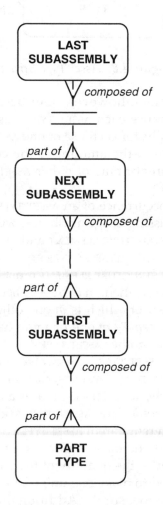

Figure 4.7: Multiple Levels of Manufacturing.

If we collapse PART TYPE and FINISHED PRODUCT TYPE into ASSET TYPE, the relationship between them becomes a many-to-many relationship between ASSET TYPE
and itself, as shown in Figure 4.8. That is, each ASSET TYPE may be now *composed of* one or more other ASSET TYPES. Similarly, each ASSET TYPE may be *part of*
one or more other ASSET TYPES.

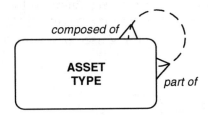

Figure 4.8: Asset Type Structure.

This model has a problem, however, both because the relationship is now
many-to-many, and because each ASSET TYPE's use in another ASSET TYPE itself
has attributes. Specifically, for each use of one ASSET TYPE in another, we want to
know the "quantity per"—the amount of the component that goes into the
assembly. This is not an attribute of either ASSET TYPE, but of the *usage* of one
ASSET TYPE in another.

To document each occurrence of an ASSET TYPE making use of another ASSET
TYPE, and to hold the missing usage attributes, we create another structure entity, like the GEOGRAPHIC STRUCTURE ELEMENT and REPORTING RELATIONSHIP of Chapter Three. This one we will call ASSET TYPE STRUCTURE ELEMENT, as shown in Figure 4.9. Each ASSET TYPE STRUCTURE ELEMENT must be *of* one ASSET TYPE *in* another
ASSET TYPE. Each ASSET TYPE, then, may be *a component in* one or more ASSET TYPE
STRUCTURE ELEMENTS, each of which is *in* one other ASSET TYPE. Similarly, each
ASSET TYPE may be *an assembly of* one or more ASSET TYPE STRUCTURE ELEMENTS,
each of which must be *of* another ASSET TYPE.

This means that an ASSET TYPE with twelve components will be *an assembly
of* twelve ASSET TYPE STRUCTURE ELEMENTS, each of which is *of* a different component ASSET TYPE. Similarly, an ASSET TYPE that is a component of four other ASSET
TYPES will be *a component in* four ASSET TYPE STRUCTURE ELEMENT occurrences,
each of which is *in* a different parent ASSET TYPE.

As mentioned above, the most important attribute of ASSET TYPE STRUCTURE
ELEMENT is "quantity per"—the quantity of the component (in the component's
unit of measure) required to make one unit of the assembly or parent ASSET TYPE
(in the parent's unit of measure). Additional attributes may include such
things as "scrap percent" (the percent of a component's usage that is typically
lost as scrap), "effective date," and so forth.

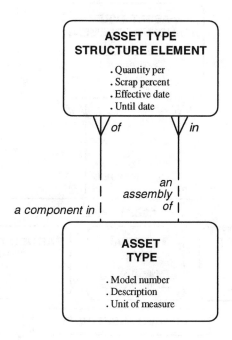

Figure 4.9: Asset Type Structure Element.

We have called this entity ASSET TYPE STRUCTURE ELEMENT because it refers to the structure of any ASSET TYPE, whatever it may be. In a discrete manufacturing environment, where ASSETS are called PRODUCTS, this entity could be called PRODUCT STRUCTURE ELEMENT.

This entity is analogous to a data file that is known commonly in the manufacturing world as the "product structure" file. The set of structures and ASSET TYPES describing all the components of an assembly is called a "bill of materials."

On the other hand, we can infer from Figure 4.10 that chemical manufacturers might call an ASSET TYPE STRUCTURE ELEMENT a MATERIAL STRUCTURE ELEMENT, and those concerned with maintenance might call it a PART/EQUIPMENT STRUCTURE ELEMENT.

Note that, as we saw when generalizing ORGANIZATION in Chapters Two and Three, generalizing here does lose any business rules about what kind of ASSETS can go into what other kinds of ASSETS, and it does not allow us explicitly to prevent "loops" (A is used in B, which is used in A). As with the ORGANIZATION example, any such business rules must be described outside the model.

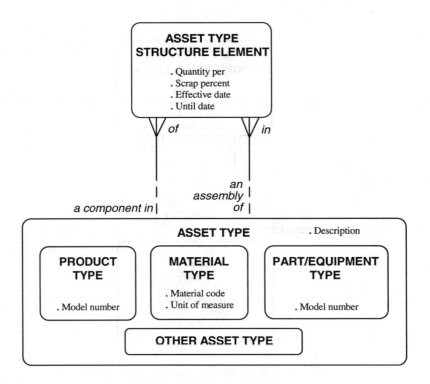

Figure 4.10: Structures of Many Things.

This approach to structure can describe relationships other than the components of ASSET TYPES. Other relationships may be defined for categories of ASSET TYPES. An ASSET TYPE RELATIONSHIP for an ASSET TYPE, for example, might show one of the following, as in Figure 4.11:

- an ASSET TYPE STRUCTURE ELEMENT, as just discussed, for any ASSET TYPE

- an ELECTRICAL CONNECTION between two PART/EQUIPMENT TYPES (as between a motor and a fuse box)

- a SAFETY CONNECTION between one PART/EQUIPMENT TYPE and any other PART/EQUIPMENT TYPE that must be turned off to work on it

- an INCOMPATIBILITY between two MATERIAL TYPES (see the discussion of material safety data sheets in Chapter Eleven)

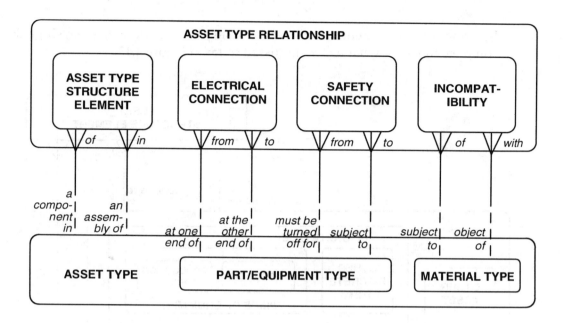

Figure 4.11: Other Connections.

Where an ASSET TYPE STRUCTURE ELEMENT defines the relationship between ASSET TYPES as designed, the relationships between real, physical objects are contained in ASSET STRUCTURE ELEMENT, as shown in Figure 4.12.

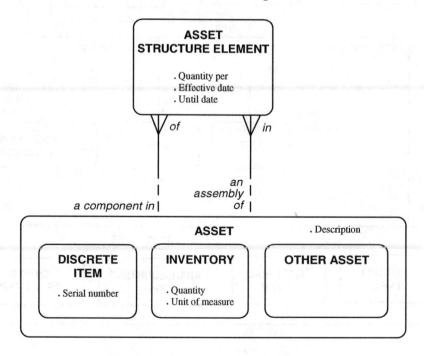

Figure 4.12: Asset Structure Elements.

Ignoring for the moment other kinds of ASSET TYPE RELATIONSHIPS, we show the complete model of what we've discussed so far in Figure 4.13.

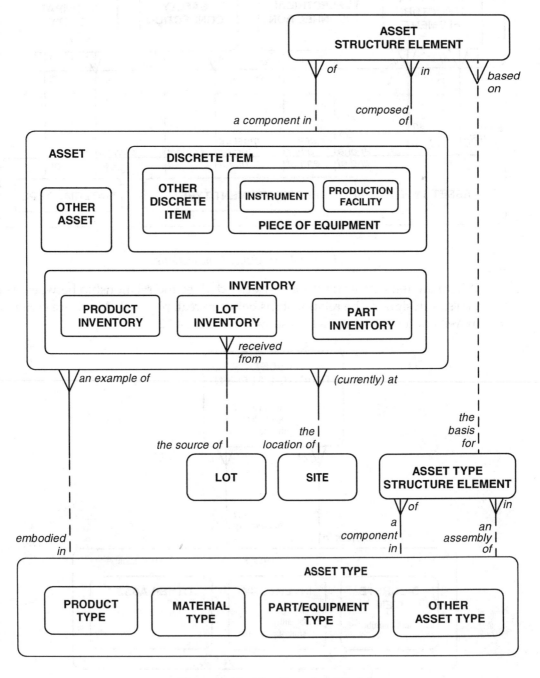

Figure 4.13: The Complete Model.

All physical things in the organization—DISCRETE ITEMS, INVENTORIES, or OTHER ASSETS, such as buildings or roads—are examples of ASSETS. The definition of each of these things exists as an ASSET TYPE. The fact that one specified ASSET TYPE is inherently part of another is an ASSET TYPE STRUCTURE ELEMENT, and the fact that one specified ASSET is actually part of another is an ASSET STRUCTURE ELEMENT. Note the connection between ASSET STRUCTURE ELEMENT and ASSET TYPE STRUCTURE ELEMENT. It is reasonable to assume that each ASSET STRUCTURE ELE- MENT is *based on* an ASSET TYPE STRUCTURE ELEMENT. Whether this is in fact so, however, depends upon your situation. In some cases, an actual ASSET STRUC- TURE ELEMENT *must be based on* an ASSET TYPE STRUCTURE ELEMENT. In other situa- tions, this is not required.

HETEROGENEOUS ENTITIES

An assumption in data modeling is that all occurrences of an entity have the same attributes. While individual occurrences may lack values for one or more attributes, the basic structure of the entity's information is expected to be the same for all.

The ASSET TYPE entity in many companies can bring this assumption into question, and dealing with it involves a modeling technique that is useful in many areas.

The problem is this: An ASSET TYPE may be of various kinds. In a power plant, for example, an ASSET TYPE might be a type of compressor, a kind of pipe segment, a brand of computer, or a type of instrument.

One way to represent this appears in Figure 4.14, which shows ASSET TYPE and ASSET TYPE CLASS (where an ASSET TYPE CLASS might be "pump," "compres- sor," "motor," and so forth). An ASSET TYPE CLASS is shown here to be *a classifi- cation for* one or more ASSET TYPES. In this case, ASSET TYPE CLASS is the category that defines the *characteristics* of the ASSET TYPE, so each ASSET TYPE must be *an example of* one and only one ASSET TYPE CLASS. Here, if new classes are needed, occurrences of ASSET TYPE CLASS are simply added. Subsequent occurrences of ASSET TYPE can then point to the new ASSET TYPE CLASS.

Unfortunately, in this model, all occurrences of ASSET TYPE must still have the same attributes—something that is unrealistic when dealing with pieces of pipe, gasoline, and sophisticated monitoring equipment. An alternative would be to model the situation as in Figure 4.15, where each subtype can have its own attributes. This is awkward, however, because new subtypes are being added all the time. With this, every time a new kind of ASSET TYPE is defined, the database derived from this model would have to be changed.

If neither of these approaches works, what can we do? The answer lies in making creative use of the ASSET TYPE CLASS from Figure 4.14. An ASSET TYPE CLASS is defined here to be the particular classification that groups ASSET TYPES into categories according to their characteristics, which in data terms are their *attributes.* With this definition, each ASSET TYPE is an embodiment of only *one*

ASSET TYPE CLASS. The SuperStar MP33/486, then, is in the ASSET TYPE CLASS "computers," since all computers have the same attributes (or at least the ones that concern us). Their being "Intel computers" or "beige computers" does not affect their attributes. All computers have "processor speed," "disk space," "RAM," and so forth. They don't have (or at least we don't care about) "length," "inside diameter," or "tensile strength," such as pieces of pipe might have.

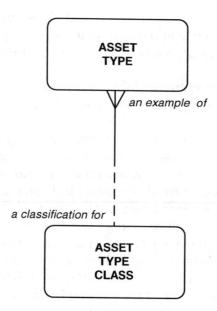

Figure 4.14: The Type Version.

In Figure 4.16, "pump" is an example of the entity ASSET TYPE CLASS, which is a *classification for* the "Jonesco Model 1650 pump."

A second part of the solution is to define an entity to contain definitions of all the ATTRIBUTES that might be used for any of the ASSET TYPES. Attributes of ATTRIBUTE include its name, format (whether it is character, numeric, or date), unit of measure, and optionally, default high and low legal values. The occurrences of this entity would include the "disk space" and "tensile strength" described above, as well as "capacity" in the pump example in Figure 4.16.

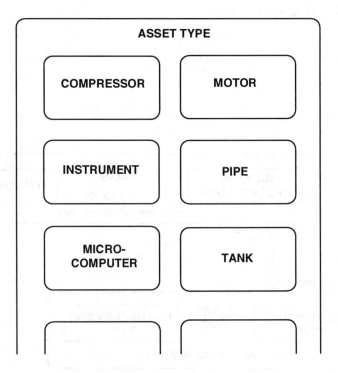

Figure 4.15: The Subtype Version.

Following this line of thought, an ATTRIBUTE ASSIGNMENT, then, is the fact that a particular ATTRIBUTE is appropriate to a particular ASSET TYPE CLASS. That is, each ATTRIBUTE ASSIGNMENT is *of* an ATTRIBUTE *to* an ASSET TYPE CLASS. Each ATTRIBUTE may be *subject to* one or more ATTRIBUTE ASSIGNMENTS, each of which is *to* an ASSET TYPE CLASS.

In the computer example above, we would have an ASSET ASSIGNMENT asserting that "disk capacity" is an attribute of "computer." Another would assert that "inside diameter" is an attribute of "pipe." In Figure 4.16, the ATTRIBUTE "capacity" is assigned to "pump."

Note that this assignment of attributes to classes does not presume that any ASSET TYPES actually exist in this ASSET TYPE CLASS. There don't have to be any actual computers or pumps. The set of ATTRIBUTE ASSIGNMENTS *to* an ASSET TYPE CLASS simply describes the format or "record layout" for all ASSET TYPES *in* that ASSET TYPE CLASS.

As mentioned, an ATTRIBUTE might be defined with limiting values ("default high value" and "default low value"), which would apply to any use of the attribute. In addition, ATTRIBUTE ASSIGNMENT might also include high and low values, which would specifically apply to this ATTRIBUTE'S use for this ASSET TYPE CLASS. That is, "capacity" might in all uses be between 0 and 100,000 gallons per minute, but when used to describe a pump, capacity can only be between 0 and 10,000 gallons per minute.

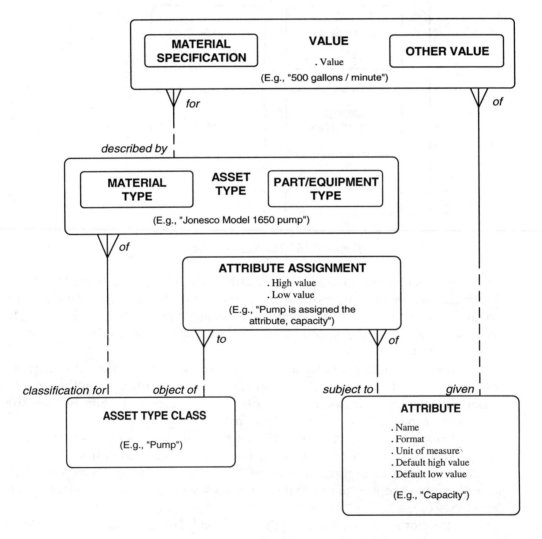

Figure 4.16: Asset Classes and Attributes.

Figure 4.16 also shows how a particular ASSET TYPE *of* this ASSET TYPE CLASS can then be *described by* VALUES for each ATTRIBUTE that is appropriate to the ASSET TYPE CLASS. For example, the "Jonesco Model 1650 pump" is *described by* a VALUE *of* the ATTRIBUTE "capacity," which in this example is "500 gallons/minute."

Of particular interest are the VALUES *of* each ATTRIBUTE *for* ASSET TYPES when the ASSET TYPES are MATERIAL TYPES. In this case, the VALUES *for* a MATERIAL TYPE constitute its MATERIAL SPECIFICATIONS, and the ATTRIBUTES *given* these values are the variables that will be measured to determine if a particular sample of material is indeed of that MATERIAL TYPE. This is discussed in detail in Chapters Eight (The Laboratory) and Ten (Process Manufacturing).

Figure 4.16 is an example of a *meta-model*—a model of models. That is, modeling elements are themselves things of significance to us. A meta-model provides such interesting things as an entity called ATTRIBUTE, which of course has attributes of its own. We will encounter more meta-models throughout the book.*

Note that the meta-model approach is very powerful as a way of describing complex data. In some cases, it is the only way to represent data accurately and cleanly. Note also, however, that data stored in this form are very difficult to retrieve. Instead of asking for the ASSET TYPES whose "capacity" is at least 300 gallons/minute, you must ask for the ASSET TYPES that are *described by* VALUES *of* the ATTRIBUTE "capacity," whose "value" (of VALUE, that is) is greater than 300 gallons/minute. Some would consider this to be unduly complicated. Typically, systems derived from such a model use it as the basis for design of the database that will gather and maintain the data, but add to the system a provision for extracting the data and storing it for retrieval in tables structured in a more familiar way.

For example, data could be extracted into a set of tables in which a separate table is defined for each ASSET TYPE CLASS, and an occurrence of each table is an ASSET TYPE. Previously, we didn't want to do that because of the resultant need to add and delete tables as the list of ASSET TYPES changes. With this model, however, we can automate the process of generating the tables themselves from the meta-model.

A VARIATION

The examples we've seen so far in this chapter are from manufacturing companies. Even though there are variations between, say, a manufacturer of pencils and one that produces heavy equipment, we have seen fundamental similarities in the descriptions of the things all manufacturers make and use.

---

* Coming soon: an attribute called "entity."

It turns out that these similarities extend beyond the world of manufacturing. A bank, for example, deals with ACCOUNTS. These are the *products* of a bank, and while the bank does not consume raw materials to produce them, the structure of the bank model looks remarkably similar in other ways to our manufacturing model. In particular, the bank has the problem we described above, where different product types (ACCOUNT TYPE) have different attributes (PARAMETERS). The resulting model, then, as shown in Figure 4.17 with parameters, parameter assignments, and values, looks remarkably like the manufacturing model of Figure 4.16.

Chapter Eleven will extend this model further.

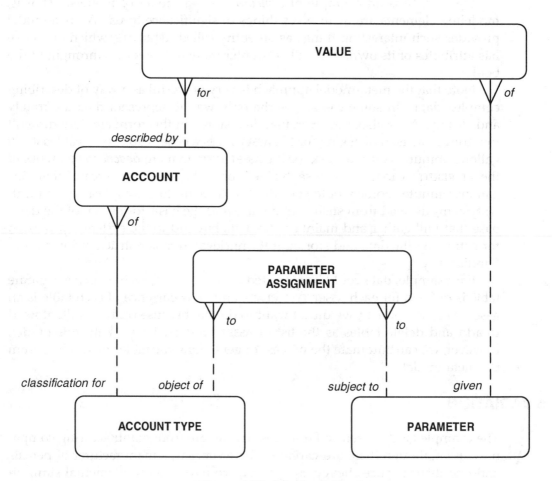

Figure 4.17: The Bank Version.

So, whatever the things an organization manipulates, the entity or entities describing them can be placed along the bottom of the drawing. This may be a single pair of entities describing ASSET and ASSET TYPE (or PRODUCT and PRODUCT

TYPE, or even ACCOUNT and ACCOUNT TYPE), or it may be a more complex construction to accommodate variations in the structure of these things. Whatever the particulars, virtually every organization will have need to model the objects of its efforts.

REFERENCES

1   International Standards Organization, "Quality management and quality system elements—part 1: Guidelines," ISO 9004-1:1994(E), p. 2.

5
PROCEDURES AND ACTIVITIES

*A*n organization must do something. A manufacturing company must make its products and maintain its equipment. If a company provides services for hire, those services are the activities of the company. A major task of the organization, then, is the planning, scheduling, and recording of activities undertaken, procedures followed, and services rendered.

This chapter will model these services, procedures, and activities. It describes internal activities and work orders, along with the consumption of labor and materials by those activities and work orders. It also discusses the similarities among and differences between various kinds of work orders—those for maintenance, production, project management, and responses to safety incidents.

SOME DEFINITIONS

Understand, by the way, that when we model actions as entities, it is not the same thing as modeling actions as functions. Rather than using the model to describe the nature of what is being done, we can use it to show that activities, procedures, and services are themselves things of significance to the business, and that they are related as things to other things. For example, these activities, procedures, and services may be related to the people, organizations, and products discussed in the previous two chapters.

Our goal in this chapter is not so much to describe the actions themselves, but to identify the data required to describe them.

As was the case with products, it is necessary to distinguish the *definition* of a service or procedure from *examples* of it. The definitions are represented by an entity that may variously be called SERVICE, ACTIVITY TYPE, or PROCEDURE. If the activity is sold to the outside, it is probably called SERVICE. If it is simply something done internally as part of doing business, it is a PROCEDURE. If the focus is on project management, it may be called more abstractly ACTIVITY TYPE. All three of these names refer to the definition of a set of steps that constitute a task. Attributes include "description," "expected duration," and so forth. For most of this chapter, we'll call the entity a PROCEDURE, but the other names would work as well.

The actual carrying out of a PROCEDURE is an ACTIVITY. Important attributes of an ACTIVITY are "scheduled start date," "scheduled end date," "actual start date," and so forth.

Figure 5.1 shows that an ACTIVITY may be *to carry out* a PROCEDURE, while a PROCEDURE may be *implemented in* one or more actual ACTIVITIES. This figure depicts an organization interested in keeping track of impromptu ACTIVITIES— as well as ones that are the execution of predefined PROCEDURES. If the *only* ACTIVITIES of interest were those *to carry out* predefined PROCEDURES, the diagram would have to be changed to show a solid line coming from ACTIVITY. That is, in some organizations, it might be more accurate to assert that each ACTIVITY *must be to carry out* a PROCEDURE.

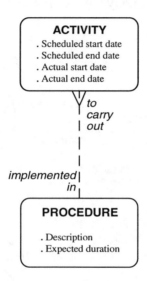

Figure 5.1: Activities and Procedures.

DIVIDING ACTIVITIES

Figure 5.2 shows two other aspects of activities: First, the steps that constitute the PROCEDURE may be called occurrences of PROCEDURE STEP, while the actual steps performed when the activity is carried out are occurrences of ACTIVITY STEP. That is, each ACTIVITY may be *composed of* one or more ACTIVITY STEPS, and each PROCEDURE may be *composed of* one or more PROCEDURE STEPS.

This is suitable when procedures and activities are clearly defined for only one level. When procedures or activities are divided into steps that are then divided further into substeps, and so forth, a second approach is needed, which is to divide each PROCEDURE into smaller PROCEDURES and each ACTIVITY into smaller ACTIVITIES. In Figure 5.2, for example, the pig's ear symbol on ACTIVITY shows that an ACTIVITY may be *composed of* one or more other ACTIVITIES, each of which in turn may be *composed of* yet more ACTIVITIES, and so forth. A project (ACTIVITY) to build a house, for example, includes an ACTIVITY to lay the foundation, which may in turn encompass the ACTIVITIES of surveying the ground, putting in footings, and so forth. When it is modeled this way, the process can be extended indefinitely.

An ACTIVITY, then, *either* may be *composed of* one or more ACTIVITY STEPS (as described above) *or* may be *composed of* one or more other ACTIVITIES.

A corresponding pig's ear appears on PROCEDURE, showing that a PROCEDURE also *either* may be *composed of* one or more PROCEDURE STEPS, *or* may be *composed of* one or more other PROCEDURES. These component PROCEDURES may be broken down into successively smaller PROCEDURES. This way of breaking things down into progressively smaller pieces is shown in Figure 5.2.

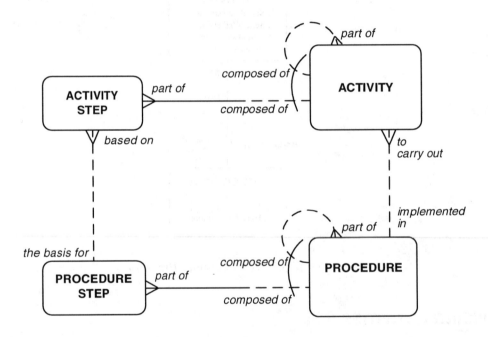

Figure 5.2: Dividing Activities.

Note that in Figure 5.2, if an ACTIVITY is *to carry out* a PROCEDURE, it is reasonable to expect that an ACTIVITY STEP may be *based on* a corresponding PROCEDURE STEP. That is, the structure of a one-time activity may be derived from the permanent structure of the procedure it is implementing. Whether this is in fact so will depend on actual circumstances.

A more compact way of showing this same configuration appears in Figure 5.3. In this drawing, an ACTIVITY STEP is a subtype of ACTIVITY, and PROCEDURE STEP is a subtype of PROCEDURE. Thus, each OTHER PROCEDURE may be *composed of* one or more PROCEDURES (either PROCEDURE STEPS or OTHER PROCEDURES), and each OTHER ACTIVITY may be *composed of* one or more ACTIVITIES (either ACTIVITY

STEPS or OTHER ACTIVITIES). This configuration allows each structure to go down as many levels as necessary. PROCEDURE STEP and ACTIVITY STEP are not required, but if they are specified, they can only be at the bottom of each respective structure.

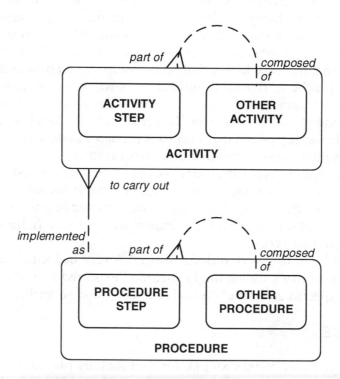

Figure 5.3: A More Compact Way to Divide Activities.

In Figure 5.3, we are asserting that each ACTIVITY (ACTIVITY STEP or OTHER ACTIVITY) may be *part of one and only one* OTHER ACTIVITY. Similarly, each PROCEDURE (PROCEDURE STEP or OTHER PROCEDURE) may be *part of one and only one* OTHER PROCEDURE. In your organization, this may be true—but then again, it may not be. It is conceivable that a PROCEDURE STEP (such as "assemble the framis") might be part of *more than one* larger procedure (such as "fix the scrope" and "calibrate the flim-flam rods"). In that case, the *part of/composed of* relationships in Figures 5.2 and 5.3 would be "many-to-many," requiring the addition of intersect entities. This would be a "structure" entity, such as the GEOGRAPHIC STRUCTURE ELEMENT discussed in Chapter Three, or the ASSET TYPE STRUCTURE ELEMENT in Chapter Four. This is less common than the one-to-many version, however, so we shall not pursue it here.

WORK ORDERS

While the work to be done is represented by ACTIVITIES and PROCEDURES, sponsorship of the work is represented by the entity WORK ORDER. (See Figure 5.4.) That is, a WORK ORDER is usually embodied in a document authorizing work to be done—the ACTIVITIES. A WORK ORDER may be *the authorization for* one or more ACTIVITIES. Note, however, that in some organizations, an activity may be carried out without being authorized by a work order. Hence, the relationship that each ACTIVITY *may be authorized by* one WORK ORDER. You will have to decide in your organization whether that relationship should be mandatory.

As with the ACTIVITIES it authorizes, a WORK ORDER may be *composed of* smaller WORK ORDERS, before ACTIVITIES are assigned to it. A WORK ORDER must be *the responsibility of* someone (usually a PERSON, but it could be an ORGANIZATION, so the relationship points to PARTY). It is probably *prepared by* a PERSON as well.

The authorization embodied in a WORK ORDER is exercised to fulfill the WORK ORDER'S purpose. Typically, the WORK ORDER may be defined *to carry out* one or more PROCEDURES, *to make* an ASSET TYPE, or *to fix, install, remove, or inspect* a specific PIECE OF EQUIPMENT. A PROCEDURE *implemented by* a WORK ORDER may itself be defined *to fix, install, remove, or inspect* an ASSET TYPE (which is most likely a PART/EQUIPMENT TYPE).

In addition to "work order number," "order quantity," and "order date," attributes of WORK ORDER might include "expected start date," "actual start date," "expected end date," "actual end date," and so forth.

LABOR USAGE

PEOPLE (and ORGANIZATIONS too, for that matter) play different roles in both individual ACTIVITIES and WORK ORDERS as a whole. These could be administrative roles (such as project secretary), or technical roles (such as chief engineer). There are several ways to represent this, as shown in Figure 5.5: A PARTY may be *given* one or more WORK ORDER ROLES *in* a WORK ORDER. Each WORK ORDER ROLE, then, is *played by* a PARTY *in* a WORK ORDER. Each WORK ORDER ROLE must be *defined by* a WORK ORDER ROLE TYPE, such as "project manager."

Alternatively, as the ACTIVITIES within a WORK ORDER are being planned, a PARTY could be *given* a specific ACTIVITY ASSIGNMENT *to* an ACTIVITY (an ACTIVITY STEP or an OTHER ACTIVITY). Each ACTIVITY ASSIGNMENT, then, is *of* a PARTY *to* an ACTIVITY. Each ACTIVITY ASSIGNMENT must be *defined by* an ACTIVITY ASSIGNMENT TYPE, such as "statistician."

In most cases, these WORK ORDER ROLES and ACTIVITY ASSIGNMENTS will be about a PERSON. ORGANIZATIONS (such as subcontractors) can also participate in WORK ORDERS and ACTIVITIES, however. So, the more conservative approach is to link WORK ORDER ROLES and ACTIVITY ASSIGNMENTS to PARTY, as is depicted in Figure 5.5.

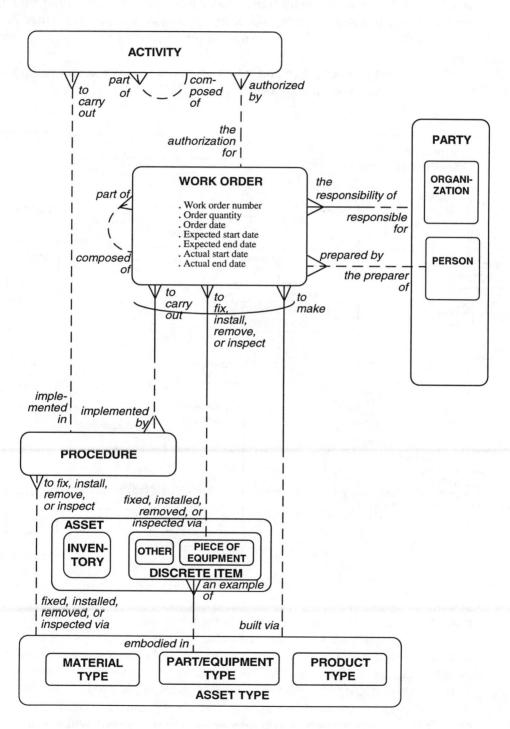

Figure 5.4: Work Orders.

The difference between a WORK ORDER ROLE and an ACTIVITY ASSIGNMENT is that WORK ORDER ROLE has the connotation that a PARTY will do something throughout the life of the WORK ORDER. An ACTIVITY ASSIGNMENT, on the other hand, describes the fact that a PARTY performs a set of actions for a single ACTIVITY only.

Both ACTIVITY ASSIGNMENT and WORK ORDER ROLE have such attributes as "start date," "end date," and so forth.

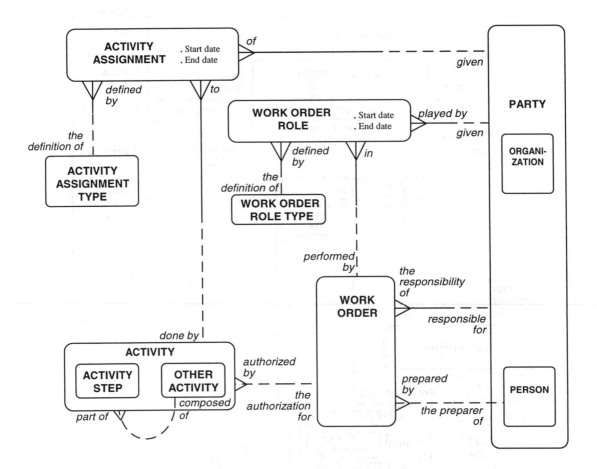

Figure 5.5: Roles and Assignments.

If roles and assignments are used to *plan* for labor usage, TIME SHEET ENTRY is the mechanism we'll use to record the *actual* hours worked by a PERSON and *charged to* either a WORK ORDER ROLE, a WORK ORDER (without a preassigned WORK ORDER ROLE), an ACTIVITY ASSIGNMENT, or an ACTIVITY (where there was not an ACTIVITY ASSIGNMENT). For the sake of this example, we will assert that TIME SHEET ENTRIES are *submitted by* a PERSON, not a PARTY, since normally that is the case. It is not impossible that you may encounter a situation where time sheets are submitted by an organization, but this is rare.

The primary attribute of interest in a TIME SHEET ENTRY is "hours worked," *submitted by* the PERSON, *charged to* the ACTIVITY, WORK ORDER, or whatever.

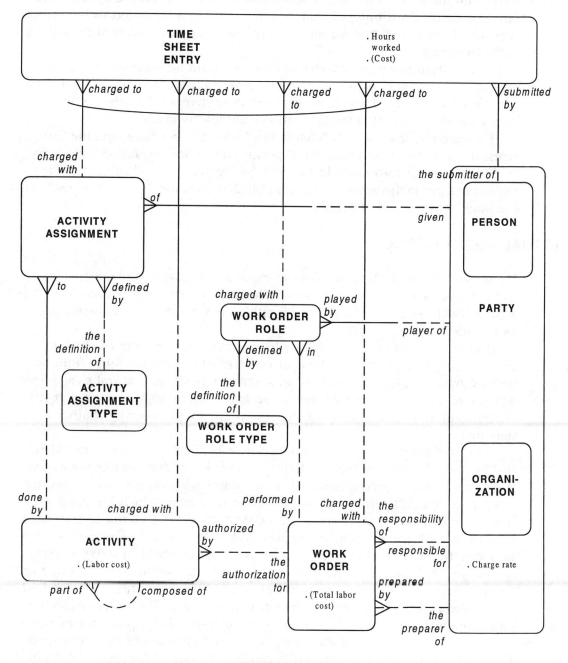

Figure 5.6: Time Sheets.

If "charge rate" is an attribute of the PERSON submitting a TIME SHEET ENTRY, this can be multiplied by the "hours worked" shown on it to arrive at the "cost," a derived attribute of that TIME SHEET ENTRY. (Note that on the diagrams, derived attributes are shown in parentheses.) The sum of these for all TIME SHEET ENTRIES for the ACTIVITY (or ACTIVITY ASSIGNMENT, or whatever) is the "labor cost" (another derived attribute) of that ACTIVITY. This can be added to the "labor cost" of all other ACTIVITIES for the WORK ORDER, in order to arrive at the latter's "total labor cost."

Obviously, if there are ACTIVITY STEPS, they would be summarized into their ACTIVITY'S "labor cost" before being made part of the WORK ORDER'S "total labor cost." Alternatively, if the TIME SHEET ENTRY is charged directly to the WORK ORDER, the ACTIVITY part of the calculation would be bypassed.

For example, if a PERSON'S "charge rate" were $35 per hour, and the "hours worked" in a TIME SHEET ENTRY for a specific WORK ORDER were "28," the "cost" of that TIME SHEET ENTRY would be $980. If the "cost" of all other TIME SHEET ENTRIES *charged to* the WORK ORDER were $10,270, then the "total labor cost" for the WORK ORDER would be $11,250.

ACTUAL ASSET USAGE

If TIME SHEET ENTRY is the labor time spent on a WORK ORDER, the materials used in the WORK ORDER are recorded in ACTUAL ASSET USAGE. (See Figure 5.7.) An ACTUAL ASSET USAGE may be *charged to* either an ACTIVITY or to the WORK ORDER as a whole.

The ACTUAL ASSET USAGE may be either *of* an identified ASSET (such as a particular PIECE OF EQUIPMENT—a kind of DISCRETE ITEM—or something from PART INVENTORY), or it may be simply *of* an ASSET TYPE (such as "natural gas"). The ACTUAL ASSET USAGE must be *expressed in* a UNIT OF MEASURE, even if it is "each"—the unit of measure for items that are simply counted, rather than measured.

That is, if the part used is a major subassembly (a PIECE OF EQUIPMENT identified by a serial number), then ACTUAL ASSET USAGE is *of* that PIECE OF EQUIPMENT. If the part used is a product that is kept in quantity in PART INVENTORY, then the ACTUAL ASSET USAGE will be *of* the PART INVENTORY from which the parts were drawn. In both cases, ASSET defines the ASSET TYPE and SITE. If the ACTUAL ASSET USAGE is of a generic material, not kept in INVENTORY (such as natural gas from a tap), then the ACTUAL ASSET USAGE is *of* an ASSET TYPE (probably a MATERIAL TYPE).

In any of these cases, the unit cost of the item used is defined either as "actual unit cost" (an attribute of ASSET), or as either "list price" or "standard cost" (one of which would be an attribute of ASSET TYPE). This unit cost can then be multiplied by the "quantity" used in the corresponding occurrence of ACTUAL ASSET USAGE, to arrive at the "cost," a derived attribute of that occurrence. The "cost" of all ACTUAL ASSET USAGES can then be added together to compute the "total material cost" of the ACTIVITY (a derived attribute), which in turn may be summed across ACTIVITIES to arrive at the derived attribute of the WORK ORDER "total material cost."

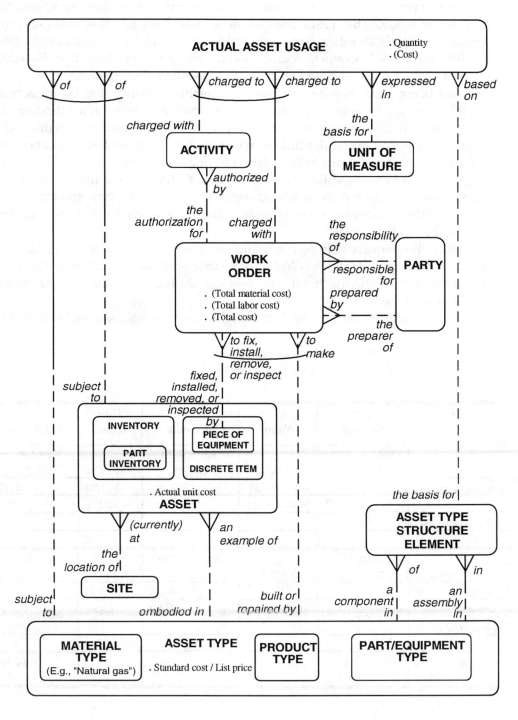

Figure 5.7: Actual Asset Usage.

As an example of these calculations, consider an ACTUAL ASSET USAGE of the MATERIAL TYPE "Whimsite" in which the "quantity" (in pounds) is 30 and the "list price" is $23. The "cost," then, of the ACTUAL ASSET USAGE is $690 ($23 multiplied by 30). If all other ACTUAL ASSET USAGES charged to a WORK ORDER total $6,024, then the WORK ORDER "total material cost" is $6,714. Note that the ACTUAL ASSET USAGE may be *based on* an ASSET TYPE STRUCTURE ELEMENT; that is, the product being used may be one that was specified. Policy (the business rule) on this will vary from company to company and from situation to situation. In some cases, it may be required that no product can be used in a work order unless it is specified in the bill of materials for the item being worked on. ("Each ACTUAL ASSET USAGE *must be based on* one ASSET TYPE STRUCTURE ELEMENT." Figure 5.7 could be modified to show this by adding a solid line in the upper half of the relationship from ACTUAL ASSET USAGE to ASSET TYPE STRUCTURE ELEMENT.) Other situations may be more relaxed, as is shown with a complete dashed line in Figure 5.7.

Note the parallel between this and the way a WORK ORDER'S "total labor cost" was computed, above. With "total labor cost" and "total material cost," we can now compute the "total cost" (another derived attribute of WORK ORDER) as the sum of the two.

To take an example, a WORK ORDER might incur the costs shown in Table 5.1:

Table 5.1.
Cost Calculations.

	Entry Number	Name	Quantity	Unit Cost	Total Cost
(Entity)	TIME SHEET ENTRY	PERSON	TIME SHEET ENTRY	PERSON	WORK ORDER
Time sheet entries	1	Joe (9/13)	10 hours	$11/hr	$110
	2	Sam (9/14)	4 hours	$20/hr	$80
(Total labor cost)					$190
(Entity)	ACTUAL ASSET USAGE	ASSET	ACTUAL ASSET USAGE	ASSET	WORK ORDER
Actual asset usage	1	Goo	4 lbs	$75/lb	$300
	2	Stuff	20 kg	$15/kg	$300
(Total material cost)					$600
(Total cost of work order)					$790

Asset Structure

In Figure 4.12 and its accompanying text, the ASSET STRUCTURE ELEMENT was defined as the fact that one ASSET is a component of another ASSET. A modified version of this is reproduced as part of Figure 5.8.

Note that if you draw a line from DISCRETE ITEM through WORK ORDER and then through ACTUAL ASSET USAGE to ASSET, this cycle is functionally equivalent to the ASSET STRUCTURE ELEMENT. That is, the fact that a WORK ORDER *to fix, install, remove, or inspect* a DISCRETE ITEM (an ASSET) may be *charged with* an ACTUAL ASSET USAGE *of* another ASSET, describes the fact that the second ASSET may be *a component in* an ASSET STRUCTURE ELEMENT that is *in* the first ASSET (in this case, a DISCRETE ITEM). The only difference is that the WORK ORDER/ACTUAL ASSET USAGE combination describes the *act of installing* the component (including the date done and any labor used, for example) not just its physical presence.

The ASSET STRUCTURE ELEMENT does allow for the description of the composition of INVENTORY, which the WORK ORDER/ACTUAL ASSET USAGE configuration does not.

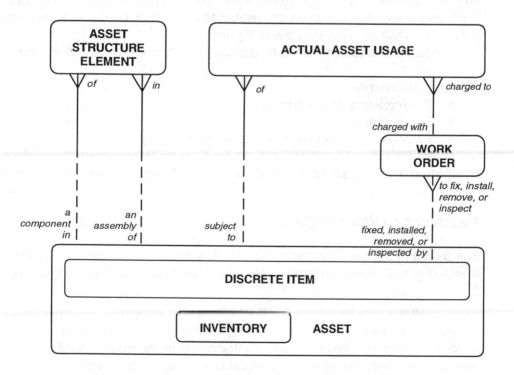

Figure 5.8: Asset Structures.

KINDS OF WORK ORDERS

Different kinds of WORK ORDERS are used to produce different kinds of things. For this reason, their models are not identical. They are very similar, however. A MAINTENANCE WORK ORDER, for example, produces working equipment. A PRODUCTION ORDER produces a product or quantity of material for sale. A PROJECT produces a building or other large-scale result. A WORK ORDER may also be issued to respond to an accident or some other safety incident. It is possible to imagine other kinds of WORK ORDERS as well.

These differences may be seen in the models that follow: a MAINTENANCE WORK ORDER is *to fix, install, remove, or inspect* a DISCRETE ITEM. (See Figure 5.9.) A PRODUCTION ORDER, on the other hand, is *to make* an ASSET TYPE, resulting in one or more PRODUCTION DELIVERIES either *of* a DISCRETE ITEM or *of* an INVENTORY (see Figure 5.10). In addition, it is usually of interest to keep track of a PRODUCTION ORDER through a plant, from WORK CENTER to WORK CENTER, while a MAINTENANCE WORK ORDER usually is not kept track of the same way. A PROJECT (such as a construction project), like a PRODUCTION ORDER, also makes something, but there is not necessarily an ASSET TYPE describing it in advance, and it is not usually as concerned with the progression of work from WORK CENTER to WORK CENTER.* Its view of the way tasks are related to each other, however, is more complex, as we shall see when we get to Figure 5.13.

The kinds of WORK ORDERS to be discussed in the following sections are

- Maintenance
- Production (manufacturing)
- Large projects
- Emergency (responses to safety incidents)

In addition, Chapter Six will describe services offered to customers under contract.

Maintenance Work Orders

The model of MAINTENANCE WORK ORDERS is similar in structure to what we've seen so far, with some variations. Usually drawn up either to fix something, or

---

* Construction companies do not, for example, usually list "Empire State Building" or "Brooklyn Bridge" in their catalogues. There are trends toward offering standardized structures, however. Modular housing, for example, is making the process of building houses more factory-like, with the customer selecting a favorite model from a catalogue. Indeed, some companies are working on designs for standardized power plants, so that many safety issues can be resolved once for the design, and only site-specific ones have to be addressed when the plant is built.

to prevent it from failing, a MAINTENANCE WORK ORDER may also be used to order the installation or removal of something, or to respond to an emergency. Figure 5.9 shows how, as with other WORK ORDERS, each MAINTENANCE WORK ORDER may be *to carry out* a single PROCEDURE or may be *the authorization for* one or more ACTIVITIES, each of which is *to carry out* a PROCEDURE. There are four types of MAINTENANCE WORK ORDERS: inspections, predictive maintenance work orders, emergency work orders, and preventive maintenance work orders.

The first of these is a WORK ORDER to authorize an INSPECTION—a diagnostic examination of a PIECE OF EQUIPMENT. An INSPECTION will probably require some labor time (TIME SHEET ENTRIES), but usually no ACTUAL ASSET USAGE. An INSPECTION may be *the trigger of* one or more PREDICTIVE WORK ORDERS.

The second type, a PREDICTIVE WORK ORDER, is issued to resolve a potential problem that has been diagnosed from an INSPECTION. That is, measurements taken from a PIECE OF EQUIPMENT may indicate that a particular part is wearing out and is due for replacement. Each PREDICTIVE WORK ORDER must be *triggered by* an INSPECTION.

An EMERGENCY WORK ORDER is the third kind of MAINTENANCE WORK ORDER. It is issued when something in the plant fails. It is the authorization to fix whatever is broken—and do it quickly! It is usually *initiated by* a call from a PERSON. Key attributes are "problem description" and "disposition." In this case, the PROCEDURES that are *implemented in* the EMERGENCY WORK ORDER are emergency procedures set up to deal with dangerous situations. EMERGENCY WORK ORDERS are discussed further in the discussion of safety-related incidents, below.

The fourth type, a PREVENTIVE MAINTENANCE WORK ORDER, authorizes work to be performed according to a schedule (every three months or every six months, for example). Like other MAINTENANCE WORK ORDERS, it is *the authorization for* one or more ACTIVITIES, each the execution of a particular PROCEDURE. Each PROCEDURE *implemented in* a PREVENTIVE MAINTENANCE WORK ORDER,* however, must have the attribute "cycle time"—the time expected between occurrences of the work. "Scheduled start date," an attribute of MAINTENANCE WORK ORDER, has special significance: Typically, the next PREVENTIVE MAINTENANCE WORK ORDER will be set up when the current one is completed, with the "scheduled start date" set to the "actual end date" of the last PREVENTIVE MAINTENANCE WORK ORDER, plus the "cycle time" of the PROCEDURES the MAINTENANCE WORK ORDER is to carry out.

As with other WORK ORDERS, MAINTENANCE WORK ORDERS may be *charged with* ACTUAL ASSET USAGES, and may be *charged with* TIME SHEET ENTRIES. "Total material cost," "total labor cost," and "total cost" may be derived as previously described and portrayed in Figures 5.6 and 5.7.

---

* That is, "each PROCEDURE *implemented in* an ACTIVITY *authorized by* a PREVENTIVE MAINTENANCE WORK ORDER . . ."

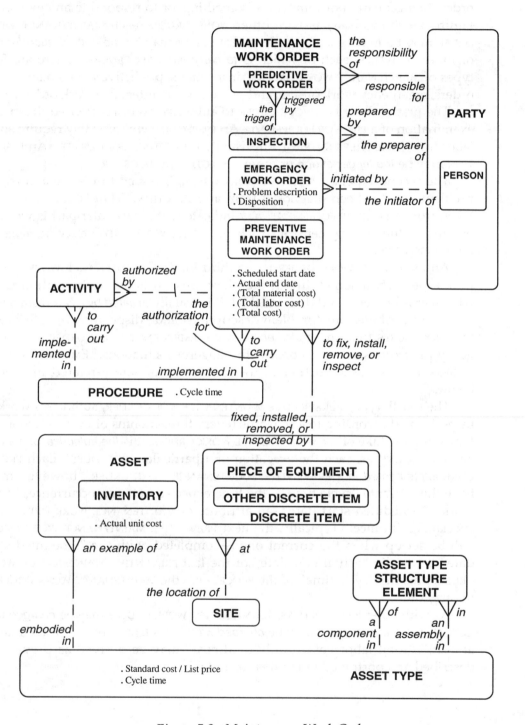

Figure 5.9: Maintenance Work Orders.

Production Orders

When the work to be done is the manufacture of a company's products, the model changes somewhat, although it retains much of the same pattern as that for maintenance.

The two primary differences between MAINTENANCE WORK ORDERS and PRODUCTION ORDERS concern the objectives of the effort, and the return of SITE, which we introduced in Chapter Three. Some names change as well.

In Figure 5.10, we've renamed WORK ORDER to PRODUCTION ORDER, and its objective, instead of being *to fix, install, remove, or inspect* a PIECE OF EQUIPMENT, is *to make* an ASSET TYPE. Upon completion, a PRODUCTION ORDER may be *the source of* one or more PRODUCTION DELIVERIES *of* an ASSET. The PRODUCTION ORDER might produce DISCRETE ITEMS or additions to INVENTORY.

To better reflect the language of the typical manufacturing plant, we have taken modeler's license and changed the name of ACTIVITY to MANUFACTURING STEP, and extended the basic model to show where each step will be performed in the plant. In the model of MAINTENANCE WORK ORDERS, the SITE of each activity is present only as the location of the DISCRETE ITEM being worked on. It may be included on the model, but it often is not required. With PRODUCTION ORDERS, however, the SITE becomes more important. In particular, a category of SITE, the WORK CENTER, is a manufacturing point in the factory.*

Actually, the organization being modeled will determine whether this is true. In some plants, WORK CENTERS may not be important. The plant also determines whether a MANUFACTURING STEP *must be to carry out* a predefined PROCEDURE. In highly controlled industries like pharmaceuticals, this would be so, but in others, the knowledge of a craftsman, rather than published procedures, may be the source of the step. Figure 5.10 takes this more craft-oriented view that each MANUFACTURING STEP *may be to carry out* a PROCEDURE.

Normally, the manufacturing sequence is defined in advance, in terms of the WORK CENTERS that a PRODUCTION ORDER must visit. The fact that an ASSET TYPE is normally processed in a particular WORK CENTER is called a ROUTING STEP. That is, each ROUTING STEP must be *to make* a particular ASSET TYPE, and this takes place *at* a particular WORK CENTER. This ROUTING STEP then may be *the basis for* one or more actual MANUFACTURING STEPS that are *part of* PRODUCTION ORDERS. Figure 5.10 shows this. For example, in the manufacture of a batch of printer's ink, a routing step places the batch of #10 blue in vessel 23. The first manufacturing step is to combine ingredients; the second is to stir for twenty minutes; and so forth.

---

* Note that WORK CENTER may be *the location of* one or more specific PIECES OF EQUIPMENT, which may in turn be *fixed, installed, removed, or inspected by* the MAINTENANCE WORK ORDERS discussed previously.

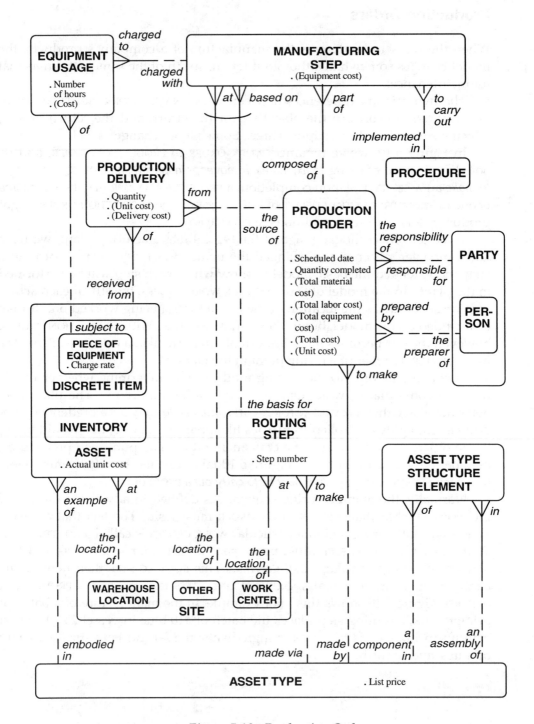

Figure 5.10: Production Orders.

A more sophisticated model than that shown would group ROUTING STEPS into ROUTINGS, so that each ASSET TYPE may be *made via* one or more ROUTINGS (sets of ROUTING STEPS), each of which is *composed of* one or more ROUTING STEPS. This allows for alternative ROUTINGS for building the same product. In either case, the same ASSET TYPE may be made in more than one WORK CENTER as alternatives, rather than as a sequence of steps. This could be controlled by assigning the same "step number" to multiple ROUTING STEPS.

Each MANUFACTURING STEP, then, either must be *at* a SITE (usually a WORK CENTER, but in some companies, it is conceivable that larger SITES may have to be identified), or it must be *based on* a ROUTING STEP (that identifies a WORK CENTER/SITE).

As with MAINTENANCE WORK ORDERS, labor usage by a PRODUCTION ORDER may be recorded via TIME SHEET ENTRIES, charged to either individual MANUFACTURING STEPS, or to the PRODUCTION ORDER as a whole. Calculation of "total labor cost" for the PRODUCTION ORDER is then done as was shown in Figure 5.6. In most organizations, however, production roles need not be defined in advance, so the WORK ORDER ROLE entity usually disappears from the production model. ACTIVITY ASSIGNMENTS could be appropriate in certain manufacturing environments, but, to keep the diagram manageable, this entity and TIME SHEET ENTRY have been left off Figure 5.10. (See them in Figure 5.6.)

A PRODUCTION ORDER certainly consumes raw materials. When we model a manufacturing plant, we may rename ACTUAL ASSET USAGE (shown back in Figure 5.7) as ACTUAL PART USAGE or ACTUAL MATERIAL USAGE, depending on what is being manufactured. Structurally, however, the ACTUAL...USAGE remains as described earlier. Consumption may be recorded for individual MANUFACTURING STEPS or for the PRODUCTION ORDER as a whole. That is, each ACTUAL ASSET USAGE must be either charged to one and only one PRODUCTION ORDER, or charged to one and only one MANUFACTURING STEP. Since the calculation of "total material cost" for the PRODUCTION ORDER is shown in Figure 5.7, it has been left off Figure 5.10.

As before, consumption may be recorded either of a physical ASSET—a DISCRETE ITEM or a quantity from INVENTORY—or of a quantity of unspecified products described as an ASSET TYPE (such as natural gas).

In addition to the consumption of labor and materials, MANUFACTURING STEPS in a PRODUCTION ORDER may also explicitly make use of one or more PIECES OF EQUIPMENT. Since each PIECE OF EQUIPMENT may also be used in one or more MANUFACTURING STEPS, it is necessary to define the entity EQUIPMENT USAGE. This enhancement is shown in Figure 5.10, where the diagram shows EQUIPMENT USAGE as the fact that a particular PIECE OF EQUIPMENT has been used in a particular MANUFACTURING STEP. That is, each MANUFACTURING STEP may be *charged with* one or more EQUIPMENT USAGES, each of which is *of* a particular PIECE OF EQUIPMENT. Conversely, each PIECE OF EQUIPMENT may be *subject to* one or more EQUIPMENT USAGES, where each of these must be *charged to* a MANUFACTURING STEP.

The cost of EQUIPMENT USAGE may be calculated the same way other costs are calculated: On Figure 5.10, the "charge rate" for a PIECE OF EQUIPMENT is multiplied by the "number of hours" of its EQUIPMENT USAGE, to produce a "cost" of the EQUIPMENT USAGE. The "cost" of all EQUIPMENT USAGES for a MANUFACTURING STEP can then be added together to produce the "equipment cost" for that MANUFACTURING STEP. Adding together the "equipment cost" for all MANUFACTURING STEPS in a PRODUCTION ORDER gives the "total equipment cost" for the PRODUCTION ORDER.

As an example, if 2 hours on a device ("number of hours" of EQUIPMENT USAGE) are used at $55 per hour ("charge rate" of PIECE OF EQUIPMENT), then "cost" for the EQUIPMENT USAGE is $110. If the sum of all other EQUIPMENT USAGES for this MANUFACTURING STEP were $3,100, the "equipment cost" for the MANUFACTURING STEP would be $3,210. If the cost of all other MANUFACTURING STEPS for this PRODUCTION ORDER were $10,450, then the "total equipment cost" for the PRODUCTION ORDER would be $13,660.

The "total cost" of the PRODUCTION ORDER, then (and by extension, of other kinds of WORK ORDERS as well), has now been expanded to the sum of "total labor cost," "total material cost," and "total equipment cost." The "unit cost" of the PRODUCTION (or other WORK) ORDER is the "total cost" divided by the "quantity completed." If the "total cost" of the PRODUCTION ORDER is $15,000 and the "quantity completed" is 1,000 units, then the "unit cost" is $15.

The example that was presented in Table 5.1 is expanded in Table 5.2 to include this calculation of equipment usage and the delivery cost.

Note that EQUIPMENT USAGE refers to the use of a PIECE OF EQUIPMENT in the production process, not to its inclusion in the finished product, as is implied by ACTUAL ASSET USAGE. The two could be combined, however, if this distinction is not important. In that case, "number of hours" would be renamed something more generic, like "quantity," and "unit of measure" ("hours" or "pieces") would have to be added as an attribute, to qualify the "quantity."

While a PRODUCTION ORDER makes something according to the specifications of an ASSET TYPE, it actually *delivers* ASSETS. That is, it is *the source of* one or more PRODUCTION DELIVERIES *of* an ASSET. (This was shown in Figure 5.10.) Each PRODUCTION DELIVERY is *of* an ASSET *from* a PRODUCTION ORDER. It is the nature of the plant and the production process that will determine whether the ASSET delivered is INVENTORY, a PIECE OF EQUIPMENT, or another DISCRETE ITEM.

The "delivery cost" of the PRODUCTION DELIVERY is calculated as the "unit cost" of the PRODUCTION ORDER multiplied by the "quantity" of the PRODUCTION DELIVERY. If, in the example above, in which the "unit cost" of 1,000 completed units was $15, only 500 units are delivered to stock, the "delivery cost" of the PRODUCTION DELIVERY is $7,500 ($15 times 500 units). In the example in Table 5.2, if the first delivery consists of 200 units of the 500 completed, it will have a "delivery cost" of $460 ($2.30 times 200).

Table 5.2.
Total Work Order Cost.

	Entry Number	Name	Quantity	Unit Cost	Total Cost
(Entity)	TIME SHEET ENTRY	PERSON	TIME SHEET ENTRY	PERSON	WORK ORDER
Time sheet entries	1	Joe (9/13)	10 hours	$11/hr	$110
	2	Sam (9/14)	4 hours	$20/hr	$80
(Total labor cost)					$190
(Entity)	EQUIPMENT USAGE	PIECE OF EQUIPMENT	EQUIPMENT USAGE	PIECE OF EQUIPMENT	WORK ORDER
Actual asset usage	1	Lathe	4 hours	$15/hr	$60
	2	Boiler	4 hours	$75/hr	$300
(Total equipment cost)					$360
(Entity)	ACTUAL ASSET USAGE	ASSET	ACTUAL ASSET USAGE	ASSET	WORK ORDER
Actual asset usage	1	Goo	4 lbs	$75/lb	$300
	2	Stuff	20 kg	$15/kg	$300
(Total material cost)					$600
(Total cost of work order)					$1150
Quantity (Completed)	500				
Unit cost	$2.30				

In the pharmaceutical and chemical industries, PRODUCTION ORDERS are often called LOTS, a term we first saw in Chapter Four. One difference between that setting and the situation of other manufacturers is that each LOT INVENTORY must be *received from* only one LOT, so there is no need for the PRODUCTION DELIVERY entity. Each LOT, of course, may be *the source of* one or more LOT INVENTORIES. (See Figure 5.11.)

Note, by the way, that the model presented in this chapter applies to PRODUCTION ORDERS in a plant manufacturing *discrete* products, such as bicycles or compressors. With the modification for lot accounting, it can also deal with process-oriented plants as long as they manufacture in discrete batches (or LOTS). *Continuous process* plants, however, such as those for producing gasoline or petrochemicals, do not use PRODUCTION ORDERS. This makes the model for them quite different, and worthy of their own chapter—specifically, Chapter Ten.

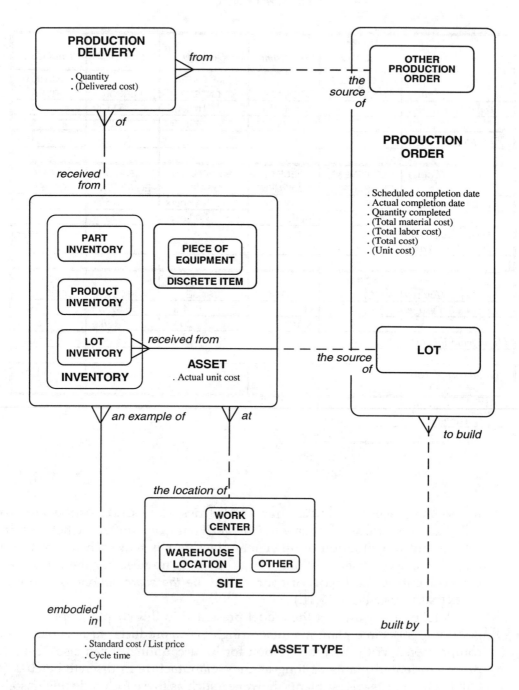

Figure 5.11: Production Orders and Lots.

Projects

Like PRODUCTION ORDERS, PROJECTS are often *the source of* a DELIVERY of an ASSET, but the ASSET is usually big, like a building or a bridge. Alternatively, a PROJECT may be simply to accomplish a specific goal, such as putting on a theatrical production. Interestingly enough, models of the various kinds of PROJECTS are not significantly different from the generic WORK ORDER model presented earlier in this chapter. A particular kind of PROJECT may vastly increase the number of occurrences of ACTIVITY/MANUFACTURING STEP, PART USAGE, or TIME SHEET ENTRY, but the fundamental meaning of these entities and their relationship to the WORK ORDER is unchanged.

Where PROJECTS are unique, however, is in their concern for the underlying structure of ACTIVITIES.

Previously, we discussed the decomposition of ACTIVITIES into progressively smaller ACTIVITIES, thereby creating what project managers call a "work breakdown structure." Modeled in Figures 5.2 and 5.3, this concept is an important part of project management. Similarly, as shown previously in the same figures, a PROCEDURE may be *composed of* one or more other PROCEDURES. In the context of projects, PROCEDURE will go by the more abstract name ACTIVITY TYPE.

A second important aspect of activity organization is the fact that one ACTIVITY or ACTIVITY TYPE may be *required to be completed before* another ACTIVITY or ACTIVITY TYPE is started. Figure 5.12, for example, contains a PERT chart that shows the sequence of steps required for the ACTIVITY TYPE "Replace power supply." The ACTIVITY TYPE "Replace power supply" is composed of

- Remove cover.
- Remove power supply.
- Remove wiring harness.

- Install new power supply.
- Install new wiring harness.
- Replace cover.

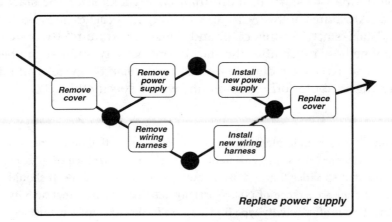

Figure 5.12: A PERT Chart for Replacing a Power Supply.

The PERT chart shows that "Remove cover" must be completed before starting either "Remove power supply" or "Remove wiring harness." Similarly, "Install new power supply" and "Install new wiring harness" must be completed before beginning to "Replace cover." In each case, the subsequent activity can be considered to be dependent upon the prior one.

A dependence may apply to a pair of ACTIVITY TYPES, or it may be true only for particular ACTIVITIES. A DESIGN DEPENDENCE is about the relationship between ACTIVITY TYPES. It expresses the fact that whenever a particular ACTIVITY TYPE is to be carried out, a specified ACTIVITY TYPE must precede or follow it. Figure 5.13 shows that each DESIGN DEPENDENCE must be *of* one ACTIVITY TYPE *on* another, and each ACTIVITY TYPE may be *subject to* a DESIGN DEPENDENCE *on* another ACTIVITY TYPE. (The first cannot start until the second is complete.)

In our example, the ACTIVITY TYPE "Replace power supply" consists of six ACTIVITY TYPES including, among others, "Remove cover" and "Remove power supply." (It is a matter of the terminology of the company involved whether the steps in the PERT chart represent ACTIVITY TYPE STEPS or simply OTHER ACTIVITY TYPES.) A DESIGN DEPENDENCE then dictates that any time the ACTIVITY TYPES are carried out, "Remove power supply" depends *on* (that is, must follow) "Remove cover," and another dictates that "Remove wiring harness" also depends *on* (must follow) "Remove cover."

An ACTUAL DEPENDENCE, on the other hand, is about the relationships between ACTIVITIES as they are expected actually to occur. It represents the fact that an ACTIVITY must happen before another ACTIVITY can be carried out. Figure 5.13 shows that an ACTUAL DEPENDENCE is *of* one ACTIVITY, *on* another ACTIVITY, so one actual ACTIVITY cannot be started before another is completed.

In our example, an *actual* schedule of activities would show that the actual ACTIVITY "Remove power supply" now scheduled for January 24 must depend *on* (follow) the actual ACTIVITY "Remove cover" scheduled for January 23.*

More subtle dependencies may also be defined. For example, an ACTIVITY may be defined to start no more than two weeks after the start of another ACTIVITY. Attributes of the (ACTUAL or DESIGN) DEPENDENCE may be "dependency type" ("start/start," in this case) and "offset maximum" (two weeks), where these define how much after the start of one activity another can begin. Similarly, if an ACTIVITY were defined to start *no less than* two weeks after the start of another, the attribute "offset minimum" would specify this.

---

* Steps must be taken in implementing this model to insure that occurrences of these dependencies are kept consistent. That is, an occurrence of ACTUAL DEPENDENCE that specifies that activity A must come before activity B should not encounter an occurrence of DESIGN DEPENDENCE that specifies that activity type A must come after activity type B. These are further examples of business rules that must be documented along with the data model, since they cannot be documented on it.

The simple power supply examples presume that the "dependency type" is "end/start," and that both the "offset maximum" and the "offset minimum" are set equal to zero. If the "dependency type" were "start/start," and the "offset maximum" were "+2 days," then the second ACTIVITY must start no more than two days after the start of the first ACTIVITY. Alternatively, if the "dependency type" were "end/start," and the "offset minimum" were "-3 days," then the second ACTIVITY must start at least three days before the end of the first ACTIVITY.

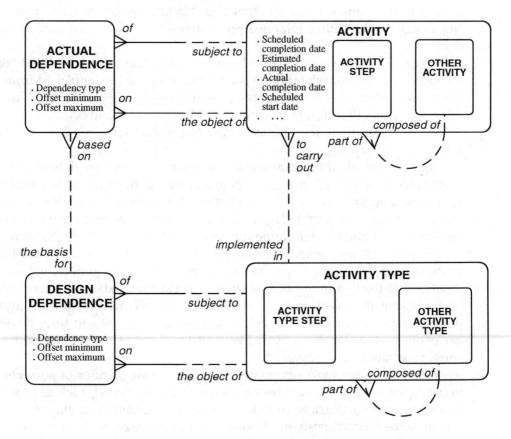

Figure 5.13: Dependence.

In the course of managing a project, the most important attributes of ACTIVITY (and, by implication, of WORK ORDER) are "scheduled completion date," "estimated completion date," and "actual completion date." (Note that comparable to these are an additional three attributes to address the project's scheduled, estimated, and actual start dates.) The "scheduled completion date" typically is defined at the beginning of a project, and the set of these for all ACTIVITIES constitutes the *base line* for the project. The "estimated completion date" is the latest best guess as to when it will be completed, and the "actual completion date," of course, is the date when the ACTIVITY is finally done.

Work Orders in Response to Safety-Related Incidents

Among the activities carried out in a plant or other large facility are those related to safety—either as protection against accidents, or in response to them. The basic work order structure applies here too, but several entities are added to fully describe the safety situation.

We have already defined an EMERGENCY WORK ORDER as a kind of MAINTENANCE WORK ORDER. In terms of its model structure, this is reasonable since it is related to the same entities as other MAINTENANCE WORK ORDERS. EMERGENCY WORK ORDERS have other relationships, however, that warrant further discussion.

Figure 5.14 shows that several kinds of INCIDENTS can occur that require response: ACCIDENTS, where there is an actual loss, are distinguished from NEAR MISSES and DANGEROUS OCCURRENCES, in which no damage was done but something was amiss that should be recorded. These are all INCIDENTS.*

An INCIDENT, then, may be *the trigger of* a WORK ORDER, as shown in Figure 5.14.

An INCIDENT must be *an example of* an INCIDENT TYPE. By defining the INCIDENT TYPES in advance, an organization can define the appropriate PROCEDURE for responding to each. A DEFINED RESPONSE is *the planned use of* a PROCEDURE *in response to* an INCIDENT TYPE. This way, when an actual INCIDENT occurs, employees can quickly determine the appropriate PROCEDURES to perform.

An INCIDENT may also be *the trigger of* an INVESTIGATION, a special kind of WORK ORDER. This will have the same structure as the generic WORK ORDER described at the beginning of this chapter, consuming labor and materials, for example, but its objective will be information, not the creation of anything physical represented in the model. The INVESTIGATION may, in turn, be *the trigger of* other WORK ORDERS—most likely OTHER MAINTENANCE WORK ORDERS—to correct any situation discovered.

Introducing INCIDENT opens the model up to all manner of subjects: For example, each INCIDENT may be *the source of* REPERCUSSIONS, such as LITIGATION, VIOLATIONS *of* a REGULATION, or ENVIRONMENTAL COMPLAINTS. It may be *subject to* one or more INVOLVEMENTS in various kinds of damage, such as BREAKAGE of a DISCRETE ITEM or EMISSION *of* a MATERIAL TYPE (such as smoke) *by* a PIECE OF EQUIPMENT. Each of these can be elaborated upon, but that is beyond the scope of this book.

---

* Be advised that in the interest of fighting Newspeak, your author has taken liberties with the true terminology used in this area. In real industrial environments, what we have called an "incident" is called a "loss event." The word "incident" is reserved for what we here have called an "accident." In real industrial environments, "accidents" never happen.

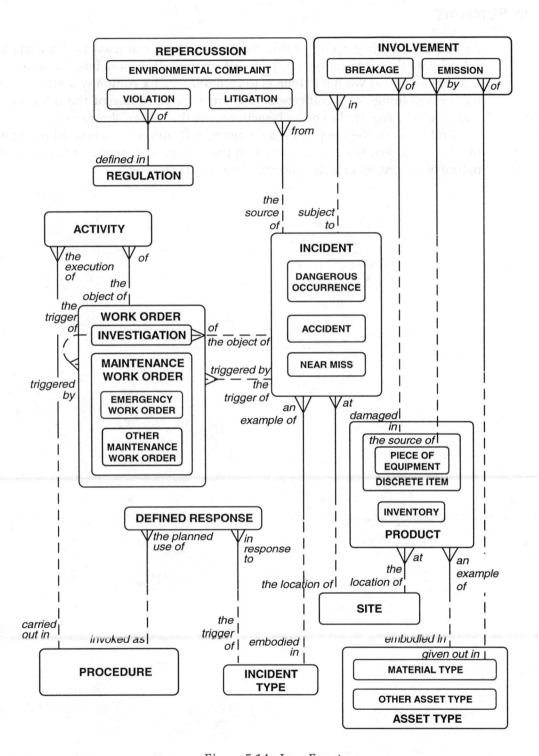

Figure 5.14: Loss Events.

IN SUMMARY

As stated at the beginning of this chapter, we have not tried to duplicate the role of data flow diagrams or any other techniques for modeling the actions of a company. What we have done is to recognize that a company's activities are themselves things of significance. We must try to represent the information that would be required to describe actions, not the actions themselves.

And, as with the people, organizations, and things presented in the previous two chapters, we can see here that there is an underlying structure to the nature of actions that can be portrayed by standard models.

6

CONTRACTS

*T*he three previous chapters have described the people and organizations that make up and concern an enterprise (Chapter Three); the things it buys, makes, or uses (Chapter Four); and the activities performed by the people in it (Chapter Five). PARTY anchors the right side of our model, while ASSET TYPE and ASSET anchor the bottom. Chapter Five began the process of filling in the center by defining the ACTIVITIES and the PROCEDURES (also known as SERVICES or ACTIVITY TYPES) the company performs. This chapter continues this filling-in by discussing the organization's relationships and transactions with the outside world.

This chapter describes the PURCHASE ORDERS and SALES ORDERS by which an organization buys and sells goods and services, and it extends these to encompass the more general concept of CONTRACT or AGREEMENT. This will be elaborated upon through refinement—first of the definitions of what is bought and sold, and then of the definition of the roles played by various PARTIES. This chapter begins to define the terms required to measure the quality of products and services delivered to customers. At the end of the chapter is a discussion of the organization of MARKETING RESPONSIBILITY.

PURCHASE ORDERS AND SALES ORDERS

The business of most organizations involves the buying and selling of goods and services. The instruments for this are the well-known purchase order and sales order. Figure 6.1 shows the model of a PURCHASE ORDER, which must be *to* a PARTY (that is, a vendor) and which must be *composed of* one or more LINE ITEMS. Each LINE ITEM, in turn, must be *for* one and only one PRODUCT TYPE—that is, for a product as specified in the company's catalogue or price list.

Astute readers will recognize PRODUCT TYPE as a kind of ASSET TYPE, described in detail in Chapter Four.

Attributes of PURCHASE ORDER include "PO number," "order date," "terms," and so forth. Attributes of LINE ITEM include the "quantity" (ordered) of the PRODUCT TYPE and its actual "price." Note that this could be the same as the "unit price," an attribute of PRODUCT TYPE (the default price), or it could be a special price for this PURCHASE ORDER. The derived attribute "extended value" is computed by multiplying "price" times "quantity" (ordered). The "extended values" of all the LINE ITEMS that are *part of* a PURCHASE ORDER then may be added together to compute the PURCHASE ORDER's "PO value."

Figure 6.2 shows the remarkably similar model of a SALES ORDER, which must be *from* one PARTY (a customer this time) and which also must be *composed of* one or more LINE ITEMS, each of which must be *for* one and only one PRODUCT TYPE. Its attributes are the same as those for PURCHASE ORDER, except, of course, for the change from "PO (purchase order) number" to "SO (sales order) number" and from the derived attribute "PO value" to "SO value."

Is there a pattern here?

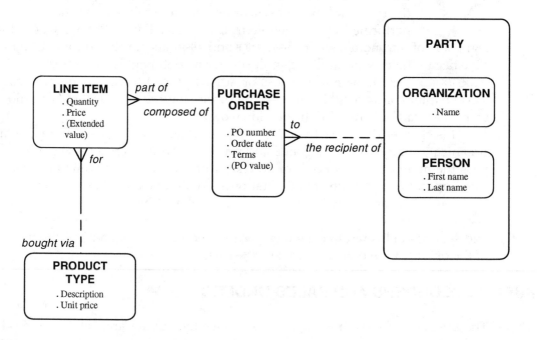

Figure 6.1: Purchase Orders.

In fact, the only difference between the two models is point of view: In the case of the PURCHASE ORDER, we are the implied *buyer*, and in the case of SALES ORDER, we are the implied *seller*. Both models describe a sales transaction, with the same attributes. This gives us the opportunity to combine them, thereby reducing by three the total number of new entities required. The result is shown in Figure 6.3, with the purchase order and sales order subsumed into CONTRACT. (It may also be called AGREEMENT.) The attributes remain the same, except that the identifier of CONTRACT is now "contract number."

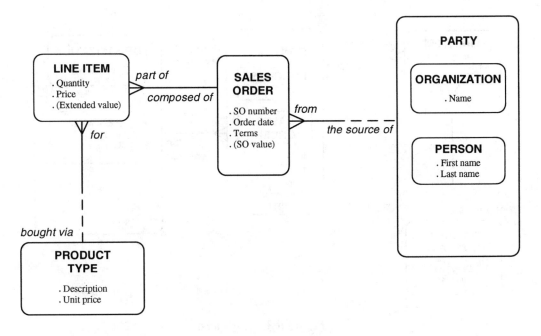

Figure 6.2: Sales Orders.

In Figure 6.3, two relationships now go between CONTRACT and PARTY: one for the seller and one for the buyer. That is, a CONTRACT must be *from* one PARTY (*the buyer in* the CONTRACT), and it must be *to* one PARTY (*the seller in* the CONTRACT).

Note the implication here that now *we* are a PARTY too, along with our vendors and customers. Once again, we see that, as modelers, it is important to step outside the immediate perspective of our clients, in order to identify what is truly going on.

As before, each CONTRACT must be *composed of* one or more LINE ITEMS, each of which must be *for* one and only one PRODUCT TYPE. Some companies deal in services, however, so it is also possible for a contract LINE ITEM to be *for* a SERVICE. (As discussed in Chapter Five, SERVICE is simply another word for PROCEDURE.) Figure 6.4, therefore, shows that each LINE ITEM must be *either for* one PRODUCT TYPE *or* it must be *for* one and only one SERVICE.

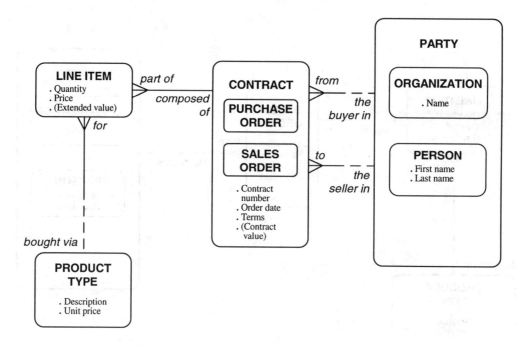

Figure 6.3: Contracts.

It is common in data models to show VENDOR as an entity that receives PUR-CHASE ORDERS, and CUSTOMER as the entity that originates SALES ORDERS. If, however, an entity is defined as "a thing of significance about which we wish to hold information," these interpretations are wrong: The *thing* is an organization or a person. A PARTY is only a vendor if it sells something. The term "vendor" includes the *relationship* to PURCHASE ORDER as part of its meaning. Similarly, a PARTY is only a customer if it buys something—it is not *inherently* a customer.

By showing a PARTY at each end of a purchasing or sales relationship, we have in fact portrayed both vendors and customers. Moreover, we have left open the possibility that the same PARTY may *both* buy from us and sell to us. If VENDOR and CUSTOMER are represented explicitly as separate entities, it is not possible to show this without duplicating the information describing the party that is "CUSTing" and "VENDing."*

---

* VENDOR could be specified as a "virtual entity," defined as a view (analogous to SQL views) of PARTY and CONTRACT. Specifically, an occurrence of VENDOR could be defined as an occurrence of PARTY, which is *the seller in* one or more CONTRACTS. For more of my thinking on this subject, see my article "Visualizing Database Structures," in *Database Programming and Design*, Vol. 7, No. 6 (June 1994), pp. 39-45.

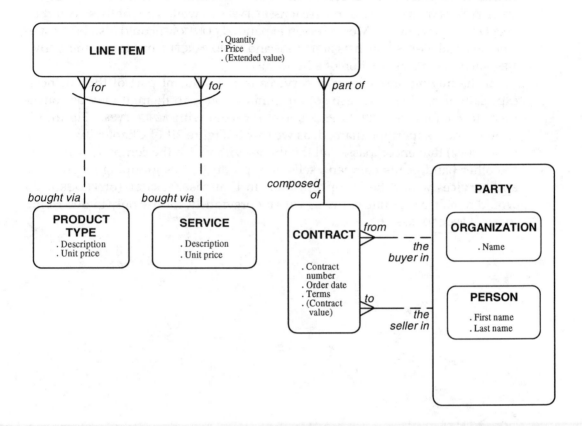

Figure 6.4: Products and Services.

This notion of the PARTY playing different roles becomes even more significant when we consider the other kinds of CONTRACTS that can be modeled, as shown in Figure 6.5. A CONTRACT might be a LEASE, in which one PARTY is the *lessor in* one or more LEASES, and one PARTY is the *lessee in* one or more LEASES. Similarly, a PERMIT may be issued by a GOVERNMENT AGENCY to a PERSON or ORGANIZATION to use a piece of land or to pollute the air. Here, too, a contractual arrangement is set up between two PARTIES and it is the CONTRACT itself, not the entities' essential nature, that makes PARTIES into *permittees* and *permit issuers*. If all the possible PARTY roles were set up as separate entities, the model would quickly become impossibly cumbersome. Because of the variety of relationships possible, those in Figure 6.5 are renamed to assert simply that each PARTY may be *on one side of* one or more CONTRACTS, and that each PARTY may be *on the other side of* one or more CONTRACTS.

Note that expanding the definition of CONTRACT also requires us to expand the definition of what is contracted *for*. The more general term, ASSET TYPE, discussed in Chapter Four, encompasses not only PRODUCT TYPE, but PART/EQUIPMENT TYPE, MATERIAL TYPE, and OTHER ASSET TYPES as well. Any of these could be *bought via* a CONTRACT.* Moreover, an expanded CONTRACT could also be *for* specific physical ASSETS,[†] such as BUILDINGS and LAND PARCELS, or for specific ACTIVITIES, such as the construction of a building.

If the buying and selling of services is a significant part of the business, especially if products are also sold in conjunction with them, it may be convenient to combine SERVICE (a PROCEDURE for sale) with ASSET TYPE. Figure 6.6 shows a new supertype (named, as we saw in Figure 2.1 of Chapter Two, CATALOGUE ITEM) that encompasses all the things with which the company deals. On the other hand, if the company sells only products, this grouping of products and services would be inappropriate. In that case, SERVICE (or PROCEDURE) would remain a separate entity as we saw previously, for use only in describing internal PROCEDURES.

---

* That is, any of these could be *bought via* a LINE ITEM that is *part of* a CONTRACT.

[†] That is, an expanded CONTRACT could also be *composed of* one or more LINE ITEMS that are *for* specific physical ASSETS. . . .

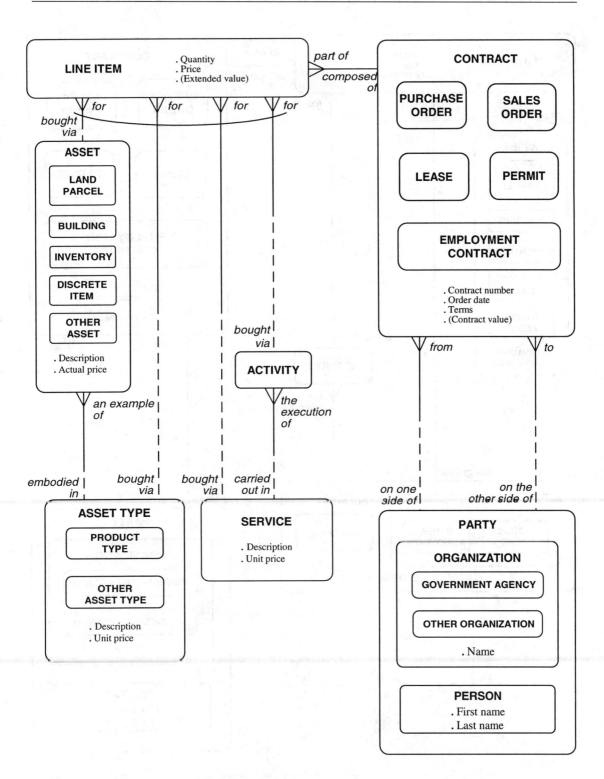

Figure 6.5: Kinds of Contracts.

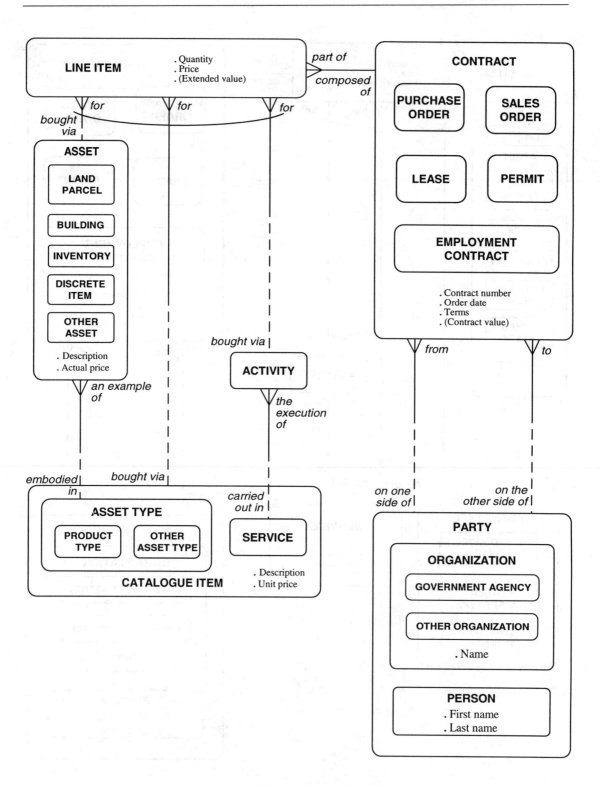

Figure 6.6: Catalogue Item Types.

USER SPECIFICATIONS

The preceding discussions and those in Chapter Four presume that the product involved is a well-defined item offered for sale. What about the situation, though, in which the physical product is not a "catalogue item," and is in fact specified either partly or completely by the customer? This has become a common situation in recent years with the industry-wide movement to improve product quality and responsiveness to customer needs. Since this is a particular issue for chemical companies and other process manufacturers who sell MATERIAL TYPES, we address it here by redefining what a "product" is. We expand the definition of MATERIAL TYPE to include not only STANDARD MATERIAL TYPES, defined by the company, but also CUSTOM MATERIAL TYPES, defined by the customer.

In addition, there is the issue of what to call a product. In many industries, this is not a problem. A bicycle is called a bicycle by nearly everyone. In other industries, however, different customers may call the same product by different names, and all of these may be different from the name used by the manufacturer. Worse than that is the case where one alias applies to more than one asset type.* If this worst case applies to your situation, the entity ALIAS USAGE is necessary to keep things straight, as shown in Figure 6.7.

In the figure, each ALIAS USAGE must be *defined by* one and only one PARTY. It may be necessary in your situation also to say that each ALIAS is *defined by* one and only one PARTY, but often this is not true.

Since the issue has arisen mostly for chemical companies, ALIAS USAGE most commonly is *for* a MATERIAL TYPE, but it is possible for PRODUCT TYPES and PART/EQUIPMENT TYPES to have aliases as well, so it doesn't cost us anything to take a more conservative approach and make each ALIAS USAGE *for* an ASSET TYPE, as is shown in Figure 6.7.

Typically, a company will offer a core set of products with specifications to cover a wide range of characteristics. An individual customer, then, may have a more specific set of requirements, which the selling organization can satisfy by mixing its standard products in various ways or by modifying its production processes. Figure 6.7 shows STANDARD MATERIAL TYPE and CUSTOM MATERIAL TYPE as subtypes of MATERIAL TYPE. Each CUSTOM MATERIAL TYPE must be *defined by* a PARTY (which is to say, a customer).

---

* Feel free to encourage your client not to allow this to happen. It causes no end of troubles to have the same name refer to more than one thing. It is far better to enforce a business rule requiring each ALIAS to be *for* one and only one ASSET TYPE.

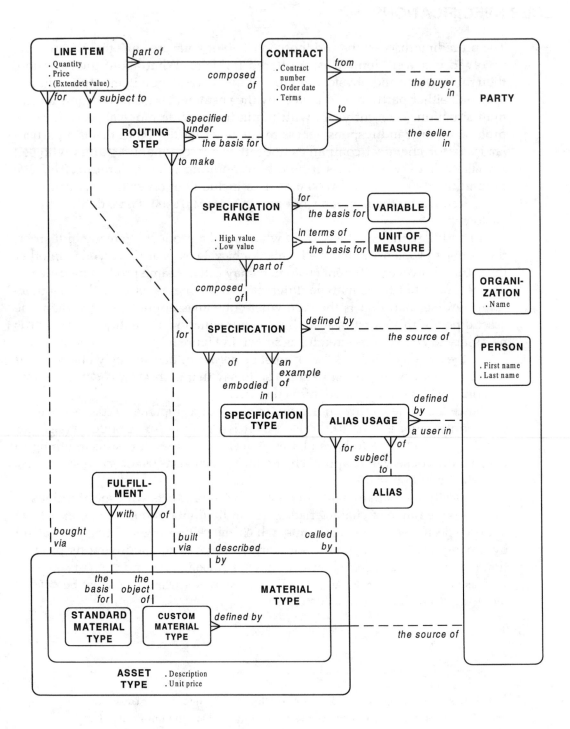

Figure 6.7: User Specifications.

Each MATERIAL TYPE (STANDARD or CUSTOM) may be *described by* one or more SPEC-IFICATIONS. A SPECIFICATION, in turn, may be *composed of* one or more SPECIFICA-TION RANGES, each of which is the high and low values *for* a particular VARIABLE, *in terms of* a UNIT OF MEASURE. That is, a SPECIFICATION RANGE must be *part of* one and only one SPECIFICATION for a CUSTOM MATERIAL TYPE.

For example, a customer may want a product with a pH of between 7.5 and 8.5, while the manufacturer has one grade (273-p) that is between 7 and 8, and another (349-y) that is between 8 and 9.

In this hypothetical case, one of the company's STANDARD MATERIAL TYPES (grade 273-p) is *described by* a SPECIFICATION with the "name" equal to "chemical properties," which is *composed of*, among others, a SPECIFICATION RANGE *for* the VARIABLE whose "name" is "pH." This SPECIFICATION RANGE has a "high value" of "8" and a "low value" of "7." Another STANDARD MATERIAL TYPE (grade 349-y) is *described by*, among others, a SPECIFICATION RANGE *for** pH with a "high value" of "9" and a "low value" of "8." The customer's CUSTOM MATERIAL TYPE, on the other hand, is *described by* a SPECIFICATION RANGE with a "low value" of "7.5" and a "high value" of "8.5." (Note that pH doesn't have a unit of measure. Had the SPECIFICATION RANGE been *of* a VARIABLE such as "particle size," then it would have also been *expressed in* a UNIT OF MEASURE, such as "micron.")

Someone now must specify which of the STANDARD MATERIAL TYPES may be *the basis for* a FULFILLMENT *of* the CUSTOM MATERIAL TYPE. Each FULFILLMENT is the fact that one of the STANDARD MATERIAL TYPES is to be used to fulfill the require-ments for the CUSTOM MATERIAL TYPE. Each FULFILLMENT must be *of* a CUSTOM MATERIAL TYPE *with* a STANDARD MATERIAL TYPE.

In our pH example, since neither of our grades is a perfect match, the cus-tomer may pick one, or it may be necessary to use a combination of the two products to meet the customer's specification. In the first case, a FULFILLMENT would be created according to the customer's wishes. In the latter case, two FULFILLMENTS would be created: One would be *of* the customer's product *with* grade 273-p, and the other would be *of* the customer's product *with* grade 349-y. Moreover, the customer's requirements may have to be fulfilled through special processing: One or more ROUTING STEPS (see Chapter Five) may be required *to make* an ASSET TYPE[†] that addresses this SPECIFICATION RANGE or SPECIFICATION.

Note that the SPECIFICATION may be *defined by* a PARTY. Where the SPECIFICA-TION was *of* a CUSTOM MATERIAL TYPE, this relationship is redundant. The specifi-er of the MATERIAL TYPE was already identified. In other cases, however, it may be useful to say that what is being purchased (the MATERIAL TYPE *bought via* the LINE ITEM that is *part of* the CONTRACT that started all this) is a STANDARD MATERIAL

---

* That is, another STANDARD MATERIAL TYPE is *described by* a SPECIFICATION that is *composed of*, among others, a SPECIFICATION RANGE *for* . . .

[†] This ASSET TYPE would be a CUSTOM MATERIAL TYPE.

TYPE, but that it is subject to this SPECIFICATION, which is not the normal one. That is, each LINE ITEM *for* a particular MATERIAL TYPE may be *subject to* a particular SPECIFICATION. Again, the specifier may be assumed to be the purchaser on the CONTRACT, but there may be reason for a PARTY to buy a MATERIAL TYPE that was specified by someone else.

The circumstances in your company will dictate which of these relationships you will use. For example, you may or may not choose to say that each LINE ITEM may be (or must be) *subject to* a SPECIFICATION.

CONTRACT ROLES

Figure 6.8 shows other roles a PARTY may play in executing a CONTRACT. Aside from the buyer and seller, there may be someone who is *the shipper in, the recipient in, the payee for,* and so forth. Each of these causes another relationship to be added between PARTY and CONTRACT. This would not be a problem, except that there seems to be a principle in systems that any time there are more than three of something there is no assurance that there will not be more.

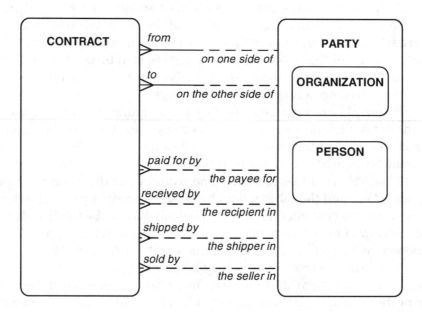

Figure 6.8: Contract Roles.

What is needed is the ability to add roles dynamically. This is accomplished by adding the entity CONTRACT ROLE, as shown in Figure 6.9. Each CONTRACT ROLE must be *for* one CONTRACT, and it must be *played by* one PARTY. Attributes include "start date" for playing the role, "end date," and contract role "type." Contract role types include those mentioned above, such as "the shipper in" and "the payee for."

Note that *the buyer in* and *the seller in* cannot be accommodated by the CON-TRACT ROLE entity, because they are *mandatory* relationships. The mandatoriness of the relationships cannot be represented for any particular occurrences of CONTRACT ROLE—the best that could be done is to say that each CONTRACT must be *served by* one or more CONTRACT ROLES, but you can't assert which one.

Note also that while a CONTRACT must always be *from* one PARTY and *to* another, this does not mean that these PARTIES can't change. The business rules controlling the ability of PARTIES to change are not documented in the model, and will vary from enterprise to enterprise. Some organization's policies may permit a PARTY to transfer its rights under a CONTRACT to another PARTY. To permit this opens the possibility of not having a record of the original contractor, so it is advisable under these circumstances to include a CONTRACT ROLE for "former buyer," "former seller," and so forth.

A more disciplined way to accomplish the same thing would be to always draw up a new CONTRACT any time the PARTIES change, and to record the fact that the second CONTRACT is *derived from* the first. This can be shown on the model, and this relationship appears as a pig's ear in Figure 6.9.

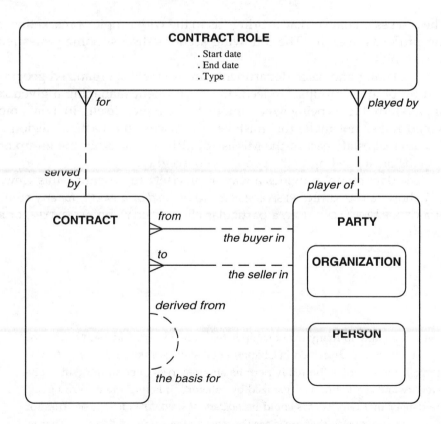

Figure 6.9: Contract Role Entity.

In Figure 6.9, only *one* CONTRACT may be *derived from* one other, and only one may be *the basis for* another. This is a matter of policy in any particular organization, and may well vary from organization to organization. It is not uncommon for this to be a one-to-many or a many-to-many relationship.

EMPLOYMENT CONTRACTS

In Chapter Three, we saw the EMPLOYMENT of a PERSON by an ORGANIZATION. It is now clear that this is simply another kind of CONTRACT. There are, strictly speaking, no LINE ITEMS, although it is probably not stretching the point too much to consider a POSITION ASSIGNMENT to be analogous to a LINE ITEM. Of course, that makes the POSITION assigned another ASSET TYPE, which is probably pushing the limits of generality. This may not be very useful in the context of a real company model (some organizations elaborate greatly on the definitions of POSITION), but Figure 6.10 shows how parallel this structure really is.

MARKETING REGIONS AND DISTRICTS

The discussion of CONTRACTS brings us to the wider topic of marketing and selling products overall. The following sections discuss some issues relative to these topics.

Marketing and sales departments are frequently organized geographically and by product groups. Indeed, the department managing a given region is often referred to as being synonymous to the region itself. In a data model, we would rather not make this mistake: To discuss the Eastern Region is not to discuss real estate east of the Mississippi River, but rather the group of people responsible for selling to the people who live there.

The data model provides a way of precisely representing this view. Figure 6.11 shows a MARKETING RESPONSIBILITY to be *held by* a PARTY, *for* any combination of a GEOGRAPHIC LOCATION, a particular client (PARTY), an ASSET TYPE, or an ASSET CATEGORY.*

---

* Note the many-to-many relationship between ASSET TYPE and ASSET CATEGORY. This structure was discussed in Chapter Four with PRODUCT and PRODUCT CATEGORY. If the organization really permits an ASSET TYPE to be in more than one category and marketing is organized by category, it is important to recognize the danger that two PARTIES could be *holders of* MARKETING RESPONSIBILITIES for two ASSET CATEGORIES that are *classifications for* the same ASSET TYPE. That is, two PARTIES could be marketing the same product. If the model is true, then the policies must be examined.

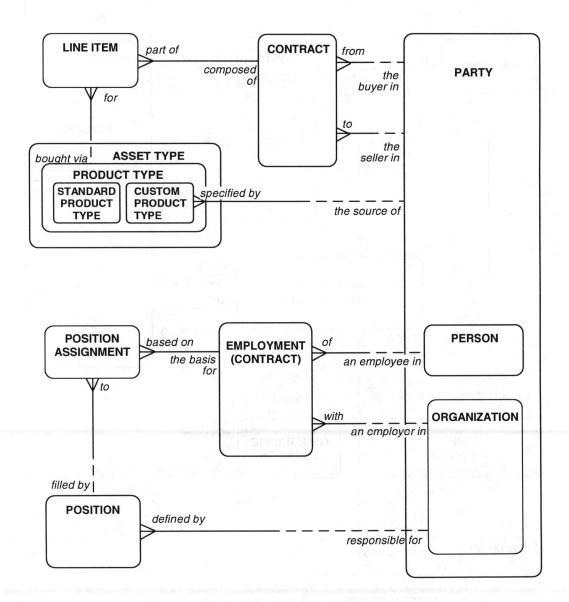

Figure 6.10: Employment Contracts.

Figure 6.11, then, makes it possible to distinguish between the *organization* responsible for the Eastern Region and the geographical *place* that is the Eastern Region.

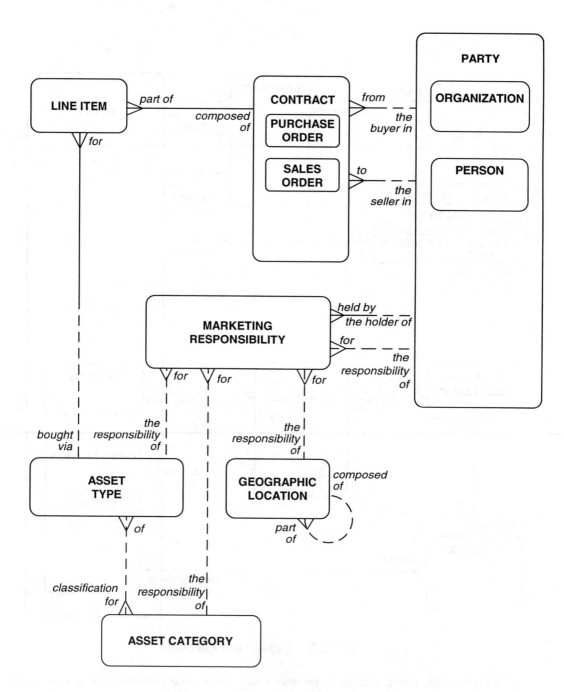

Figure 6.11: Marketing Responsibilities.

DELIVERIES OF PRODUCTS AND SERVICES

Figure 6.12 shows that either the CONTRACT as a whole or individual LINE ITEMS may be *for delivery to* a specified SITE. That is, the delivery site may be specified in advance. Each LINE ITEM may be actually *delivered as* one or more CONTRACT DELIVERIES. Where the LINE ITEM was *for* either an ASSET or ASSET TYPE, a CONTRACT DELIVERY must always be *of* a particular ASSET. Note that the definition of a particular INVENTORY includes the SITE where it is located. For this reason, CONTRACT DELIVERIES *of* INVENTORY do not have to specify the SITE. While DISCRETE ITEMS are also always currently located *at* one SITE, they can move. Indeed, the CONTRACT DELIVERY is the act of moving them into place. For this reason, CONTRACT DELIVERIES of DISCRETE ITEMS must specify the SITE being moved *to.* Hence, the general statement that each CONTRACT DELIVERY *may be to* one and only one SITE.

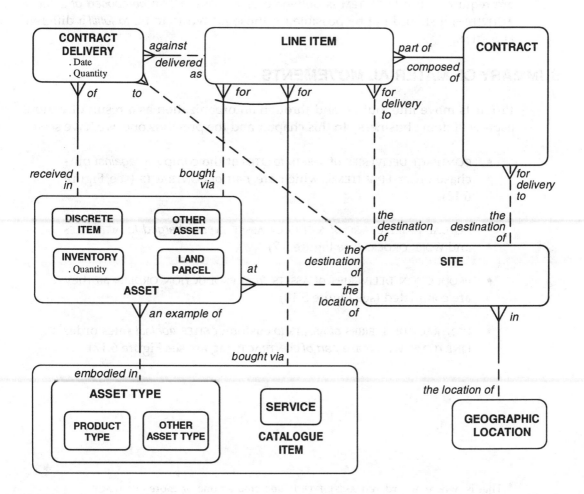

Figure 6.12: Deliveries.

Note that, in a common but nonrelational step, the transaction creating a CON-TRACT DELIVERY to INVENTORY would probably update the "quantity" attribute of INVENTORY as well. Strictly speaking, "quantity" is a derived field, computed from the sum of all CONTRACT DELIVERY, ACTUAL ASSET USAGE, and PRODUCTION DELIVERY transactions. (In addition to Figure 6.12, see Figures 5.7 and 5.10 in Chapter Five.) The impracticality of summarizing the company's history of inventory transactions, however, plus overwhelming popular opinion, has bent the "no computed attributes" rule a bit in this case.

Where an ordered ASSET TYPE is *delivered as* an actual ASSET,* so an ordered SERVICE is *delivered as* an actual ACTIVITY—or as a WORK ORDER, which is a set of ACTIVITIES. Alternatively, as shown in Figure 6.13, a WORK ORDER may be *to fulfill* either a CONTRACT or a LINE ITEM that is *part of* a CONTRACT. For simplicity's sake, we'll constrain an ACTIVITY to be *to fulfill* an individual LINE ITEM. Note that business rules will probably be required here to specify exactly which combinations are required: If a LINE ITEM is delivered as a WORK ORDER *composed of* a set of ACTIVITIES, it should not be possible for those ACTIVITIES to be *to fulfill* a different LINE ITEM.

SUMMARY OF MATERIAL MOVEMENTS

Products move into, out of, and through an organization as a result of various aspects of doing business. In this chapter and the previous one, we have seen

- CONTRACT DELIVERIES *of* ASSETS *to* SITES at the company *against* purchase order LINE ITEMS, which are *part of* CONTRACTS (see Figure 6.12)

- ACTUAL ASSET USAGE *of* ASSETS or ASSET TYPES *charged to* ACTIVITIES and WORK ORDERS (see Figure 5.7)

- PRODUCTION DELIVERIES *of* ASSETS *from* PRODUCTION ORDERS as they are completed (see Figure 5.10)

- CONTRACT DELIVERIES *of* ASSETS *to* customer SITES *against* sales order LINE ITEMS, which are *part of* CONTRACTS (again, see Figure 6.12)

---

* That is, where an ordered ASSET TYPE is *delivered as* one or more CONTRACT DELIVERIES *of* an actual ASSET . . .

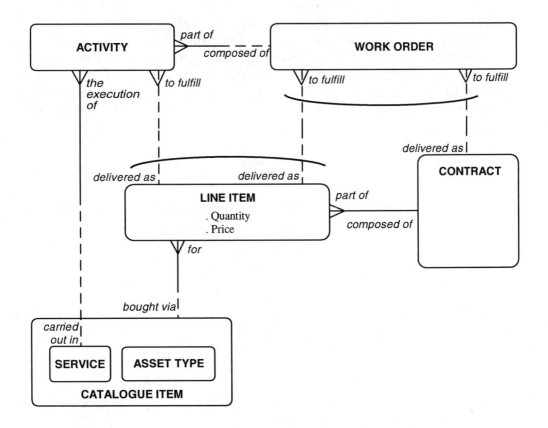

Figure 6.13: Deliveries of Services.

The consumption of ASSETS could also be represented as a movement from the SITE where they are located to the SITE that is a WORK CENTER. Similarly, the production of ASSETS could be recast as a movement from the WORK CENTER SITE to the WAREHOUSE LOCATION SITE.

Figure 6.14 summarizes this and, in so doing, captures CONTRACT DELIVERY, PRODUCTION ORDER DELIVERY, and ACTUAL PRODUCT USAGE in a supertype called MATERIAL MOVEMENT.

In Figure 6.14, each MATERIAL MOVEMENT

- may be *from* one PARTY (such as a vendor) or *from* one SITE (such as a WAREHOUSE LOCATION or a WORK CENTER)

- may be *to* one PARTY (such as a customer) or *to* one SITE (such as a WAREHOUSE LOCATION or a WORK CENTER)

The relationships are optional, so that the same transaction can also be used for INVENTORY ADJUSTMENTS, which are either MATERIAL MOVEMENTS *from* a SITE into the ether, or MATERIAL MOVEMENTS *to* a SITE from the ether.

Note that the PLACEMENT *of* a PARTY *at* a SITE (originally described in Chapter Three) allows inferences to be drawn about the source and destination of the MATERIAL MOVEMENT. If the MATERIAL MOVEMENT is *to* a PARTY, it is likely to be *to* one of the SITES that are *the location of* the PARTY.* Similarly, if the MATERIAL MOVEMENT is *to* a SITE, it is, by definition, *to* one of the PARTIES that are *at* the SITE.[†]

---

* That is, it is likely to be *to* one of the SITES that are *the location of* the PLACEMENT *of* the PARTY.

[†] That is, it is, by definition, *to* one of the PARTIES that are *subject to* PLACEMENT *at* the SITE.

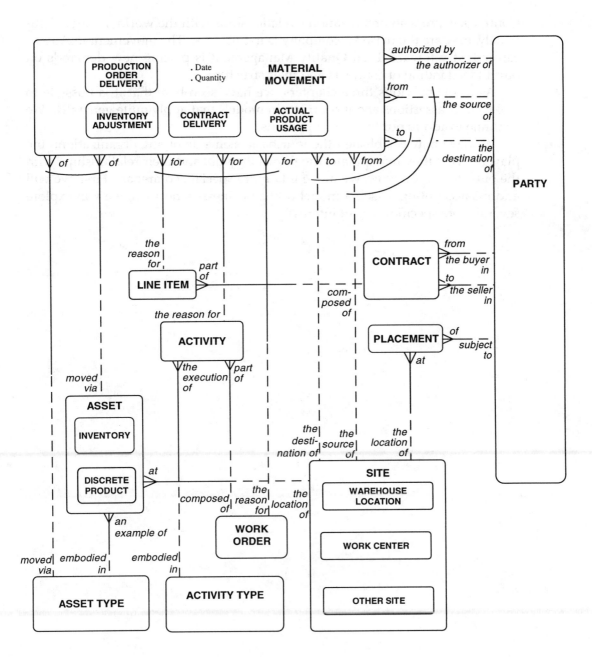

Figure 6.14: Material Movements.

IN SUMMARY

Contracts express an organization's relationships with the world at large. Ultimately, they are the reason a company is in business. The movement in American industry toward Total Quality Management is placing new demands on our understanding of contracts and their structures.

As in the previous three chapters, we have seen here that it is possible to make many assertions about contracts in models that apply quite generally. We continue to add to our toolbox of patterns.

We have now established the four basic elements of any organization: the players; what they manipulate; the things they do; and their relationships with the outside world. Now, we move into more specialized arenas. First, we will address accounting—itself a model of the business—and then, we will explore several more specific areas of interest.

7

ACCOUNTING

"*A*ccounting may be viewed broadly as a systematic means of writing the economic history of an organization. Its purpose is to provide information that can be drawn upon by those responsible for decisions affecting the organization's future."[1]

Accounting is itself a model of an organization. It represents the organization's activities and resources in a highly structured way, as does any model. It is in fact *better* at representing certain kinds of situations than is data modeling. To try to draw a data model of the accounting model is fraught with problems. This is not only because of the problems inherent in representing the abstract accounting model in an even more abstract data model, but also because many of the dimensions of a company's accounting data are not inherent in the nature of the business; rather, they are the results of particular attitudes and objectives held by company management.

Bookkeeping, on the other hand, has more specific rules, and can therefore be modeled more easily, but bookkeeping is not accounting. "Accountants do little or none of the actual recording of a firm's history. That is the function of bookkeeping, and the rules under which accounting history is written permit the delegation of this task to clerks and to an increasing extent to giant electronic computers. The accountant, on the other hand, designs the system and deals with the nonroutine items, the transactions that cannot be handled without the exercise of judgment. Furthermore, as a member of the management team, his analysis and interpretation of financial statements and other accounting data contribute to an understanding of the past and the prediction of the future."[2]

Modeling the fundamental structures of bookkeeping must be done at several levels to appreciate the richness of the accounting model. The first level, which asserts only that all accounting transactions consist of debits and credits, is not robust enough to be very informative. The second level approximates the way bookkeepers and accountants see transactions, but it is cumbersome because it requires creating a separate model for nearly every type of transaction—and there are an almost unlimited number of these. Only by moving to a third level of abstraction can accounting be represented in a single, simple model, but this is more abstraction than most people are accustomed to seeing.

The problem is that even if we document bookkeeping successfully, the resulting model is not of interest to most people in the organization concerned with "accounting" as defined above. They work with summaries of the data, and while it is possible to model any particular summary, that is by definition a model only of a particular view. The goal of this book—to identify fundamental structures—will fail when discussing summarized data.

Unless you are about to build a general ledger system, you will probably have little direct use for the detailed bookkeeping models, but you are very likely to encounter people looking for better financial reports. It is worthwhile, therefore, to understand the underlying structures of accounting, as well as the strategies you can take for dealing with the less-well-defined aspects of financial reporting. Besides, dealing with the particular problems of modeling bookkeeping yields interesting insights into the modeling process itself.

This chapter, then, first presents the general model of bookkeeping transactions, followed by specific models of the more common kinds of transactions; it then presents the bookkeeping meta-model (the abstract one). The chapter concludes with a discussion of the thornier problem of modeling accounting's manipulations to achieve management purposes. In this latter case, no standard models are possible, but the chapter presents some of the kinds of assignments and summarizations that can be found in typical organizations.

BASIC BOOKKEEPING

The general ledger is the record of a company's assets and liabilities, and of the flow of money into or out of the company. The basic rules and transactions for recording this flow are well-defined by the principles of double-entry bookkeeping.

At the heart of the system is an ACCOUNT. (See Figure 7.1.) An ACCOUNT is "a place in which to record particular kinds of effects of the firm's transactions."[3] That is, it is the basis for recording accounting activities. An ACCOUNT must be *for* one and only one corporate ORGANIZATION, although this may be an entire company, a subsidiary, or a corporate entity at a SITE. In addition, an ACCOUNT may refer to any of several other elements of the organization—an ASSET, a SITE such as a WORK CENTER, a department (an ORGANIZATION within the corporation), and so on. Which kinds of things are referred to depends on the kind of account it is. This will be discussed further, below.

Double-entry bookkeeping has been set up so that each basic transaction, whether it pertains to revenue, expense, or investment, represents an addition to or a subtraction from at least two accounts. More complex transactions are composed of combinations of the basic transactions.

Each ACCOUNT may be one of three basic kinds—*asset*, *liability*, and *equity*, as shown in Figure 7.1, and defined as follows:

- An ASSET ACCOUNT is "any [set of] rights that has value to its owner."[4] Occurrences of this type might be cash, accounts receivable, or equipment. An ASSET ACCOUNT may also describe such things as the headquarters building, automobiles, or avail-

able labor. Available labor will be discussed in conjunction with
LABOR USAGE, below.

- A LIABILITY ACCOUNT is any amount owed to another party.
  Examples of this might be credit-card debt, notes payable, or
  employee withholding.

- An EQUITY ACCOUNT is the amount of the company's assets held
  by the company's owners. This is usually either owner-held
  stock or retained earnings. Among the EQUITY ACCOUNTS are two
  subcategories of accounts that have special significance: revenue
  and expense.

  - A REVENUE ACCOUNT describes one or more assets contributed
    to the firm by customers in exchange for goods or services.
    This might be, for example, professional service revenue or
    product sales. Each dollar of income represents *an increase in*
    the organization's equity.

  - An EXPENSE ACCOUNT describes assets spent by the company
    to acquire goods and services. This is the money spent for
    salary, hotel, airfare, purchase of equipment, and similar
    expenses. Each dollar of expense represents *a decrease in* the
    organization's equity.

Each ACCOUNT must be *an example of* an ACCOUNT TYPE. (Each ACCOUNT TYPE
may be *embodied in* one or more ACCOUNTS.) ACCOUNT TYPES include such things
as accounts receivable, cash, owner's equity, and so forth. These are specific
categories within the more general categories of ASSETS, LIABILITIES, and EQUITIES.
There are some general principles in the definition of ACCOUNT TYPES, but the
organization has wide latitude in setting up the specific list. This latitude cre-
ates data modeling problems, as we shall see below, since the meaning of the
ACCOUNT TYPE affects the way transactions are structured.

ACCOUNTS may be aggregated into larger ACCOUNTS. That is, each ACCOUNT
may be *composed of* one or more other ACCOUNTS. ACCOUNT TYPE has a corresponding hierarchical structure.

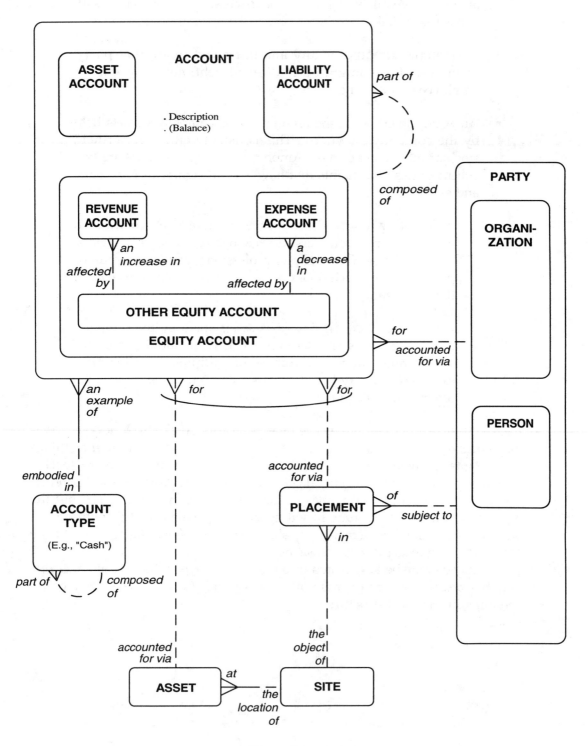

Figure 7.1: Accounts.

ACCOUNT has one-and-a-half attributes: The one is "description," which is the name of the ACCOUNT; the half is "balance." All ACCOUNTS have "balance" as an attribute—sort of. It is half an attribute because, like the "quantity" of inventory described in Chapter Four, it is derived from all transactions against it. In theory, it is nothing but the sum of all additions to and subtractions from the account since it was established. Because these transactions could happen over a very long period of time, however, a "beginning balance" (as of a particular date) is sometimes defined as a stored attribute (with "beginning balance date" also as an attribute), but this is a gimmick, since even "beginning balance" is derived from transactions that went before. Even doing this, then, still makes the "current balance" derived, if only from the transactions since the "beginning balance date," so the problem has not gone away.

As a matter of convenience, then, "balance" may be considered an attribute. (This is assumed to be the current balance, as of the time the ACCOUNT is examined.) Because it is treated as a stored attribute, each transaction must update "balance" when it occurs. As with the INVENTORY "quantity" balance described in Chapter Four, the benefits of this violation of relational rules outweigh its disadvantages.

The ACCOUNTS other than EXPENSE ACCOUNTS and REVENUE ACCOUNTS make up the company's *balance sheet.* They describe the *value of* the organization at a given point in time, and how much of that value is either owned by the stockholders or owed to others.

EXPENSE ACCOUNTS and REVENUE ACCOUNTS, on the other hand, are categories of EQUITY ACCOUNTS, and are not like other ACCOUNTS—even other EQUITY ACCOUNTS. Where other ACCOUNTS describe the *state* of the organization, EXPENSE and REVENUE ACCOUNTS describe the *flow* of money into and out of the firm. These ACCOUNTS in effect collect separately the transactions that increment and decrement the EQUITY ACCOUNT "retained earnings," or its equivalent. They are considered EQUITY ACCOUNTS because they represent increases and decreases in equity.

EXPENSE and REVENUE ACCOUNTS and their transactions are held separately, so that they can be reported together as the organization's *income statement.* This is an itemization of the expenses and revenues, along with the contribution to "net earnings" for a given period.

By definition, the total of the "balances" of an organization's ASSETS must equal the sum of the "balances" of its LIABILITY and EQUITY ACCOUNTS. That is, the total resources available to the company must equal the sum of those owed by the company plus those contributed by the company's owners. This means that any ACCOUNTING TRANSACTION that *increases* the "balance" of an ASSET ACCOUNT must also either *decrease* the "balance" of another ASSET ACCOUNT, *increase* the "balance" of one or more EQUITY ACCOUNTS, or *increase* the "balance" of one or more LIABILITY ACCOUNTS—or some combination of the three. Similarly, *decreases* to any ACCOUNT must be balanced.

This balancing is accomplished by requiring each transaction to be composed of two kinds of ACCOUNTING ENTRY—DEBITS and CREDITS. DEBITS and CRED-

ITS are additions to or subtractions from different kinds of accounts, and have been cleverly defined so that if you have at least one of each, you will have done the balancing. Table 7.1 shows how a DEBIT or a CREDIT is either *an increment in* or *a decrement in* (the "balance" of) an ACCOUNT, depending on what kind of ACCOUNT it is.

For example, a transaction that debits an asset (say, "cash") and credits a liability (say, "short-term loans") increases both the asset and the liability. On the other hand, a transaction that debits one asset (say, "cash" again) and credits another asset (say, "inventory") has just added to one and subtracted from the other—converting one asset into another.

Table 7.1.
Debits and Credits.

Assets		**Liabilities**		**Equity**	
Debit	Credit	Debit	Credit	Debit	Credit
+	-	-	+	-	+

In its most general form, then, the data model of an ACCOUNTING TRANSACTION looks like that shown in Figure 7.2. Each ACCOUNTING TRANSACTION must be *composed of* at least two ACCOUNTING ENTRIES—which is to say, one or more DEBITS and one or more CREDITS, each of which is either *an increment in* or *a decrement in* exactly one ACCOUNT. This is summarized by the relationship, which says that each ACCOUNTING ENTRY must in turn be *an effect on* one and only one ACCOUNT. As can be seen in Table 7.1 and Figure 7.2, different kinds of DEBITS and CREDITS have different effects on different kinds of ACCOUNTS:

- An ASSET DEBIT must be *an increment in* (+) an ASSET.

- An ASSET CREDIT must be *a decrement in* (-) an ASSET.

- A LIABILITY DEBIT must be *a decrement in* a LIABILITY.

- A LIABILITY CREDIT must be *an increment in* a LIABILITY.

- An EQUITY DEBIT must be *a decrement in* an EQUITY.

- An EQUITY CREDIT must be *an increment in* an EQUITY.

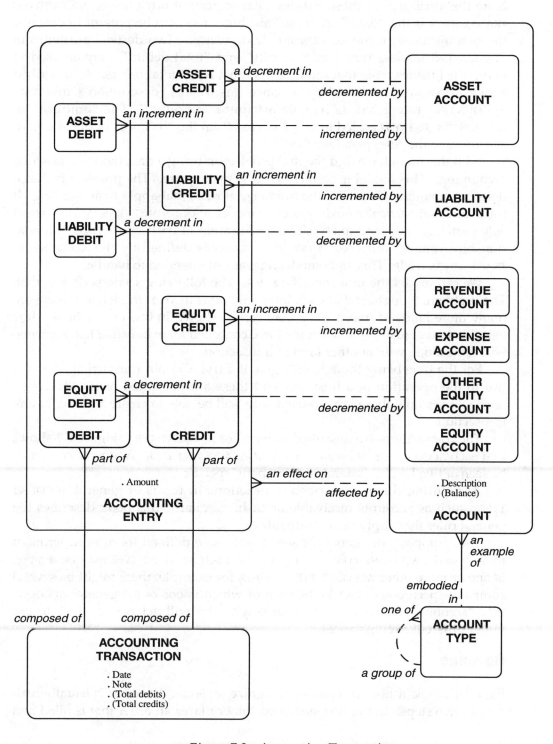

Figure 7.2: Accounting Transactions.

Note the attributes of these entities: An important attribute of ACCOUNTING TRANSACTION is the "date." A "note" attribute may also be present to describe the circumstances of the ACCOUNTING TRANSACTION. Two derived attributes in ACCOUNTING TRANSACTION ("total credits" and "total debits") may be used to verify the business rule that total credits must equal total debits. As described above, ACCOUNT is described by "balance" (as well as "description"), and each ACCOUNTING ENTRY has as its sole attribute "amount." The "amount" in ACCOUNTING ENTRY is added to or subtracted from the "balance" of the ACCOUNT, according to the rules just described.

With this model, we find the first problem in using a data model to describe accounting: This model is correct, but it is inadequate. The problem is that it does not adequately describe the full *range* of rules that apply to accounting. It turns out that *particular kinds of occurrences* of ACCOUNTING TRANSACTION affect *only* particular ACCOUNT TYPES. The specification of each occurrence of a relationship from ACCOUNTING ENTRY to ACCOUNT is defined by the ACCOUNTING TRANSACTION itself. This, data modeling was not intended to handle.

We can model the more specific rules. The following sections do just that. The problem, though, is that each transaction has its own model, and there are many more kinds of transactions than can be shown in this or any book. It is very likely that just as we think we have compiled an exhaustive list, someone will come along with another kind of transaction.

For the time being though, let's give it a try: Certain transactions are central to the operation of a business, and these are presented here. Moreover, once you see how these are modeled, you will be able to create a model of any transaction.

The transactions are described in terms of ACCOUNT TYPE. Figure 7.2 shows that each ACCOUNT must be *an example of* an ACCOUNT TYPE. ACCOUNT TYPES may be seen at two levels: general and company-specific.

Accounting theory describes transactions in terms of general ACCOUNT TYPES, such as accounts receivable or cash. Similarly, this book describes the general rules that apply to all companies.

Your company or agency, however, will have defined its rules in terms of more specific ACCOUNT TYPES. In Figure 7.2, each ACCOUNT TYPE may be *a group of* one or more other ACCOUNT TYPES. Thus, for example, there might be several company-specific ACCOUNT TYPES, each of which is *one of* the general ACCOUNT TYPE "accounts receivable." The company's rules will determine which to use under different circumstances.

Revenue

First, let's look at how companies recognize revenue. Revenue is usually realized in two steps: In the first step, a customer places an order that is filled and an invoice is sent out. In the second step, the customer pays the balance shown on the invoice. There are alternative points at which to recognize that revenue has occurred. Among them is the distinction between recording revenue on an "accrual basis," where revenue is recognized at the time the invoice is cut, and on a "cash basis," where revenue is not recognized until the invoice has been paid. For our purposes, we will assume the accrual situation wherein revenue occurs when the invoice is issued.

Figure 7.3 shows the transaction for recording an INVOICE. In this example, each INVOICE must be *composed of* one or more ASSET DEBITS, each of which must be *an increment in* the ASSET ACCOUNT of ACCOUNT TYPE *ACCOUNTS RECEIVABLE*, and it must be *composed of* one or more EQUITY CREDITS, each of which must be *an increment in* a selected REVENUE ACCOUNT (which one depends on the company). This REVENUE ACCOUNT increase in turn represents *an increase in* an OTHER EQUITY ACCOUNT—probably of ACCOUNT TYPE *RETAINED EARNINGS*.

Note that in this diagram and the ones to follow, we have extended the data modeling notation to describe a pseudo-entity: This is any occurrence of an ACCOUNT that is *an example of* the specified ACCOUNT TYPE. For example, in Figure 7.3, *ACCOUNTS RECEIVABLE* is shown as a pseudo-entity. This refers to a specific subset of ASSET ACCOUNTS that are of ACCOUNT TYPE "accounts receivable." A pseudo-entity is shown as a subtype, but with a dashed border. Both on the diagram and in the text, the name of a pseudo-entity will be shown in small-capital italics. The notation indicates a business rule that requires the use of a particular kind of ACCOUNT (that is, a particular ACCOUNT TYPE).

The pseudo-entity *ACCOUNTS RECEIVABLE* may refer either to a specific ACCOUNT or to one of several ACCOUNTS that are *examples of* the ACCOUNT TYPE "accounts receivable." If this information were left in ACCOUNT TYPE, it would be impossible in the data model to show that this is the particular ACCOUNT TYPE affected by the INVOICE transaction. We don't want to make it a subtype either, however, since there are going to be many kinds of accounts addressed in this chapter, and it is virtually impossible to create a definitive list. In a real system based on this model, the business rules implied by this pseudo-entity would be implemented in program code.

Returning to our example, when a customer pays for goods, a PAYMENT RECEIPT is created, which must be *composed of* one or more ASSET DEBITS, each of which must be *an increment in* a *CASH* ASSET ACCOUNT, and it must be *composed of* one or more ASSET CREDITS, each of which must be *a decrement in* the *ACCOUNTS RECEIVABLE* ASSET ACCOUNT already incremented by the INVOICE transaction described above. (See Figure 7.4.)

If this were a cash purchase in the first place, the two transactions would have been combined: The ASSET ACCOUNT debited at the time the sale was recognized would have been *CASH*. The *ACCOUNTS RECEIVABLE* ACCOUNT would have been bypassed. (See Figure 7.5.)

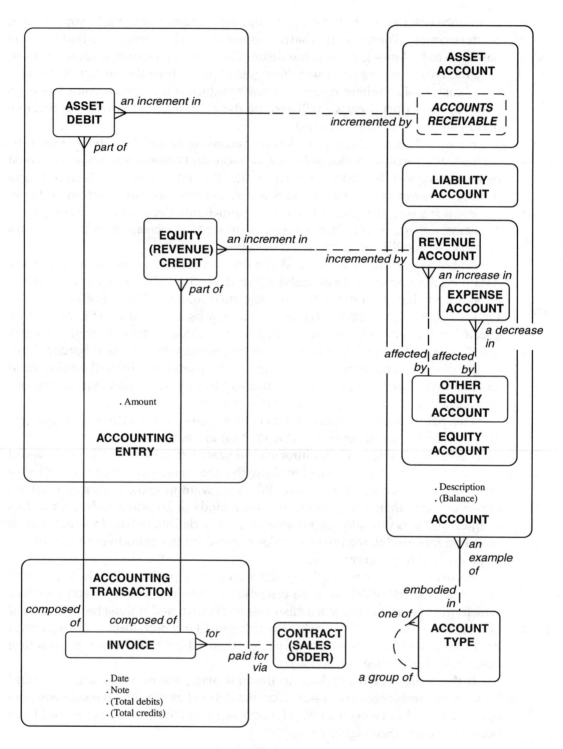

Figure 7.3: Revenue.

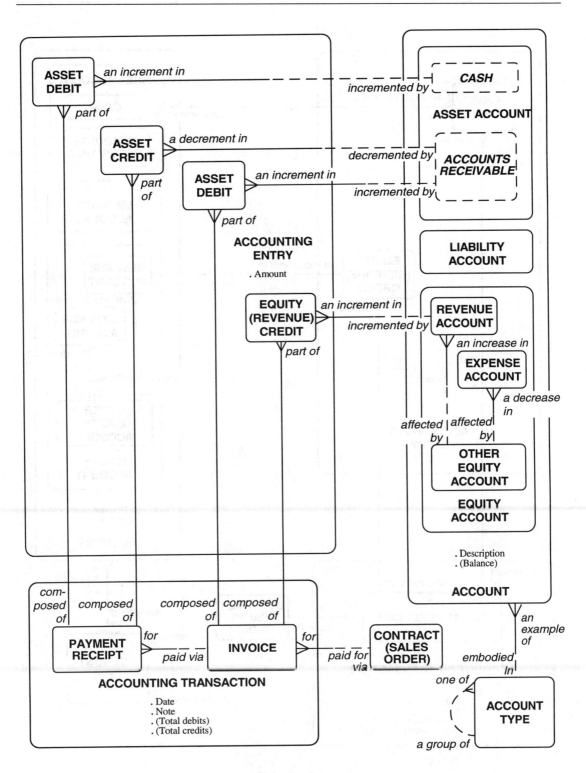

Figure 7.4: Receipts.

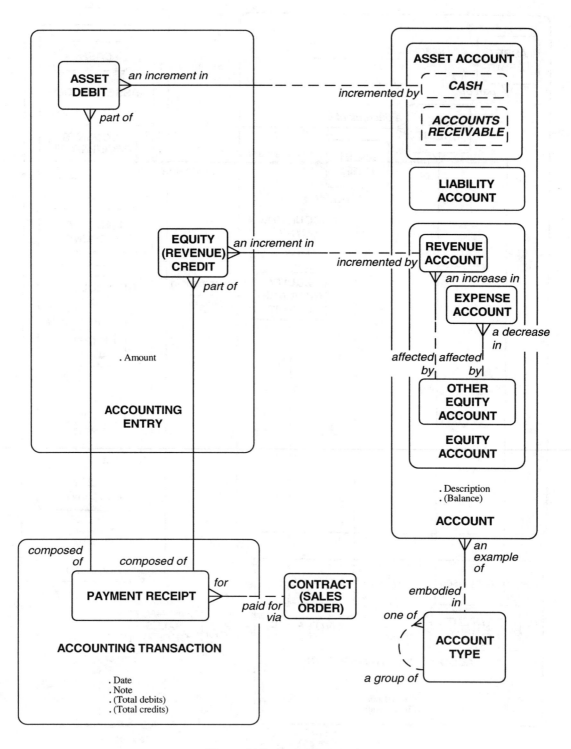

Figure 7.5: Cash Transactions.

Expense

Expenses are the mirror image of revenues. As shown in Figure 7.6, when the company buys something and receives an invoice for it, a VENDOR BILL (or a transaction with a similar name) is created. This transaction must be *composed of* one or more EQUITY (EXPENSE) DEBITS, each of which is a *decrement in* an EXPENSE ACCOUNT.* The VENDOR BILL must also be *composed of* one or more LIABILITY CREDITS, each of which must be *an increment in* an ACCOUNTS PAYABLE LIABILITY ACCOUNT.

When the organization pays its bills, through a VENDOR PAYMENT, one or more LIABILITY DEBITS are involved, each of which must be *a decrement in* the ACCOUNTS PAYABLE LIABILITY ACCOUNT just mentioned. The VENDOR PAYMENT must also be *composed of* one or more ASSET CREDITS, each of which must be a *decrement in* a CASH ASSET ACCOUNT.

Investment

A company is originally established by someone's putting up capital (usually money) to pay for its initial expenses. This puts money into one or more ASSET ACCOUNTS (specifically, CASH and related ACCOUNTS), and establishes a balance in an OTHER EQUITY ACCOUNT. The transactions shown in Figure 7.7 show how an EXTERNAL INVESTMENT TRANSACTION debits a CASH ASSET ACCOUNT, and credits an EQUITY ACCOUNT (in this example, OWNER'S EQUITY). That is, both CASH and the OWNER'S EQUITY "balances" are increased.

---

* Non-accountants, please note the *decrement* in the EXPENSE ACCOUNT, even though we are *increasing* expenses. This is because we are also *decreasing* the OTHER EQUITY ACCOUNT with which the EXPENSE ACCOUNT is associated.

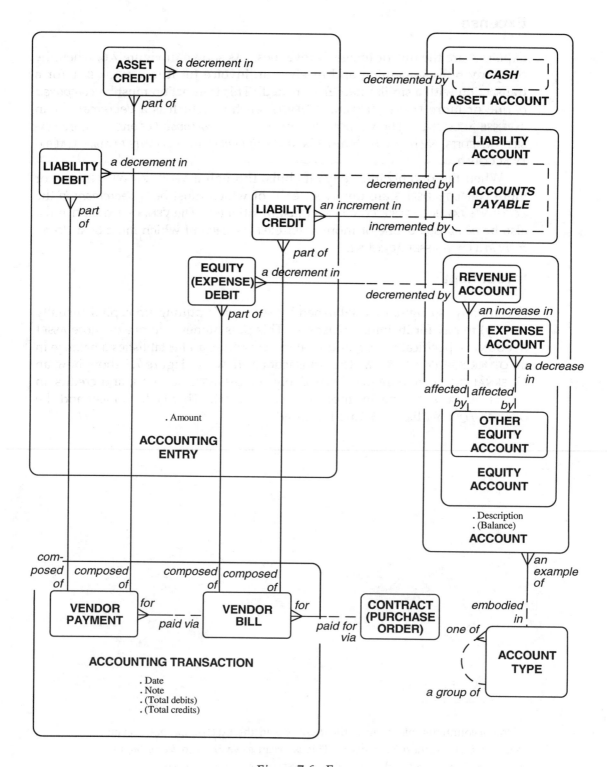

Figure 7.6: Expenses.

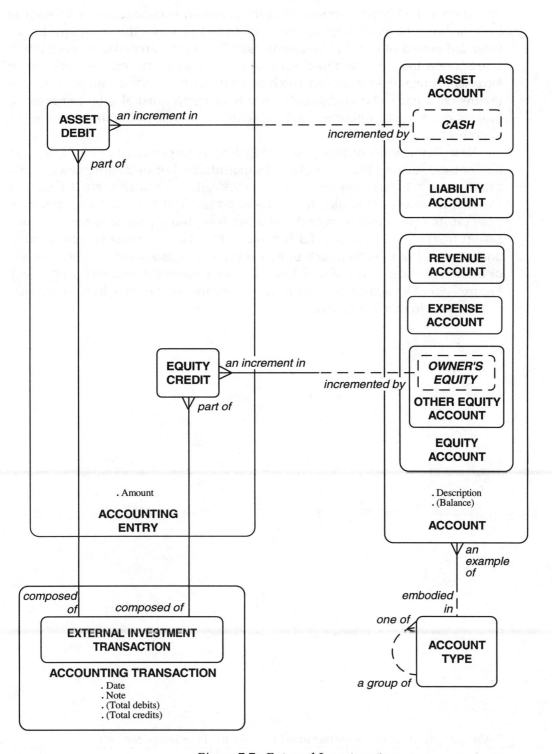

Figure 7.7: External Investments.

An INTERNAL INVESTMENT occurs when the company exchanges an ASSET such as *CASH* (a "current asset") for an ASSET intended to serve the company for an extended period of time (a "long-term asset"). That is, an INTERNAL INVESTMENT TRANSACTION must be *composed of* one or more ASSET DEBITS, each of which is *an increment in* one ASSET ACCOUNT (such as *EQUIPMENT, INVENTORY,* or, as shown in Figure 7.8, a particular *MACHINE A*). The transaction must also be *composed of* one or more ASSET CREDITS, each of which is *a decrement in* a *CASH* ASSET ACCOUNT.*

Note that a kind of INTERNAL INVESTMENT is important to labor-intensive businesses, such as those involved in manufacturing or maintenance. This INTERNAL INVESTMENT is in an ASSET ACCOUNT called *AVAILABLE LABOR.* That is, a PAYROLL TRANSACTION is like an INTERNAL INVESTMENT TRANSACTION, spending *CASH* (or its equivalent) to obtain, not a machine, but a pool of labor (*AVAILABLE LABOR)* from which to draw. Each PAYROLL TRANSACTION must be *composed of* one or more ASSET CREDITS, each of which must be *a decrement in* *CASH*, plus one or more ASSET DEBIT, each of which must be *an increment in* *AVAILABLE LABOR*. (See Figure 7.9.) The significance of this will become apparent when we discuss LABOR USAGE in manufacturing.

---

* Alternatively, if money were borrowed to make the investment, the CREDITS would be LIABILITY CREDITS, *incrementing* a LIABILITY ACCOUNT.

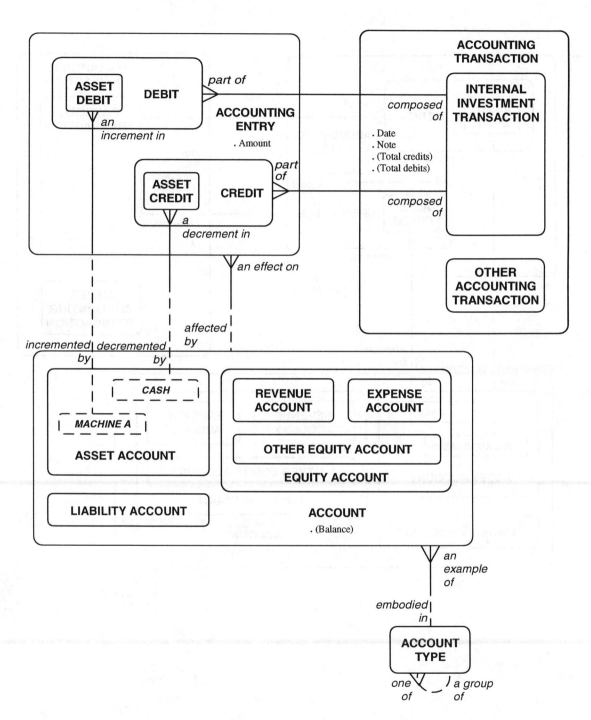

Figure 7.8: Internal Investments.

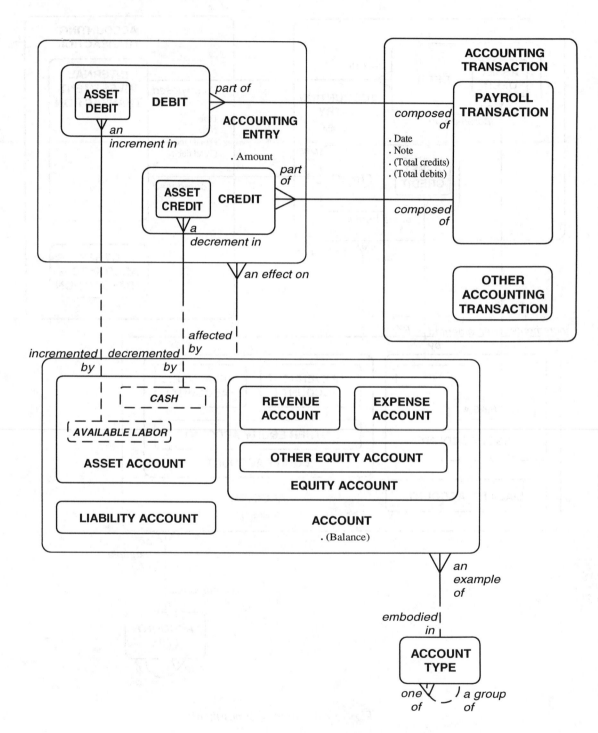

Figure 7.9: Investment in Labor.

Depreciation

Once a piece of equipment has been purchased (if it is to be treated as an ASSET), it has to be depreciated over time, so that the expense of consuming it can be recognized. Figure 7.10 shows that a DEPRECIATION EXPENSE must be composed of one or more EQUITY (EXPENSE) DEBITS, each of which is *a decrement in* an EQUITY ACCOUNT of ACCOUNT TYPE *DEPRECIATION EXPENSE*. (Again, this is an increase in the negative balance of an EXPENSE ACCOUNT.) Each DEPRECIATION EXPENSE must also be *composed of* one or more ASSET CREDITS, each of which is *a decrement in* the ASSET ACCOUNT for the asset which is being depreciated. (In Figure 7.10, this is shown, for example, as *MACHINE A*.)

Manufacturing and Maintenance

The activities described in Chapter Five all involve transforming labor and materials into some result—either a product or a condition of the plant or equipment in it. This process is reflected directly in accounting. So far in this chapter, we have described how assets are consumed when expenses are incurred, and how assets can be converted to other assets by means of internal investments. In the example shown in Figure 7.8, we converted cash into the asset *MACHINE A*, and in Figure 7.9, we converted cash into *AVAILABLE LABOR*.

Using the internal investment approach, we could also use cash to buy raw-material inventory. Manufacturing accounting can then convert the assets raw-material inventory and available labor into other assets. First, we will convert raw-material (RM) inventory into work-in-process (WIP) inventory (Figure 7.11); then, we will convert available labor into work-in-process inventory (Figure 7.12); and then finally, we will convert the WIP inventory into finished-goods (FG) inventory (Figure 7.13).

As we saw in Chapter Five, a WORK ORDER (specifically, a PRODUCTION ORDER) is *charged with* material consumption in ACTUAL ASSET USAGES, labor in TIME SHEET ENTRIES, and, optionally, equipment time in EQUIPMENT USAGES. It then is *the source of* one or more PRODUCTION DELIVERIES *of* an ASSET. The accounting analogy to the process of *consuming* resources in the course of manufacturing appears as the movement of value from the ACCOUNTS describing the ASSETS *RM INVENTORY* and *AVAILABLE LABOR*, to the ACCOUNTS describing *WIP INVENTORY*.

The accounting analogy to the process of *producing* products appears as the movement of value from *WIP INVENTORY* to *FG INVENTORY*. The following section describes how this is done.

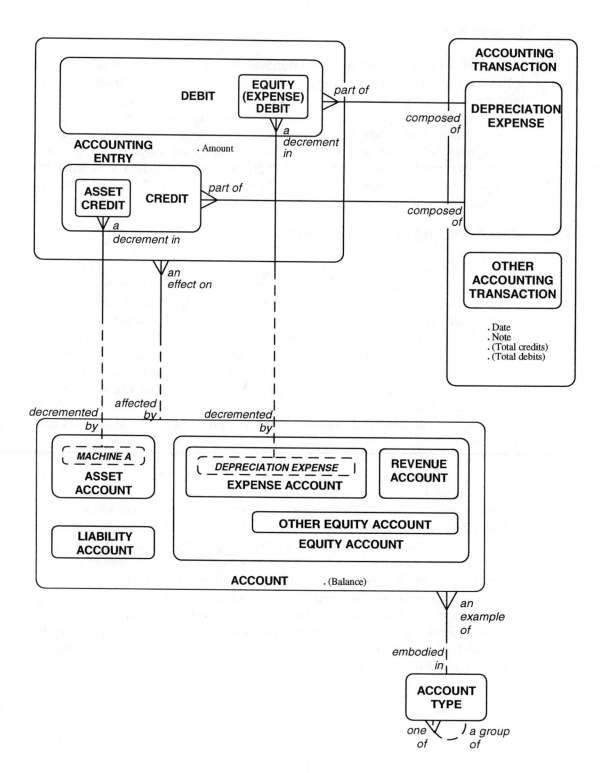

Figure 7.10: Depreciation.

Asset usage

First, we'll consume materials. Figure 7.11 shows that the value of raw materials is maintained in the ACCOUNTS for *RM INVENTORY*. Each (in this case, raw material) INVENTORY may be *accounted for in* one financial *RM INVENTORY*. This value is moved to the *WIP INVENTORY* ACCOUNT by means of the ASSET USAGE (accounting) TRANSACTION. Note that this financial transaction is directly *derived from* the ACTUAL ASSET USAGE, described in Chapter Five.

In a pure system, these transactions would be identical—that is, the real-world event ACTUAL ASSET USAGE would be equivalent to the accounting event ASSET USAGE TRANSACTION. In practice, however, one or more manufacturing transactions may be aggregated for accounting purposes. It is also possible that in some companies, a single ASSET USAGE may be split into separate accounting ASSET USAGE TRANSACTIONS.

It may, for example, be a policy to allocate ASSET USAGE charges to more than one account. To keep our explanation simpler, however, we'll assume that this is not the case. Here, groups of ACTUAL ASSET USAGE physical transactions are grouped into a single ASSET USAGE (accounting) TRANSACTION.

In practice, each ACTUAL ASSET USAGE (or any real-world transaction, for that matter) *may be accounted for in* the appropriate ASSET USAGE TRANSACTION. Some time may pass before the accounting transaction takes place, so we have to be able to record the physical transaction before the accounting one. To be sure, though, the activity must eventually be accounted for.*

Looking at the relationship from the other direction, the ACCOUNTING TRANSACTION *must be derived from* real transactions, such as ACTUAL ASSET USAGE.[†]

---

* This argues for a hitherto-uninvented modeling symbol representing a relationship that "initially may be, but eventually must be. . . ." Perhaps a wavy line would do it.

[†] The Internal Revenue Service, investors, and others frown on financial transactions that are not derived from real transactions.

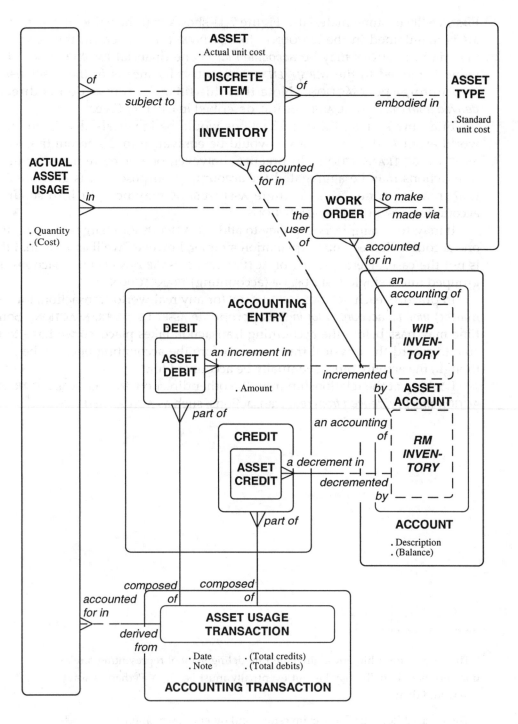

Figure 7.11: Asset Usage.

Each ASSET USAGE TRANSACTION must be *composed of* one or more ASSET CREDITS, each *a decrement in* the ASSET ACCOUNT *RM INVENTORY*—and it must be *composed of* one or more ASSET DEBITS, each *an increment in* another ASSET ACCOUNT—*WIP INVENTORY*. The "amount" of the ACCOUNTING ENTRY is the "cost" calculated for the ACTUAL ASSET USAGE being recorded. You will recall from Figure 5.7 in Chapter Five that this was the "quantity" (used) attribute of the ACTUAL ASSET USAGE, multiplied by either the "actual unit cost" of the ASSET or the "standard cost" or "list price" of the ASSET TYPE used. The *RM INVENTORY* being credited must be *an accounting of,* among others, the ASSET being used. The WORK ORDER in which the usage occurred must be *accounted for in* the *WIP INVENTORY* that was debited.

Note that, in Figure 7.11, all ACTUAL ASSET USAGE is *of* an ASSET—either a DISCRETE ITEM or an INVENTORY. In Chapter Five, we raised the possibility that an occurrence of ACTUAL ASSET USAGE could be *of* an ASSET TYPE, such as natural gas from a pipe. In that case, not shown here, the credit would not be an ASSET CREDIT, decreasing INVENTORY, but a LIABILITY CREDIT, increasing its liability to the gas company. Or, if the company had arranged with the gas company to dip directly into its checking account, the ASSET CREDIT would be to *CASH,* decrementing that.

Figure 7.12 shows that labor usage is handled in the same way as asset usage. Each LABOR USAGE (accounting) TRANSACTION must be *derived from* one or more TIME SHEET ENTRY transactions, while each TIME SHEET ENTRY may be *accounted for in* one and only one LABOR USAGE TRANSACTION. The record of actual labor usage is TIME SHEET ENTRY. The corresponding consumption of value is recorded with a LABOR USAGE TRANSACTION.

Each LABOR USAGE TRANSACTION must be *composed of* one or more ASSET DEBITS, each of which is *an increment in* the "balance" of the ASSET ACCOUNT *WIP INVENTORY* and one or more ASSET CREDITS, each of which is *a decrement in* the "balance" of the ASSET ACCOUNT *AVAILABLE LABOR*. (This is the *AVAILABLE LABOR* we bought with the INTERNAL INVESTMENT TRANSACTION shown in Figure 7.9.) Since the LABOR USAGE TRANSACTION must be *derived from* one or more TIME SHEET ENTRIES, so the "amount" of each CREDIT and DEBIT is the sum of the "costs" of the corresponding TIME SHEET ENTRIES. ("Cost," you will recall, was a derived attribute of TIME SHEET ENTRY, calculated as the "hours worked" on the TIME SHEET ENTRY multiplied by the "charge rate" of the PERSON involved.)

The *AVAILABLE LABOR* involved must be *an accounting of* one or more PEOPLE, and the *WIP INVENTORY,* as before, must be *an accounting of* at least the WORK ORDERS recorded in this transaction.

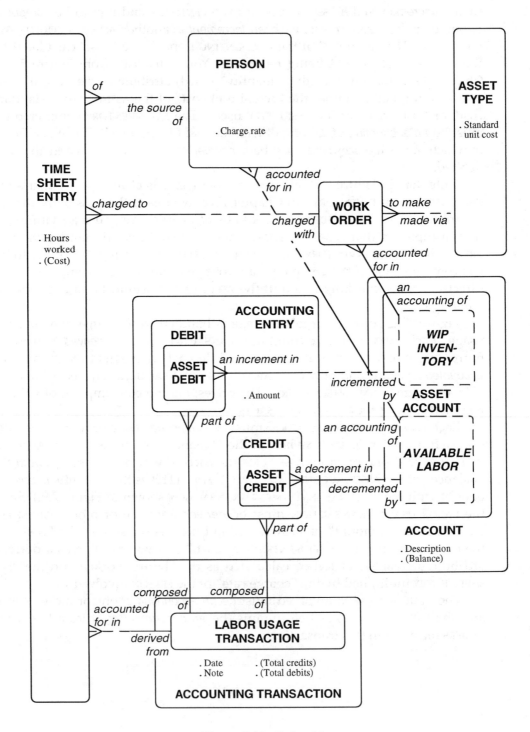

Figure 7.12: Labor Usage.

Delivery of product to finished-goods inventory completes the process. In Figure 7.13, a WORK ORDER COMPLETION TRANSACTION moves the "amount" of the DEBIT and CREDIT from *WIP INVENTORY* to *FG INVENTORY*. That is, each WORK ORDER COMPLETION TRANSACTION must be *composed of* one or more ASSET CREDITS, each of which must be *a decrement in WIP INVENTORY*—plus one or more ASSET DEBITS, each of which must be *an increment in FG INVENTORY*.

Each WORK ORDER COMPLETION TRANSACTION (a financial transaction) must be *derived from* one or more PRODUCTION DELIVERIES (the corresponding physical transactions), and the sum of the "amount" of all the debits and credits that are *part of* the WORK ORDER COMPLETION TRANSACTION must be equal to the "delivery cost" of the PRODUCTION DELIVERY. This is consistent with what we saw in Chapter Five, where the labor, material, and equipment costs were accumulated for a work order, and then "delivery cost" in PRODUCTION DELIVERY was set to the "unit cost" from the WORK ORDER ("total cost" divided by the "quantity" manufactured) multiplied by the "quantity" delivered. See the next section for what we do with "delivery cost."

In Figure 7.13, *WIP INVENTORY* must be *an accounting of* one or more WORK ORDERS, and each *FG INVENTORY* must be *an accounting of* one or more ASSETS. Note that both *RM* and *FG INVENTORY* can be each *an accounting of* DISCRETE ITEMS as well as INVENTORIES, since some of the ASSETS that are DISCRETE ITEMS from the point of view of the production floor, may be grouped together as one *FG INVENTORY* for accounting purposes. Other DISCRETE ITEMS may remain distinct on the books and have their own ACCOUNTS. In other words, in some cases, an *FG INVENTORY* (ACCOUNT) must be *an accounting of* one or more ASSETS (either DISCRETE ITEMS or INVENTORIES), as must an *RM INVENTORY*.

We now see that some ASSETS may be *accounted for in* either *FG INVENTORY* ASSET ACCOUNTS or *RM INVENTORY* ASSET ACCOUNTS. This suggests that the arced relationship in Figure 7.13 could be combined into the more general statement that each ASSET may be *accounted for in* one and only one ASSET ACCOUNT. Some organizations are not able to accept the "one and only one" requirement, as is discussed later in this chapter.

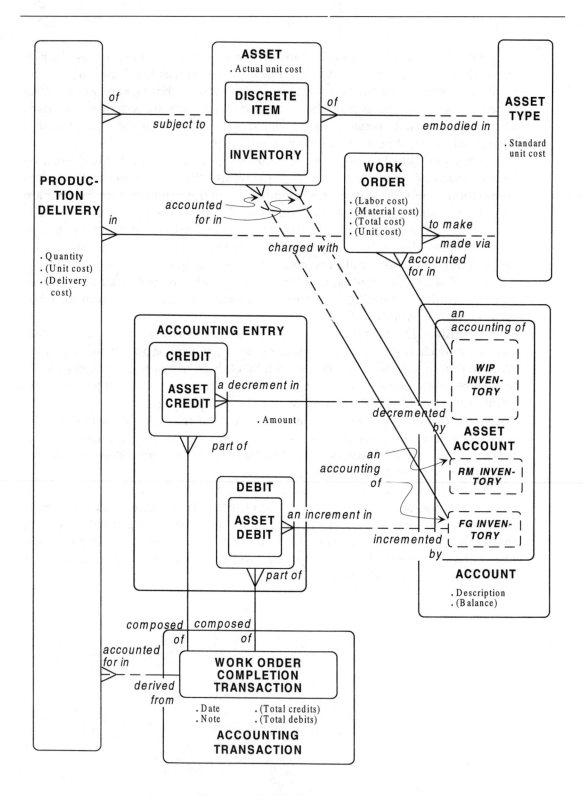

Figure 7.13: Work Order Completion.

Cost of Goods Sold

In the preceding discussions, the value delivered to finished-goods inventory (through work-in-process inventory) is the sum of the value of the raw material plus the labor used (plus, optionally, the cost of the equipment used). That is, if 50 Part A's are used, at $2 each, then $100 is moved from RM INVENTORY to WIP INVENTORY as shown in Figure 7.11, above. If 50 Part B's are used, at $1 each, then $50 is moved from RM INVENTORY to WIP INVENTORY in the same way. Similarly, if 5 hours of labor are invested in this process at $10 per hour, then $50 is moved from AVAILABLE LABOR to WIP INVENTORY, as shown above in Figure 7.12. Altogether in this example, then, a total of $200 has been added to the "balance" of WIP INVENTORY by the time the job is complete.

If 100 widgets are manufactured, the "unit cost" of each is $2, which is the $200 in accumulated production costs, divided by 100 widgets. If 70 widgets were delivered in one ACTUAL ASSET USAGE as represented by Figure 7.13, the "delivery cost" is $140 (70 widgets multiplied by $2 per widget). This $140 is also the amount moved from WIP INVENTORY to FG INVENTORY with the WORK ORDER COMPLETION TRANSACTION. When an ACTUAL ASSET USAGE records the last 30 widgets being delivered, the remaining $60 is moved from WIP INVENTORY to FG INVENTORY via another WORK ORDER COMPLETION TRANSACTION.

When finished goods are sold, a SALE (ACCOUNTING TRANSACTION) will use a DEBIT and CREDIT to convert a quantity of FG INVENTORY to the cost of the product sold, or COST OF GOODS SOLD. That is, if 40 widgets are sold, a "cost of goods sold" of $80 ($2 multiplied by 40) will be recognized. This amount is deducted from the "balance" of FG INVENTORY and is added to that for the ACCOUNT COST OF GOODS SOLD.

The transaction to do this is shown in Figure 7.14. Each SALE must be *composed of* one or more ASSET CREDITS, each of which is *a decrement in* FG INVENTORY, and it also must be *composed of* one or more EQUITY DEBITS, each of which is *a decrement in* equity by increasing COST OF GOODS SOLD.

Note that this SALE is none other than the INVOICE we saw in Figure 7.3 at the beginning of the chapter. That is, the recording of the INVOICE is equivalent to recording the SALE. For this reason, Figure 7.14 also shows the ASSET DEBIT and EQUITY CREDIT we saw at the beginning of the chapter. That is, the *increments in* ACCOUNTS RECEIVABLE and REVENUE ACCOUNT happen concurrently with the determination of COST OF GOODS SOLD.

Note that the "amount" in the EQUITY CREDIT to a REVENUE ACCOUNT (and the corresponding ASSET DEBIT) is the revenue from the sale. From this may be subtracted the "amount" of the EQUITY DEBIT to COST OF GOODS SOLD (and the corresponding ASSET CREDIT), to determine the profit from the sale.

This is, of course, much too simple an example for real companies, where inventory policies, standard costing procedures, and so forth undoubtedly make calculating unit costs much more complex—but it will do for our demonstration.

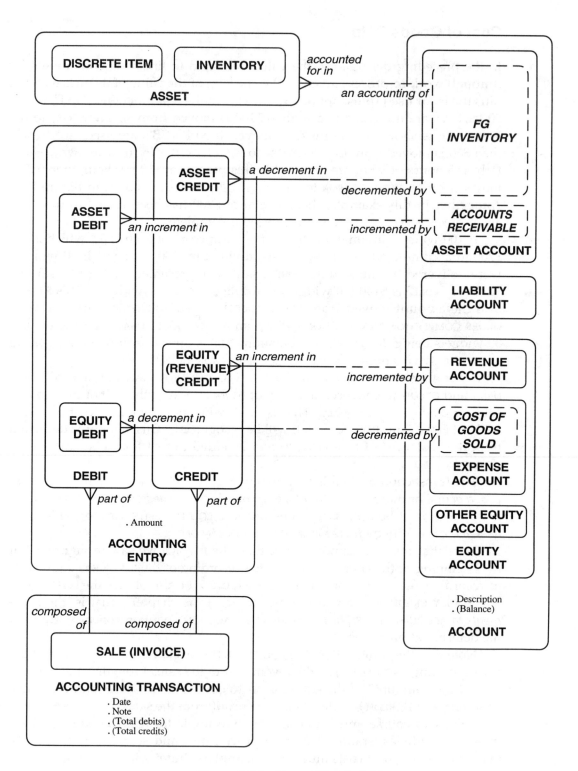

Figure 7.14: Cost of Goods Sold.

The Meta-model

Figure 7.15 shows a composite of all the ACCOUNTING TRANSACTION types that we have seen so far. These ACCOUNTING TRANSACTIONS are representative of what a typical company or government agency can expect to see. The list is not exhaustive, however, and OTHER ACCOUNTING TRANSACTION remains an undefinably big box.

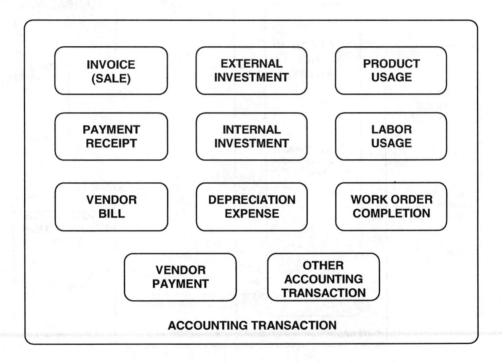

Figure 7.15: Accounting Transaction Subtypes.

To address the dynamic nature of this structure, instead of showing each kind of transaction as a subtype, we could simply portray them all as a single separate entity, ACCOUNTING TRANSACTION TYPE, as shown on the lower right side of Figure 7.16. This has the advantage of allowing us easily to add new ACCOUNTING TRANSACTION TYPES whenever necessary.

Earlier, however, we observed that accounting theory describes rules in terms of ACCOUNT TYPES. Different rules make use of different ACCOUNT TYPES. In any given organization, its policies dictate that each transaction be defined in terms of the specific accounts affected. We can define the rules governing transactions as ACCOUNTING RULE ENTRIES, showing them at two levels.

First, Figure 7.16 shows that an ACCOUNTING TRANSACTION TYPE must be *composed of* at least one CREDIT RULE ENTRY and at least one DEBIT RULE ENTRY. Each of these ACCOUNTING RULE ENTRIES, then, must be *to* an ACCOUNT TYPE. Thus, if you have an ACCOUNTING TRANSACTION TYPE, such as the "internal investment" shown earlier in Figure 7.8, for example, you can look here to discover that it is *composed of* a CREDIT RULE ENTRY *to* the ACCOUNT TYPE "cash," and a DEBIT RULE ENTRY *to* the ACCOUNT TYPE "fixed assets."

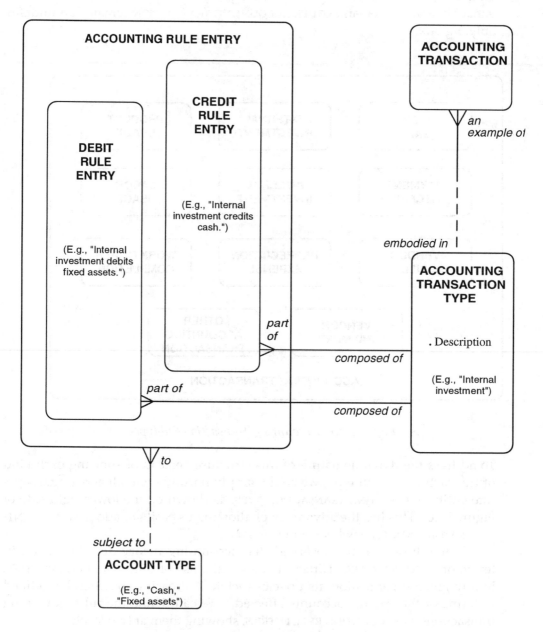

Figure 7.16: Accounting Transaction Types.

In a particular company, however, the rules have to be described at a second level, in more detail. This is shown in Figure 7.17.

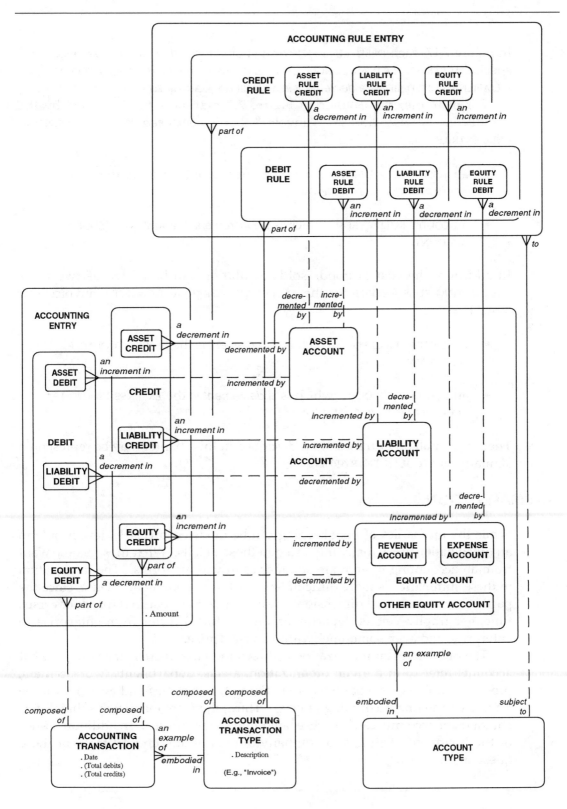

Figure 7.17: Accounting Rule Entries.

In Figure 7.17, each DEBIT RULE ENTRY must be *an increment in* or *a decrement in* a specific ACCOUNT. (An ASSET RULE DEBIT is *an increment in* an ASSET ACCOUNT, and a LIABILITY RULE DEBIT is *a decrement in* a LIABILITY ACCOUNT.)

For example, the INVOICE in Figure 7.3 may now be described by the ACCOUNTING TRANSACTION TYPE "invoice" that is *composed of* two ACCOUNTING RULE ENTRIES:

- an ASSET RULE DEBIT, which specifies *an increment in* the ASSET ACCOUNT *ACCOUNTS RECEIVABLE*

- an EQUITY RULE CREDIT, which is *an increment in* a REVENUE (EQUITY) ACCOUNT

In addition, the cost-of-goods-sold calculation can be added as two more ACCOUNTING RULE ENTRIES for the ACCOUNTING TRANSACTION TYPE "invoice" (or "sale"):

- an ASSET RULE CREDIT, which is *a decrement in* the ASSET ACCOUNT *FG INVENTORY*

- an EQUITY RULE DEBIT, which is *a decrement in* the EXPENSE (EQUITY) ACCOUNT *COST OF GOODS SOLD*

The rules for all other transactions described in this chapter may be represented similarly as ACCOUNT ENTRY RULES.

SUMMARIZATION

While the mechanics of bookkeeping can be modeled precisely, few people in an organization are actually interested in those details. What most people want from an accounting system are summaries in various forms. The information in these summaries is more difficult to model in a fundamental sense, since the particular methods and dimensions of summarization required (product versus time, geography versus department, and so forth) differ from enterprise to enterprise, and even sometimes within an enterprise.

The problem of summarization is threefold. First, there is the issue of what accounts refer to in a given organization: assets, departments, work centers, products, projects, or what have you. Second, companies and agencies can be arbitrary in setting accounting policies. Third, there are many ways that different kinds of accounts can be aggregated into larger groups. In addition, issues of the treatment of time and company budgets transcend all three of these questions.

What are we referring to?

The first acute problem is the identification of accounts in the first place. For example, Chapter Four introduced the concept of ASSET as a physical thing owned by the company. In principle, an asset described by the entity ASSET should be the same as an asset that represents the value the company holds in a corresponding ASSET ACCOUNT. The difficulty lies in mapping one to the other. In a *tidy* company, each ASSET (inventory, building, or piece of equipment, for example) would be represented by *exactly one* ASSET ACCOUNT, as shown in the upper part of Figure 7.18 (The Ideal).

The Ideal

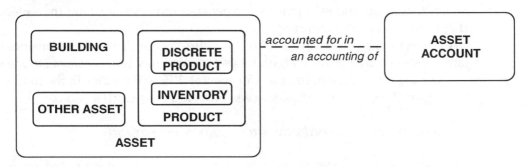

The Real

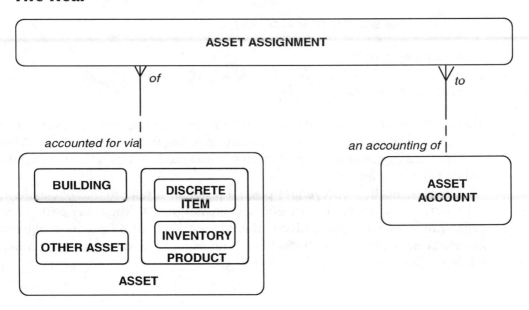

Figure 7.18: Assets.

In a *real* company, however, an ASSET ACCOUNT may be *an accounting of one or more* ASSETS (as we asserted earlier), and an ASSET might be *accounted for in one or more* ASSET ACCOUNTS. This requires an ASSET ASSIGNMENT *of* an ASSET *to* an ASSET ACCOUNT, giving the more complex view shown in the lower part of Figure 7.18 (The Real). Here, each ASSET ACCOUNT may be *an accounting of* one or more ASSET ASSIGNMENTS *of* an ASSET, and each ASSET may be *accounted for via* one or more ASSET ASSIGNMENTS *to* an ASSET ACCOUNT. Accumulation of transaction data by asset, then, requires specification of which kind of asset (physical or financial) is of interest.

Another problem with identifying what accounts refer to is the issue of "cost centers" and "revenue centers." Many companies aggregate expenses by cost center. That is, in the model represented by Figure 7.19, each EXPENSE ACCOUNT must be *for* a COST CENTER. A COST CENTER is defined to be a part of the business that accumulates expenses. Expenses (and revenues) are then identified as to the cost center involved.

A problem arises, however, with the definition of "part of the business." Again, as shown by Figure 7.19, each COST CENTER may be *to account for* one or more COST CENTER ASSIGNMENTS *of* any of several different entities in the model.

In Figure 7.19, a COST CENTER ASSIGNMENT is *to* a COST CENTER and *of*

- a PLACEMENT *of* an INTERNAL ORGANIZATION *in* a SITE, or

- an INTERNAL ORGANIZATION, including all SITES where it is located, or

- a WORK CENTER, including all INTERNAL ORGANIZATIONS assigned to it, or

- a PIECE OF EQUIPMENT or a PRODUCT, or

- a PROJECT, or

- (something else)

This list is not complete. Because the possibilities for allocating expenses are so broad, COST CENTER could refer to virtually anything in the organization. Which aspect of the organization a COST CENTER is assigned to depends on accounting policies of the organization.

The classification of revenues poses a problem similar to that of classifying expenses. In principle, revenues could be assigned to the same parts of the organization as expenses. Indeed, often departments or offices are designated as profit centers, to denote the fact that both expenses and revenues are collected there. (See Figure 7.20.)

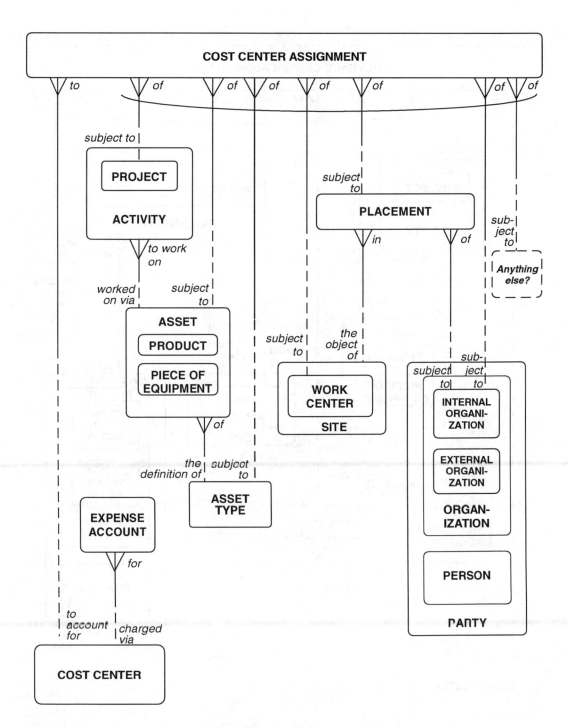

Figure 7.19: *Allocating Expenses.*

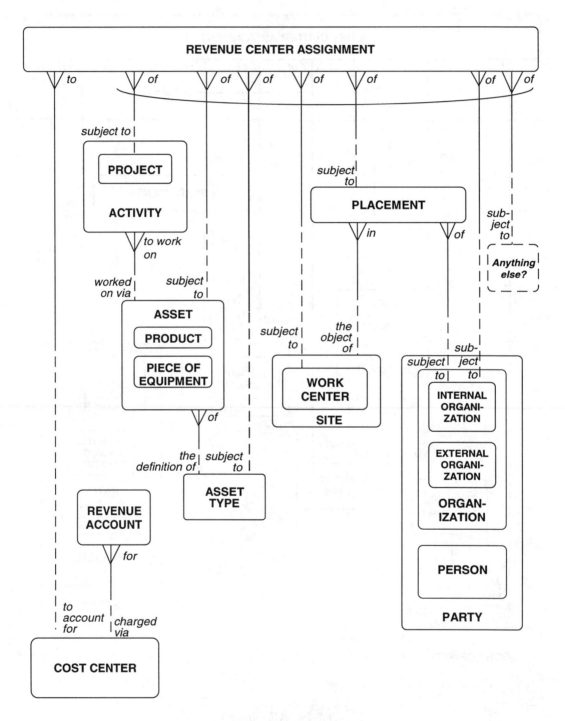

Figure 7.20: *Attributing Revenue.*

What is the company's (or agency's) accounting policy?

The second problem in summarizing accounting information is that the *policies* that determine such things as when revenue is recognized, how depreciation is determined, and so forth, are defined by the organization. The underlying accounting system, as modeled above, is flexible enough to accept many different kinds of policies, but any particular company would like to see the model constrained to reflect its own. The problem with this is that while these policies may be justified by current circumstances, they remain arbitrary in the sense that they may be changed at will. If they are incorporated in the model, the model is vulnerable to future changes. By definition, there are no standard data model patterns of accounting policy.

What are the account groups?

The third part of the account summarization problem is that the *grouping* of accounts into categories for reporting is arbitrary. Figure 7.1 showed that each ACCOUNT must be *an example of* one and only one ACCOUNT TYPE, such as "cash," for example. We also saw that an ACCOUNT TYPE could be *composed of* one or more other ACCOUNT TYPES. In large corporations with multiple subsidiaries, an ACCOUNT TYPE may be *embodied in* more than one ACCOUNT. This is one kind of classification of accounts, based on the nature of the transactions applied to the ACCOUNTS in each ACCOUNT TYPE.

If other kinds of classification are needed, ACCOUNTS may be grouped into ACCOUNT CATEGORIES, as shown in Figure 7.21. Since one ACCOUNT may be *in* more than one ACCOUNT CATEGORY, and one ACCOUNT CATEGORY may be a classification for more than one ACCOUNT, it is necessary to create the entity ACCOUNT CLASSIFICATION, in which each ACCOUNT CLASSIFICATION is *of* an ACCOUNT *into* an ACCOUNT CATEGORY.

An alternative way of grouping accounts is to define the account group itself as a higher-level ACCOUNT. That is, an ACCOUNT may be *part of* another ACCOUNT. ACCOUNT balances may then be rolled up (summed together) into larger balances of more comprehensive ACCOUNTS. Again, the particular definitions of roll-up rules will depend on the enterprise,* but the essential structure is shown by the pig's ear in Figure 7.21.

Note that this is a hierarchical way of grouping ACCOUNTS, and it does not allow an account to be in more than one higher-level account. If a company wanted to allow for multiple roll-up paths, changing the model would be easy: All that would be required would be simply to replace the loop with a "structure" entity. Administering such an arrangement, however, would be extremely difficult.

---

* Indeed, in one company, the definitions for roll-up rules differed from department to department. *That* posed an interesting modeling challenge! Drawing that model is left as an exercise for the reader.

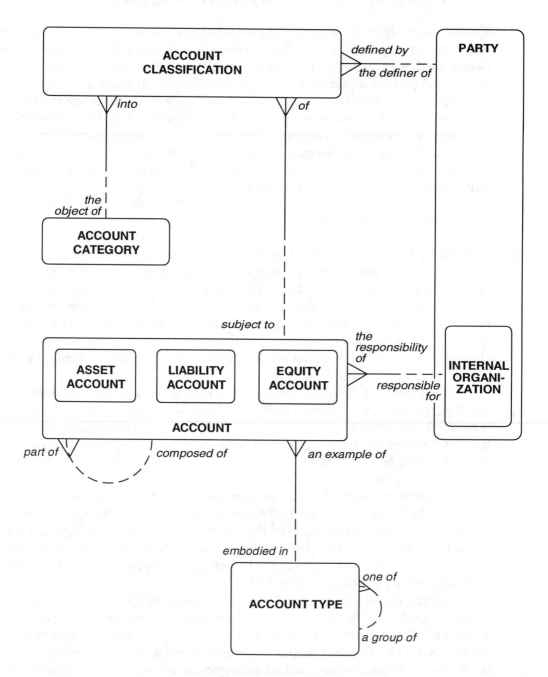

Figure 7.21: Account Categories and Structure.

Again, the actual combination of ACCOUNT TYPES, ACCOUNT CATEGORIES, and ACCOUNT roll-up schemes will depend on the company or agency. All structures, however, will be made up of the elements we have seen here.

Time and Budgets

One dimension that is present in all accounting data is time. Every ACCOUNTING TRANSACTION, and therefore every summarization of ACCOUNTING TRANSACTIONS, is placed in time. An important attribute of ACCOUNTING TRANSACTION is "date" (see Figure 7.17, for example). This means that the future and the past can be dealt with in equivalent ways. A budget in principle is nothing other than a set of ACCOUNTING TRANSACTIONS dated in the future. (See Figure 7.22.)

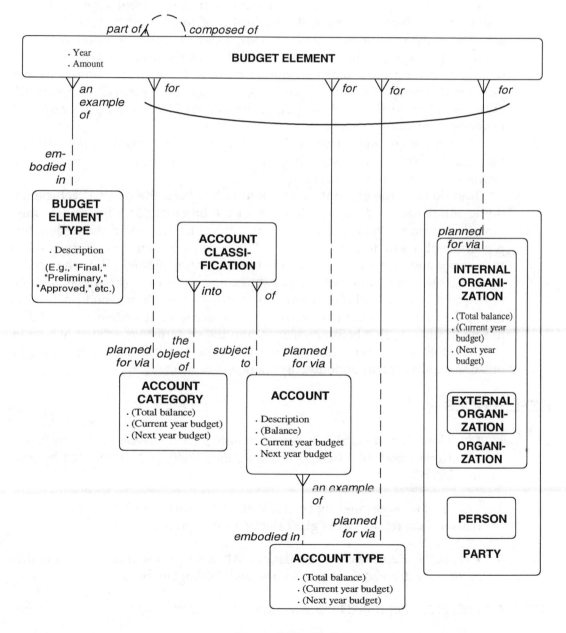

Figure 7.22: Budgets.

The problem in dealing with organizational time is that the basic data that describe the company's history are collected at the ACCOUNTING TRANSACTION level, while budgeting is done with aggregates. Budgets for groups of accounts or for departments, for example, are broken into their components only after the basic framework of the budget has been defined. The process of developing budgets begins at a corporate level, or at least at the level of groups of accounts. Only later is it driven down into more detail.

As shown in Figure 7.22, a simple way of keeping track of budgets at the account (or any other) level, then, is to simply make "current year budget" or "next year budget," for example, attributes of the ACCOUNT, ACCOUNT TYPE, ACCOUNT CATEGORY, or INTERNAL ORGANIZATION. A more rigorous approach would require something like a BUDGET ELEMENT, as shown in the figure. A BUDGET ELEMENT for a particular year allows there to be different budgets in that year for different BUDGET ELEMENT TYPES, such as "preliminary," "approved," "final," and so forth. Each aggregate BUDGET ELEMENT may be *composed of* lower-level BUDGET ELEMENTS.

Thus, a budget might first be developed for an ORGANIZATION, then broken down by ACCOUNT TYPE, ACCOUNT CATEGORY, or both, until eventually it is expressed in terms of the ACCOUNT.

Traditionally, the accounting mechanism has been the original vehicle for doing summaries and aggregations about the organization's financial status. Now, however, more integrated systems, gathering data about the underlying physical realities of an organization, will be able to do more and more of these summaries and aggregations—outside the accounting system. With the appropriate lists of CONTRACTS, LINE ITEMS, PARTIES, and so forth, it should be possible to determine exactly who sold how much of what to whom—and how much they paid for it—without ever going into the accounting system. This ability has not been available before, when accounting systems were the only way to get the information. Now that it is available, however, the role of accounting in business reporting will undoubtedly change.

REFERENCES

1 M.J. Gordon and G. Shillinglaw. *Accounting: A Management Approach*, 4th ed. (Homewood, Ill.: Richard D. Irwin, Inc., 1969), p. 1. Reprinted by permission.

2 *Ibid.*, p. 14. Reprinted by permission. Note this 1969 book's publication date and the reference to "giant electronic computers."

3 *Ibid.*, p. 28. Reprinted by permission. All descriptions of accounting in this section are derived from the Gordon and Shillinglaw book.

4 *Ibid.*, p. 22. Reprinted by permission.

8

THE LABORATORY

*M*any companies and government agencies use laboratories to analyze materials for various purposes. A laboratory could be used by a regulatory agency to identify salmonella in eggs, by a chemical manufacturer to determine a product grade, or by a quality assurance department to identify contaminants in a product. Whatever the purpose of the laboratory, the underlying model is common to them all.

SAMPLES, TESTS, AND OBSERVATIONS

The laboratory process begins with a SAMPLE. (See Figure 8.1.) A SAMPLE could be *taken from* a SITE, or it could be more specifically *taken from* an ASSET—a PIECE OF EQUIPMENT or an INVENTORY. Here, a PIECE OF EQUIPMENT may be a tank, a machine, or even a spigot. The ASSET is itself currently at a SITE.*

The SAMPLE must be *drawn according to* a predefined SAMPLE METHOD that in turn may be *composed of* one or more SAMPLE METHOD STEPS. The extent to which the identity of the SAMPLE is known depends upon the laboratory and the circumstances of drawing it. A SAMPLE may be *assumed to be of* a MATERIAL TYPE (as when, for example, a pharmaceutical lot is being tested for purity), it may be *to be tested for the presence of* a MATERIAL TYPE (as when a chemical that may be one of several grades is being tested), or its composition may be completely unknown (as when polluted water is being tested).

Depending on the laboratory, a sample may be *taken by* an individual PERSON or by an ORGANIZATION. Whether this relationship points to PERSON or more generally to PARTY depends upon the organization. (In Figure 8.1, it is shown to be *taken by* a PERSON.)

---

* This is a simplified view of the sources of SAMPLES. A more sophisticated model is presented in Chapter Ten.

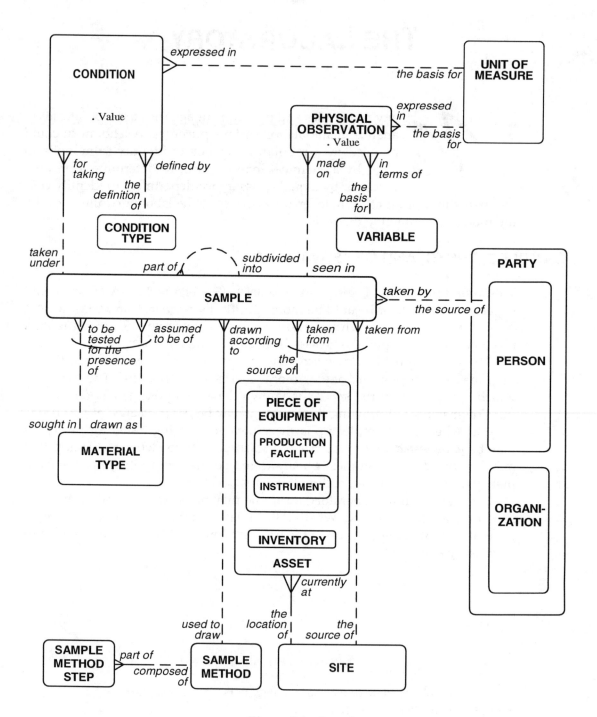

Figure 8.1: Samples.

The SAMPLE may be *taken under* one or more CONDITIONS, in which each CONDITION must be *defined by* a CONDITION TYPE. A CONDITION TYPE may describe such things as humidity, temperature, or pressure, and the "value" of the CONDITION tells how much (humidity, temperature, or pressure, for example) was present when the sample was taken. CONDITION may be *expressed in* a UNIT OF MEASURE.

Once collected, it is possible that a SAMPLE may be *subdivided into* one or more smaller SAMPLES.

One or more PHYSICAL OBSERVATIONS (color or texture, for example) must be *made on* the SAMPLE. The "value" of the PHYSICAL OBSERVATION, then, might be "blue," or "soft." Each PHYSICAL OBSERVATION must be *in terms of* a VARIABLE, such as the "color" or "texture" mentioned above. In some cases, the PHYSICAL OBSERVATION may be *expressed in* a UNIT OF MEASURE, such as "feet."

Figure 8.2 shows that each SAMPLE may be *subject to* one or more TESTS, in which each TEST is *an example of* a TEST TYPE. That is, the TEST TYPE may be *embodied in* the TEST being *conducted on* the SAMPLE. The process of conducting any TEST that is *an example of* that TEST TYPE may entail one or more of the TEST METHOD STEPS that are *part of* that TEST TYPE. That is, each TEST TYPE may be *composed of* one or more TEST METHOD STEPS.

Each TEST may be *the source of* one or more TEST OBSERVATIONS. As with PHYSICAL OBSERVATIONS, each TEST OBSERVATION must be *in terms of* a VARIABLE—where the "name" of that VARIABLE might be "temperature," "viscosity," "pH," or such, and the "value" of the TEST OBSERVATION could be "92," "1.7," "7.5," and so forth. A TEST OBSERVATION may also be *expressed in* a UNIT OF MEASURE. TEST OBSERVATIONS and PHYSICAL OBSERVATIONS are two principal kinds of OBSERVATION.

An OBSERVATION must be *made by* a PARTY. In the case of TEST OBSERVATIONS, this is typically the same PERSON that is *responsible for* the TEST, but it doesn't have to be. The OBSERVATION may be *made by* an assistant, or it may be simply credited to the laboratory (ORGANIZATION) as a whole, hence the relationship's attachment to PARTY rather than PERSON. The "date" and "time" of the OBSERVATION may also be recorded.

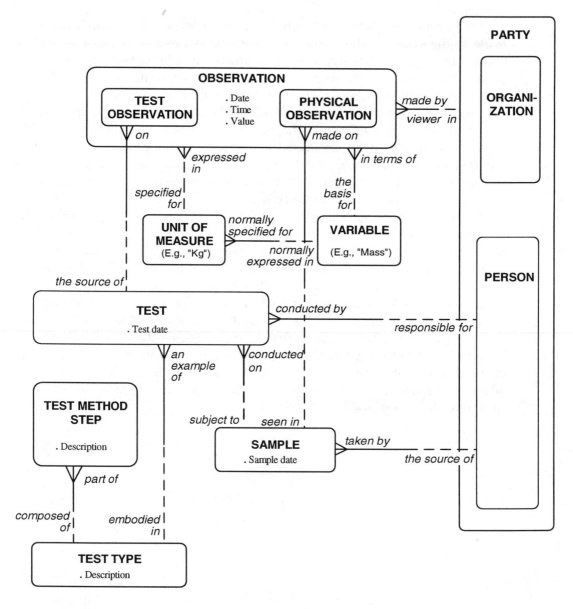

Figure 8.2: Tests and Observations.

DERIVED OBSERVATIONS

In addition to TEST OBSERVATIONS and PHYSICAL OBSERVATIONS, DERIVED OBSERVATIONS are *calculated from* one or more other OBSERVATIONS (either TEST OBSERVATIONS or other DERIVED OBSERVATIONS*), as shown in Figure 8.3. A DERIVED OBSERVATION may be a total, an average, or some other function. The "expression" for calculating the DERIVED OBSERVATION is its principal attribute.

Since the same OBSERVATION may be used to calculate more than one DERIVED OBSERVATION, the entity SUMMARIZATION is *the use of* an OBSERVATION in *the calculation of* a DERIVED OBSERVATION.

For example, a DERIVED OBSERVATION might be the sum of ten readings. It may be *calculated from* ten SUMMARIZATIONS (each of which is *the use of* another OBSERVATION), plus a "constant." The main attribute of SUMMARIZATION is "operator," which tells the role that this particular SUMMARIZATION plays in the calculation. In the case of the sum, the "operator" for each SUMMARIZATION that is *the use of* another OBSERVATION is "plus."

A derived attribute of DERIVED OBSERVATION is "number of summarizations." An average may then be computed from the sum previously calculated, by dividing it by the "number of summarizations" of that DERIVED OBSERVATION. That is, the SUMMARIZATION would represent *the calculation of* the average, and would be *the use of* the sum described above. The "operator" would be "divide by the sum's number of summarizations."

Often the algorithm for this summarization is defined for all occurrences of OBSERVATIONS on the VARIABLE being observed. A set of SUMMARY RULES *to derive* the VARIABLE describes that algorithm.

In a similar structure to that of SUMMARIZATION, each SUMMARY RULE *to derive* a VARIABLE must be *the use of* another VARIABLE.

For example, if "mass" and "volume" were normally determined from TESTS, and "density" were the VARIABLE desired, a SUMMARY RULE *to derive* "density" would be *the use of* "mass" (with the attribute "operator" whose value is "plus"), and another would be *the use of* "volume" (with "divided by" as the value of the attribute "operator"). The value of the attribute "expression" for the DERIVED VARIABLE "density" would be "mass/volume."

---

* The model permits you also to base a DERIVED OBSERVATION on a PHYSICAL OBSERVATION. This seems an unlikely occurrence, however, but if you need it, you can do it.

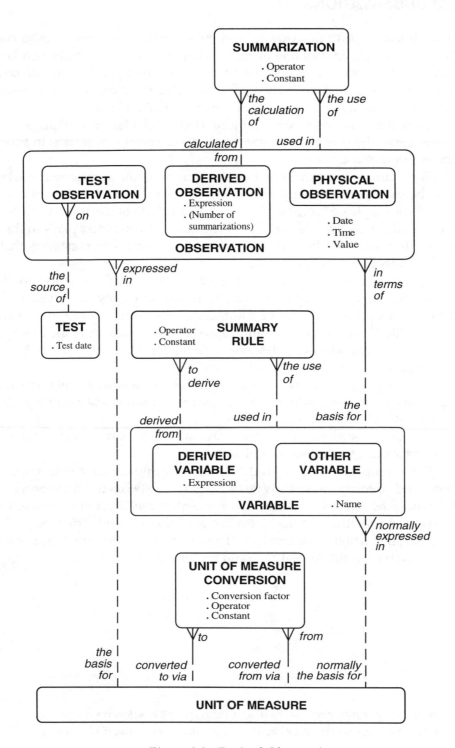

Figure 8.3: Derived Observations.

As mentioned above, for each OBSERVATION, the UNIT OF MEASURE may be specified. Alternatively, the VARIABLE that is *the basis for* the OBSERVATION may be *normally expressed in a* UNIT OF MEASURE. (A VARIABLE such as "mass," for example, may be *normally expressed in* "kilograms.") If the UNIT OF MEASURE that is *the basis for* a particular OBSERVATION is not different from the UNIT OF MEASURE that is *normally the basis for* the VARIABLE (which is *the basis for* the OBSERVATION), then it needn't be specified explicitly. Note that some VARIABLES such as "pH" and "color" have no UNIT OF MEASURE at all, but a business rule not shown on the diagram would assert that other VARIABLES require that a UNIT OF MEASURE be specified either generally for the VARIABLE, or for each OBSERVATION.

A later analyst may want to see an OBSERVATION *in terms of* different UNITS OF MEASURE. The entity UNIT OF MEASURE CONVERSION describes the relationships between pairs of occurrences of UNIT OF MEASURE. Its primary attribute is "conversion factor," although some conversions also need a "constant." That is, an occurrence of UNIT OF MEASURE CONVERSION must be *from* one UNIT OF MEASURE *to* another, with the "conversion factor" multiplied by the one to get the other, and, optionally, the "constant" either added to or subtracted from the result.

For example, if one occurrence of UNIT OF MEASURE were "pounds" and another were "kilograms," an occurrence of UNIT OF MEASURE CONVERSION pointing *from* the "kilograms" UNIT OF MEASURE *to* the "pounds" UNIT OF MEASURE would have "2.2" as the value of its attribute "conversion factor."

As a second example, to convert from "degrees Celsius" to "degrees Fahrenheit," we establish that the "conversion factor" is "1.8," and the "constant" is "+32."*

To summarize, in order to convert a "value" of an OBSERVATION to a different UNIT OF MEASURE, it is necessary only to multiply the original "value" by the "conversion factor" in the UNIT OF MEASURE CONVERSION *from* the original UNIT OF MEASURE *to* the UNIT OF MEASURE desired. If necessary, you must also add the "constant" (which may be negative) in the same UNIT OF MEASURE CONVERSION.

TEST TYPES

As shown above in Figure 8.2, a TEST TYPE may be *embodied in* one or more TESTS. Its definition includes the TEST METHOD STEPS that are *part of* the TEST TYPE. Figure 8.4 shows that also included in the definition of the TEST TYPE are the EXPECTED OBSERVATIONS (or, to some, the BASE LINE) *for* that TEST TYPE. An EXPECTED

---

* This is a convoluted way to say that to get "degrees Fahrenheit" you multiply the "degrees Celsius" amount by 1.8 and add 32.

OBSERVATION is the fact that TESTS that are examples of a particular TEST TYPE are expected to be *the source of* OBSERVATIONS *in terms of* a particular VARIABLE, *expressed in* a UNIT OF MEASURE. A particular TEST TYPE, for example, might be a method for determining the boiling point of a material. The "description" of an EXPECTED OBSERVATION would be "boiling point," and it would be *in terms of* "temperature" (the VARIABLE) *expressed in* "degrees Celsius" (the UNIT OF MEASURE).

Note that while the EXPECTED OBSERVATIONS are *for* a TEST TYPE, actual OBSERVATIONS are *on* actual TESTS. The "value" of a OBSERVATION *on* a particular TEST (with a test "date" of "12/9/95") in the boiling point example might be "150." Here, each OBSERVATION *may be against* an EXPECTED OBSERVATION. In your organization, you may want to make that mandatory.

Since the EXPECTED OBSERVATION is *for* a TEST TYPE, you would expect that EXPECTED OBSERVATIONS would only be *seen in* TEST OBSERVATIONS (not DERIVED OBSERVATIONS or PHYSICAL OBSERVATIONS). It is not out of the question, however, that a TEST TYPE could be *defined in terms of* the expectation that PHYSICAL OBSERVATIONS would also be made as a TEST is being conducted. Similarly, specific DERIVED OBSERVATIONS that are significant to the TEST TYPE may be *calculated from* one or more TEST OBSERVATION(s) *on* TESTS that are *examples of* that TEST TYPE.* Thus, an EXPECTED OBSERVATION *for* a TEST TYPE might be *seen in* one or more DERIVED OBSERVATIONS or one or more PHYSICAL OBSERVATIONS, as well as one or more TEST OBSERVATIONS.

Hence, Figure 8.4 shows that each EXPECTED OBSERVATION may be *seen in* one or more OBSERVATIONS of any kind.

SAMPLE METHODS

Laboratory activities are often organized around SAMPLE METHODS. A SAMPLE METHOD may determine not only the procedures for collecting the sample, but also the kinds of tests appropriate for samples drawn according to that method.

---

* That is, specific DERIVED OBSERVATIONS that are significant to the TEST TYPE may be *calculated from* one or more SUMMARIZATIONS, each of which is *the use of* TEST OBSERVATION(S) *on* TESTS . . .

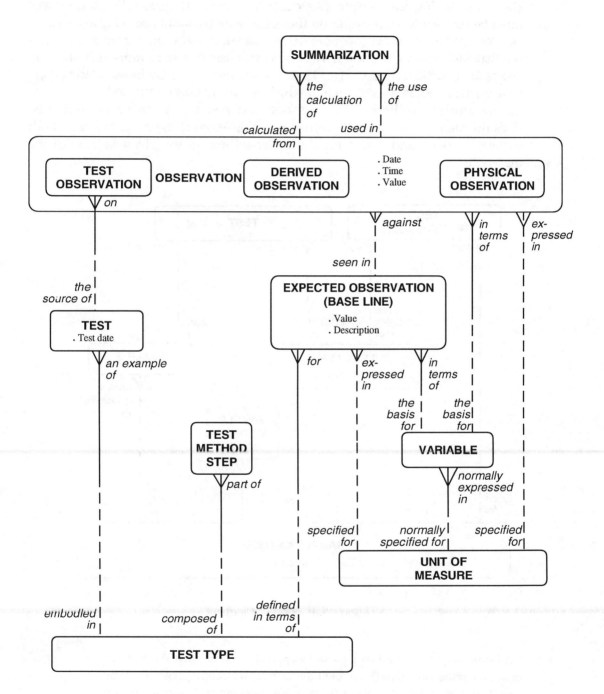

Figure 8.4: Expected Observations.

In some cases, different kinds of tests are required, depending on the circumstances of taking the sample. As described above (Figure 8.1), each SAMPLE must be (or *may be*, depending on the organization) *drawn according to* a SAMPLE METHOD, *composed of* one or more SAMPLE METHOD STEPS. In Figure 8.5, we can see that each SAMPLE METHOD may also be *the basis for* one or more TEST REQUIREMENTS *for* a particular TEST TYPE. That is, each TEST TYPE may be *the object of* one or more TEST REQUIREMENTS, each of which is *from* a SAMPLE METHOD.*

An attribute of both SAMPLE METHOD and TEST TYPE is "medium"—that is, does the method apply to the sample in solid, semi-solid, or liquid form? Both SAMPLE METHODS and TEST TYPES differ depending on the physical state of the material.

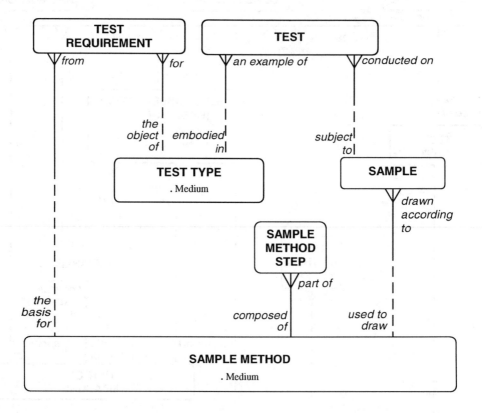

Figure 8.5: Sample Methods.

* A business rule would then have to be applied to ensure that the TEST TYPE *embodied in* the TESTS (which were on the SAMPLE) was appropriate, given the TEST REQUIREMENTS *from* the SAMPLE METHOD that the SAMPLE was *drawn according to.* That is, in Figure 8.5, there are two paths to TEST TYPE from SAMPLE METHOD. Occurrences of the TEST TYPE and SAMPLE entities have to be defined to ensure that they are consistent with each other.

TESTING FOR MATERIAL COMPOSITION

In Figure 8.1, we saw that a SAMPLE may be *assumed to be of* a MATERIAL TYPE, or it may be *to be tested for the presence of* a MATERIAL TYPE. As a third alternative, the content of the sample may be completely unknown.

In the first case, the underlying material is completely known, and the testing is for the purpose of discovering characteristics (such as its purity, for example) that don't affect the definition of that material. In the second and third cases, the content of the material is unknown to some degree.

In these latter cases, as shown in Figure 8.6, an OBSERVATION (TEST, PHYSICAL, or DERIVED) may be *an indication of the presence of* a MATERIAL TYPE. The presence of an occurrence of this relationship is actually the result of an evaluation:* To determine whether the OBSERVATION (*in terms of* a particular VARIABLE) is or is not *an indication of the presence of* the MATERIAL TYPE in question (either CUSTOM or STANDARD), simply compare the "high value" and the "low value" of each SPECIFICATION RANGE *of* the MATERIAL TYPE[†] (which is *in terms of* a VARIABLE and *expressed in* a UNIT OF MEASURE) with the "value" of the OBSERVATION (*in terms of* the same VARIABLE and *expressed in* the same UNIT OF MEASURE).[‡]

If enough (as defined by the laboratory) OBSERVATIONS are in fact *indications of the presence of* a MATERIAL TYPE, the laboratory can then assert that the SAMPLE in fact contains that MATERIAL TYPE.

We now have the ability to determine if the MATERIAL we are delivering under CONTRACT to a customer meets that customer's SPECIFICATIONS, as described in Chapter Six.

---

* The act of comparing, of course, is a process and is not shown on the data model.

[†] That is, compare the "high value" and the "low value" of each SPECIFICATION RANGE that is *part of* the SPECIFICATION *of* the MATERIAL TYPE . . .

[‡] If necessary, use the UNIT OF MEASURE CONVERSION to make the UNITS OF MEASURE comparable.

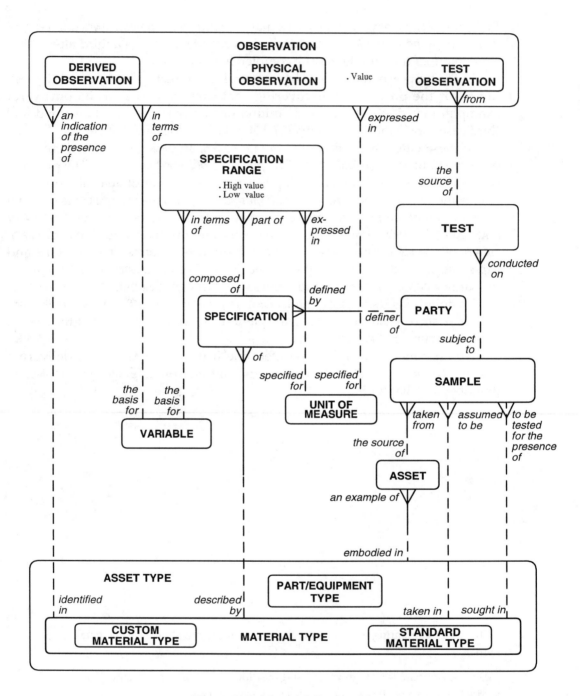

Figure 8.6: Material Composition.

TESTS AS ACTIVITIES

Both TESTS and TEST STEPS can be construed as ACTIVITIES, as we described them in Chapter Five. As with other ACTIVITIES described in Chapter Five, the conduct of TESTS uses resources.

Figure 8.7 introduces the entity INSTRUMENT (a kind of PIECE OF EQUIPMENT) and INSTRUMENT TYPE (a kind of PART/EQUIPMENT TYPE). It shows that each TEST must be *conducted with examples of* an INSTRUMENT TYPE, or *conducted with* a specific INSTRUMENT. An INSTRUMENT is a particular kind of PIECE OF EQUIPMENT, which is to say, an ASSET, as discussed in Chapter Four.

Similarly, a TEST TYPE is *defined to require* either a single INSTRUMENT TYPE or it is *defined to require* one or more INSTRUMENT USAGES, each of which is *of* an INSTRUMENT TYPE.* Note that this INSTRUMENT USAGE looks suspiciously like the EQUIPMENT USAGE shown in Figure 5.10 of Chapter Five. The difference is that that was the usage of equipment for a specific activity, while INSTRUMENT USAGE is the general requirement that, whenever a TEST TYPE is *embodied in* a TEST, it will require this INSTRUMENT. The assumption in the laboratory model is that any single TEST will require only one INSTRUMENT, while the models in Chapter Five assumed that an ACTIVITY could require more than one PIECE OF EQUIPMENT.

---

* Here, again, is our slightly redundant notation for "mostly one but sometimes more than one." In your organization, you may use this model, or by policy, you may assert either that it may always be only one INSTRUMENT or that it may always be more than one.

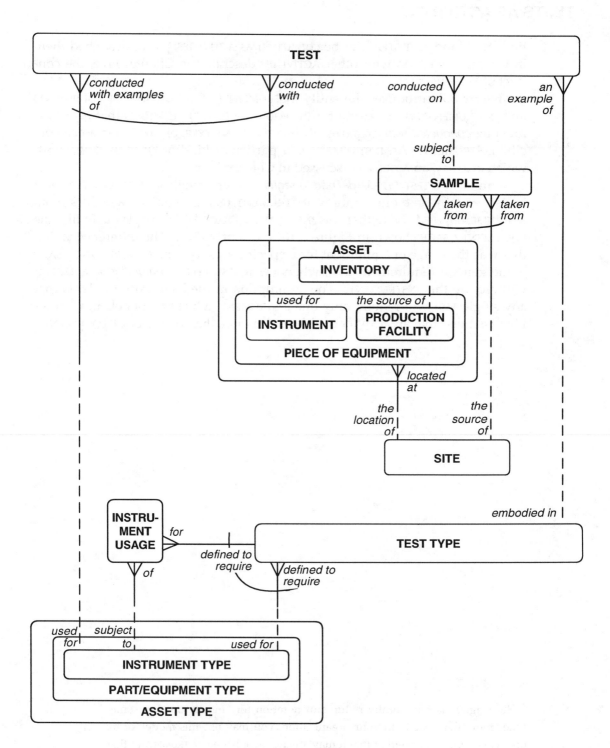

Figure 8.7: Instruments.

Figure 8.8 shows the combination of the two patterns. Here, we see that a TEST is indeed a kind of ACTIVITY, potentially *charged with* all the same resource usages that any ACTIVITY might be charged with: equipment, assets, and labor time. The special requirements of the laboratory are also shown, however. Rather than requiring an intersect entity like EQUIPMENT USAGE, a TEST would probably be *conducted with* only a single PIECE OF EQUIPMENT. Note that while this assertion seems to be true in general, it may not be true for your organization. In your organization, indeed, a TEST might require more than one PIECE OF EQUIPMENT.

(Note that to keep the Figure 8.8 diagram manageable, the relationships shown in Figure 8.7 between TEST and INSTRUMENT TYPE and directly between TEST TYPE and INSTRUMENT TYPE are not shown. These may, of course, be added back.)

In the ACTIVITY model, we didn't make any statements about what PART/EQUIPMENT TYPES an ACTIVITY TYPE might be defined to use in advance, although we could have. It seems particularly important to do so in the case of laboratory TEST TYPES, but this could be made more general if your organization requires it.

Thus, we can see that the patterns developed earlier in the book can be combined as requirements become more subtle and extensive. This process will continue when we take up process manufacturing in Chapter Ten.

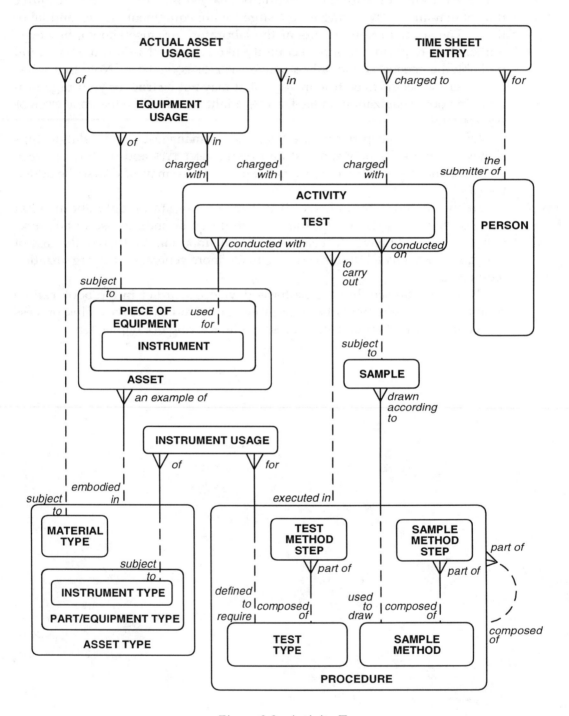

Figure 8.8: Activity Types.

9

MATERIAL REQUIREMENTS PLANNING

*C*hapter Four presented models of the manufacturing process, showing how to record the definitions of products and their structures, as well as the manufacturing activities and their consumption of resources. This chapter extends that model to describe one kind of process for *planning* manufacturing: Material Requirements Planning, or MRP.

MRP is, in effect, a simulation of one aspect of a plant's operations—albeit a relatively simple one. As such, it provides a unique challenge to the data modeler, who must now represent the forecasted, simulated world, in addition to the current real one.

During the second half of the 1970s, the manufacturing world discovered that the computer could dramatically improve the coordination of activities in a plant. It was now possible to schedule production and then have the computer translate the schedule into corresponding schedules for raw-material purchases and for work centers. More significantly, as circumstances in a plant changed, the computer could quickly update the finished-goods schedules and, in turn, automatically update those for purchasing and the work centers.

The software to support this tended initially to be very complex and expensive. Only mainframe computers were large enough to support it, and large projects usually were required to train all the workers in a plant as to its implications on their jobs. Over time, the underlying structure of the information became clearer, software became more modular, and computers became smaller, easier to use, and more distributed throughout a plant. Large projects are still required, however, to train everyone in the nature and implications of this new way of doing things. To that end, a data model provides a useful way of explaining the underlying nature and structure of the planning process.

As with any new technology, MRP systems were built by various software vendors in various ways—and some vendors were more successful than others. The more successful ones had a better understanding of the underlying data structures involved. Data models help clarify these underlying structures.

Since this book makes no assumption that you already know about MRP, a brief description of the planning process itself follows.

PLANNING FINISHED PRODUCTS

The planning process begins with the development of a Master Production Schedule. This is simply a list of products, with work orders scheduling them to be released to the production floor over a planning horizon of, say, the next few weeks. Table 9.1 shows a production schedule for a Model 22-xz bicycle. Note that this schedule is described as a series of expected quantities to be released to production over time—in this case, an order for 75 bicycles is to be started in week one, and another is to be started in week three. Note as well that, by policy, 75 bicycles is the standard order size.

A production schedule may be arrived at in several ways, the simplest of which is to analyze a product's supply and demand in terms of a sales forecast, inventory currently on hand, and any production currently in process. This analysis is the heart of the MRP.

Table 9.1.
Master Production Schedule.

Bicycles (Model 22-xz)						
	wk 1	*wk 2*	*wk 3*	*wk 4*	*wk 5*	*wk 6*
Planned Orders	75		75			
Order quantity: **75**						

Table 9.2 shows the MRP product supply-and-demand analysis for our bicycle example. Each column in the table represents a time period—in our case, one week. The demand for each week is defined as the sum of sales forecasts and committed orders ("scheduled shipments"). To compute each week's ending inventory, derived demand is subtracted from the sum of the current production of inventory to be received that week ("scheduled receipts") and the previous week's (ending) inventory.

In our example, the inventory at the end of week one is 10, obtained by subtracting the scheduled shipments (30) from the beginning inventory (40). The inventory at the end of week two is 20 (the prior period's ending inventory of 10 *minus* forecast demand of 20 *minus* scheduled shipments of 10 *plus* a scheduled receipt of 40).

As of the end of week three, orders exceed the inventory, leaving a projected inventory of -10, representing the point at which new production should be made available. If we wanted to describe negative inventory without using the minus sign, we would refer to it as a "net requirement." This is in contrast to the "gross requirement," which is the sum of scheduled shipments and the sales forecast. Thus, the gross requirement in week 3 is 30, but the net requirement is 10. (The net requirement of 10 is the gross requirement of 30 less the previous week's closing inventory of 20. Since the inventory was positive, the net requirement in earlier weeks was zero.) Based on the lead time for a production order, which is defined in this example as two weeks, and the standard order quantity, which is 75, a new order ("planned order") of 75 bicycles is scheduled to begin in week one. It is a *planned* order, because a real work order will not be released until week one.

Table 9.2.
Material Requirements Planning.

Bicycles (Model 22-xz)						
	wk 1	*wk 2*	*wk 3*	*wk 4*	*wk 5*	*wk 6*
Sales Forecast		20	30	50	30	30
Scheduled Shipments	30	10				
Scheduled Receipts		40				
Inventory (40)	10	20	**-10**/65	15	**-15**/60	30
Planned Orders	75		75			
Lead time: **2 weeks**		Order quantity: **75**			Initial inventory: **40**	

Since, by policy, production is to be done in lots of 75 and the net requirement for week three was only 10, the resulting inventory is now greater than zero for that week. The inventory line shows the effect of the planned order. If this plan is carried out, 65 more bicycles will be manufactured than are expected to be needed.

The 65 bicycles can of course be used to meet demand in subsequent weeks, so the cycle repeats until the amount of the expected balance is again negative (-15) in week five, triggering a second planned order of 75 to begin two weeks earlier in week three.

DETERMINING COMPONENT REQUIREMENTS

Once the plan for finished products is determined, the next task is to determine the requirements for the component materials.

Figure 9.1 diagrams part of the "bill of materials" for the Model 22-xz bicycle and for the Model 44-xz bicycle. The diagram shows some of the components required to build each kind of bicycle. Note that one bicycle of either model requires, among other things, one each of its own frame, plus one each of common front wheels and back wheels. Making 75 bicycles of either model, then, will require 75 of each component shown in the first row below the top-most row of model names in Figure 9.1.

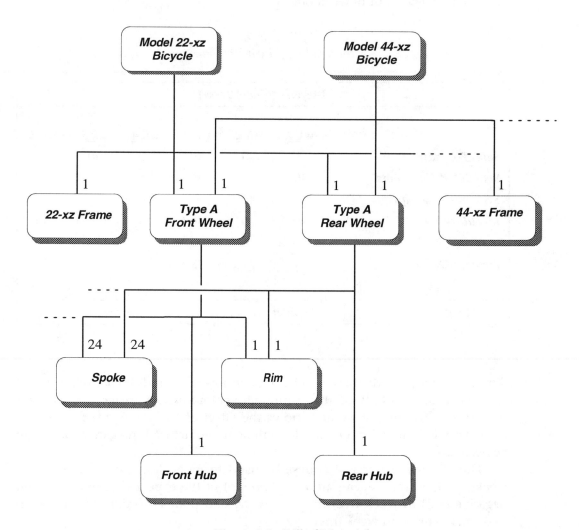

Figure 9.1: Bill of Materials.

A component's "dependent demand" is defined as the sum of requirements for a component derived from the planned orders of all assemblies that use the component. This dependent demand may be contrasted with the "indepen-dent demand" for bicycles represented by the sales forecast. Indeed, if frames and wheels are sold as spare parts, they could have sales forecasts for indepen-dent demand as well. Both independent demand and dependent demand may be used as the basis for planning the production for each component—using the method described above for the original bicycle. Note that a Model 44-xz bicycle uses the same kind of front wheel as does Model 22-xz. This means that the total dependent demand for the front wheel will be the sum of the demands for the two kinds of bicycles.

Table 9.3 shows the planning for the front wheel. In this case, the two orders for 75 Model 22-xz bicycles in weeks one and three (shown above in Table 9.2) turn into dependent demands for 75 front wheels in the same weeks. These are added to other demands for front wheels that we haven't seen before. We can assume that they were generated by the production plans for Model 44-xz bicycles (50 each in weeks two, three, and five).

Table 9.3.
Component Planning.

Front Wheels						
	wk 1	*wk 2*	*wk 3*	*wk 4*	*wk 5*	*wk 6*
Dependent Demand	75	50	125		50	
Sales Forecast	5	5	5	5	5	5
Scheduled Receipts	80					
Inventory (55)	55	0	**-130**/20	15	**-40**/110	5
Planned Orders		150		150		
Lead time: **1 week**		Order quantity: **150**		Initial inventory: **55**		

Independent demand, for use of the front wheels as spare parts, has also been added at this level. This is shown as a sales forecast of 5 per week.

As before, the demand for the front wheel is subtracted from prior period's inventory and scheduled receipts for each successive period, until the projected balance goes negative (in this case, to -130). Since the lead time for building a front wheel is (in this example) one week, planned orders for 150 wheels (the standard order quantity) are created for the period one week before each requirement.

Note that the planned orders may be *either* for production of the component *or* for its purchase from the outside. Currently, front wheels are being purchased from an outside vendor, so the scheduled-receipts line refers to pending purchase orders.

FIRM PLANNED ORDERS

If, on the other hand, front wheels were manufactured by our company, the planned orders for front wheels could now be exploded to determine the requirements for rims, spokes, and so forth. The analysis process would then be repeated. Note in the bill of materials that, among other things, both the front wheel and the rear wheel each need 24 spokes. Assuming that the plan for back wheels looks like the plan for front wheels shown in Table 9.3 (a very weak assumption, but it will do for our purposes here), 150 back wheels will also be ordered in week two.

This means that the need for 150 front wheels and 150 back wheels in each of the order periods, together generate a demand in each period for 7,200 spokes (two kinds of wheels multiplied by 150 wheels needed of each kind multiplied by 24 spokes per wheel).

At each level, the order is moved back by the lead time at that level. Note that, while finished-goods planning may be going on many weeks into the future, the plant is right now dealing with previous plans. The original need for 10 bicycles in week three (shown in Table 9.2), for example, resulted in a demand for 75 front wheels (shown in Table 9.3), which can't be met by additional planned orders. It must be met by the current inventory of 55 and a scheduled receipt of 80. Fortunately, these wheels are available.

Note, however, that if the sales forecast for finished bicycles were to go to 100 in week three (as shown in Table 9.4), the net requirement would be for 80 bicycles, not 10. This would cause the planned launch to be two 75 bicycle orders instead of one—generating a requirement for a planned order of 150 front wheels. Looking back at Table 9.3, we see that only 135 wheels (55 on hand, plus a scheduled receipt of 80) are available. Since the demand would be in the first week, and the lead time is one week, it is too late for the wheel manufacturer to respond to this demand. This means that the first planned order for bicycles could not be produced.

In short, if circumstances change in the near term, and the finished-goods plan changes dramatically, this can put undue pressure on the people making components. In some cases, increased demand can be accommodated through extraordinary efforts, but this should only be done rarely, and as a conscious management decision, not because the computer says so.

For this reason, a planning horizon may be defined for the finished product, typically at its cumulative lead time. That is, while it might take only two weeks to assemble a bicycle from its components ("lead time"), it might take two months to create it from raw steel ("cumulative lead time").

Imposition of a "time fence" at a point "cumulative lead time" in the future, fixes the planned orders within it as "firm planned orders." Any recommendations that might be made within this time period by a computer performing this analysis are communicated to the planner, but they are *not* automatically reflected in a revised schedule. The computer can recommend changes, but it will not make them. Those looking at lower-level reports will not know of the recommendation unless the manager at the upper level manually changes the planned release date—presumably with the advice and cooperation of the people affected. It is the user, not the computer, who controls the schedule.

Table 9.5 shows the effect of firm planned orders. In this case, firm planned orders have already been specified for weeks one and four, before the inventory analysis was done. The analysis reveals that the one currently scheduled to be released in week four should in fact be released in week three to cover the shortfall in week five. Rather than moving the firm planned order, however, the computer simply prints a message recommending the change.

When appropriate, the computer may also recommend the rescheduling of scheduled receipts as well.

Note that the techniques shown here for planning are demand driven. Some companies make use of linear programming and other optimizing techniques in order to take into account other factors, such as the cost of idleness, set-up time, and so forth. Such techniques can be used comfortably in conjunction with the MRP approach, by entering the resulting plans into this matrix as firm planned orders.

THE MANUFACTURING PLANNING MODEL

Chapter Five showed the models for the manufacturing process itself. The entities in these prior models that are of interest to the planning process are shown in Figure 9.2, and include primarily the entities that describe the products made by the plant:

- An ASSET TYPE, which is the definition of a thing, identified by a "model number" or a "part number." A Model 22-xz bicycle is an example of an ASSET TYPE, as is the specification for a spoke. ASSET TYPES are what we plan. Note that an ASSET TYPE may be a finished product, a component, or a subassembly.

- An ASSET is an *example of* an ASSET TYPE. A particular Model 22-xz bicycle (serial number 34256-765) is an ASSET. Each ASSET must be one of the following: a discrete item, an inventory, or an asset structure element.

  - A DISCRETE ITEM, such as the particular bicycle just described, is a single physical example of an ASSET TYPE. A DISCRETE ITEM has "serial number" as an identifying attribute.

Table 9.4. MRP Done Too Late.

Bicycles (Model 22-xz)							
		wk 1	**wk 2**	**wk 3**	**wk 4**	**wk 5**	**wk 6**
Sales Forecast			20	30(100)	50	30	30
Scheduled Shipments		30	10				
Scheduled Receipts			40				
Inventory	(40)	10	20	-10 (-80)/**70**	15	-15/**60**	30
Planned Orders		75 (150)		75			
Lead time: **2 weeks**		Order quantity: **75**			Initial inventory: **40**		

Table 9.5. Firm Planned Orders.

Bicycles (Model 22-xz)							
		wk 1	**wk 2**	**wk 3**	**wk 4**	**wk 5**	**wk 6**
Sales Forecast			20	30	50	30	30
Scheduled Shipments		30	10				
Scheduled Receipts			40				
Inventory	(40)	10	20	65	15	**-15**	30
Planned Orders		75(f)			< = 75(f)		
Recommendation: **Reschedule FPO in week 4 to week 3.**							
Lead time: **2 weeks**	Order quantity: **75**		Initial inventory: **40**		Time fence: **8 wks**		

- An INVENTORY is a quantity *of* an ASSET identified only in groups. That is, an INVENTORY could be the 1,000 spokes on a shelf, considered only as a group. The primary attribute of inventory is "quantity." (Chapter Five also discussed various kinds of INVENTORY, but to keep this discussion manageable, these will not be considered here.)

- An ASSET TYPE STRUCTURE ELEMENT is the fact that a particular ASSET TYPE is required to make another ASSET TYPE. The set of ASSET TYPE STRUCTURE ELEMENTS in which an ASSET appears as the *assembly* constitutes that ASSET's "bill of materials." The set of ASSET TYPE STRUCTURE ELEMENTS where it appears as the *component* is its "where-used list." Table 9.6 shows the table created from the ASSET TYPE STRUCTURE ELEMENT entity for our bicycle's bill of materials.

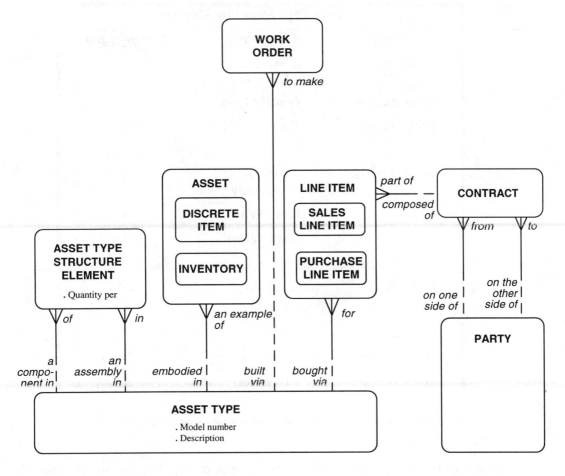

Figure 9.2: The Manufacturing Planning Data Model.

The primary attribute of ASSET TYPE STRUCTURE ELEMENT is "quantity per"—the amount of the component required to make one unit of the assembly. For example, if a bicycle wheel requires 24 spokes, the wheel and spoke each would be occurrences of ASSET TYPE, while the requirement for 24 spokes in a wheel would be an example of an ASSET TYPE STRUCTURE ELEMENT. (The value of "quantity per" would be "24.")

The ASSET TYPE's "description" is *not* an attribute of ASSET TYPE STRUCTURE ELEMENT even though this is shown in Table 9.6. In the table, the "model number" represented in each relationship from ASSET TYPE STRUCTURE to ASSET TYPE is replaced by the ASSET TYPE's "description."

Table 9.6.
Asset Type Structure Elements.

Asset Type Structure Elements		
Assembly	*Component*	*Quantity per*
22-xz Bicycle	22-xz Frame Assembly	1
22-xz Bicycle	Front Wheel	1
22-xz Bicycle	Back Wheel	1
...		
44-xz Bicycle	44-xz Frame Assembly	1
44-xz Bicycle	Front Wheel	1
44-xz Bicycle	Back Wheel	1
...		
Front Wheel	Spoke	24
Front Wheel	FW Hub	1
...		
Back Wheel	Spoke	24
Back Wheel	BW Hub	1
...		

Other entities in Figure 9.2 were modeled in previous chapters and describe the transactions of selling, manufacturing, and buying products:

- A WORK ORDER is the authorization to manufacture a quantity of a material. Among its attributes are "order quantity," "order date," "expected end date," and "actual end date."

- A PARTY is a person or organization of interest to our company. In this case, a PARTY may be either the buyer in or the seller in one or more CONTRACTS.

- A CONTRACT for the sale of one or more ASSET TYPES is *from* one PARTY *to* another. Each CONTRACT may be *composed of* one or more LINE ITEMS, each of which, in this version, is *for* an ASSET TYPE. From the point of view of our company, some CONTRACTS are PURCHASE ORDERS and some are SALES ORDERS. By extension, therefore, a LINE ITEM must be either a SALES LINE ITEM or a PURCHASE LINE ITEM.

THE PLANNING MODEL

Figure 9.3 shows how the manufacturing data model can be expanded to include the inputs to the planning process. This expansion requires some redefinition of previously presented entities. The PURCHASE LINE ITEM and the SALES LINE ITEM, for example, have now been separated, since the former represents a kind of SCHEDULED RECEIPT, while the latter represents a SCHEDULED SHIPMENT.

WORK ORDER has been combined with PURCHASE LINE ITEM as another kind of SCHEDULED RECEIPT, since the two represent alternative ways that materials come into the plant.

Both SCHEDULED RECEIPT and SCHEDULED SHIPMENT have as attributes the "quantity" involved and the planned "date" of the event.

The new entities FIRM PLANNED ORDER and FORECAST have been added. Both of these also have "quantity" and planned "date" as attributes.

What does not show on this version of the model are the calculated values: PLANNED ORDERS, DEPENDENT DEMAND, and PROJECTED INVENTORY. Relational theory frowns upon including such ethereal items in a data model. Several arguments can be made for including them here, however: First, they, along with FIRM PLANNED ORDER, SCHEDULED RECEIPT, and SCHEDULED SHIPMENT, all have the same attributes, "quantity" and planned "date." Second, they are usually examined as a set. It is not reasonable to look for the PROJECTED INVENTORY (as shown in Figure 9.4) for July 23 and expect it to be derived on the spot. The body of data undergoes a significant transformation when the MRP program is run, and the complete set of calculations must be produced concurrently.

In other words, we are not modeling the current world, but a simulated world. By definition, the attributes in the simulated world are calculated (they are not captured from real events)—even though from the point of view of that world, they are real.

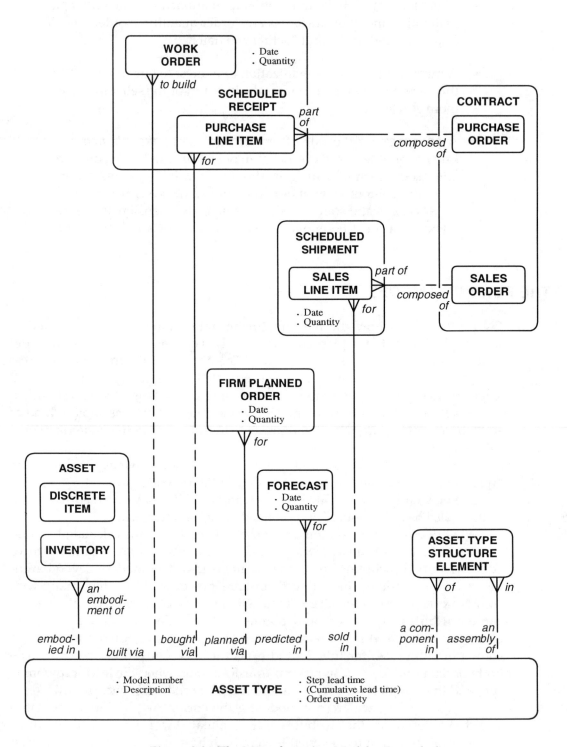

Figure 9.3: The Manufacturing Model—Reworked.

In addition, it should be noted that a single PURCHASE LINE ITEM or WORK ORDER might in fact result in more than one SCHEDULED RECEIPT. Accommodating this and the desire to look at the set of MRP data together produces the model shown in Figure 9.4. Here, a single SALES LINE ITEM is shown potentially to be *delivered as* one or more SCHEDULED SHIPMENTS, and similarly, each WORK ORDER or PURCHASE LINE ITEM may be *delivered as* one or more SCHEDULED RECEIPTS. (This harkens back to Figure 5.11 in Chapter Five, where each OTHER PRODUCTION ORDER was *the source of* one or more PRODUCTION DELIVERIES. This is that model with the names changed.) Separating the SCHEDULED RECEIPT and SCHEDULED SHIPMENT entities from the LINE ITEMS they came from allows us to return the rest of the model to its previous form (grouping SALES LINE ITEMS and PURCHASE LINE ITEMS again).

In addition, each ASSET TYPE may be expected to have one or more PROJECTED INVENTORIES.

Since they all have the same attributes (again, "quantity" and planned "date"), it makes sense to group the SCHEDULED RECEIPTS and SHIPMENTS, PROJECTED INVENTORY, and the various demands and plans into a single supertype, PLANNING ITEM.

The set of PLANNING ITEMS, then, is the domain of MRP. With this model, a run of the MRP program will perform the analysis and update all the calculated values, so that various reports can be produced quickly for all who need them.

Note that the distinction between DISCRETE ITEM and INVENTORY may change during the planning process. In the case of our bicycles, when they are defined, each may be entered as a DISCRETE ITEM, but for planning purposes, a bicycle's PROJECTED INVENTORY will be treated as if it were an INVENTORY.

Note also that both SCHEDULED SHIPMENT and SCHEDULED RECEIPT are in fact kinds of MATERIAL MOVEMENTS, as presented in Chapter Six. They, along with other planned demands and supplies, may be together considered a new subtype of MATERIAL MOVEMENT, which we can call PLANNED MATERIAL MOVEMENT.

Considering PROJECTED INVENTORY also to be a PLANNED MATERIAL MOVEMENT would allow us to simply rename PLANNING ITEM to PLANNED MATERIAL MOVEMENT, the subtype of MATERIAL MOVEMENT. Considering PROJECTED INVENTORY to be an example of PLANNED MATERIAL MOVEMENT may seem a little arcane, but leaving it out would require PLANNING ITEM to be different from PLANNED MATERIAL MOVEMENT, and this would require multiple inheritance—PLANNED DEMAND and PLANNED SUPPLY would each be a subtype of two different supertypes.

If multiple inheritance makes you uncomfortable,* then PLANNING ITEM must be a subtype of MATERIAL MOVEMENT, with all that that implies.

This chapter continues building the models of manufacturing and purchasing that were begun in Chapters Five and Six. All of these, however, are based on the premise that the manufacturer is making discrete, countable items in

---

*   . . . as it does your author . . .

discrete, countable batches. Models of the manufacture of chemicals and similar products, however, cannot use those premises and, therefore, they are very different. Chapter Ten shows just how different this can be.

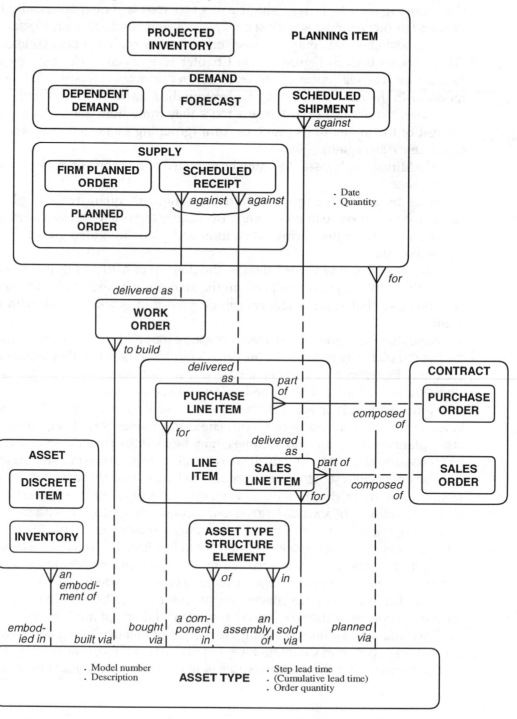

Figure 9.4: The Planning Model.

10

PROCESS MANUFACTURING

*C*hapter Four described the products a company manufactures, sells, and uses. Chapter Five then went on to describe how these products might be made, and Chapter Nine described how to plan that production. The entity ASSET encompassed both products made and products used in the manufacturing process, including liquids and powders, as well as solid objects such as products or pieces of equipment. The assumption in the manufacturing chapters, however, was that the products being made were *discrete* (either uniquely identified or countable), or at least made in discrete quantities.

Manufacturing that uses *continuous processes* introduces different modeling problems. In some cases, if the product is produced in batches, a process manufacturer can use the discrete model. (Pharmaceutical "lots" described in Chapter Five are examples of this.) Batches can be treated like PRODUCTION ORDERS, with specified quantities of material used and produced. Some organizations, however, such as oil refineries or other chemical plants, produce continuously, and to define batches for them would add artificial constraints that are not useful. What is needed is a different model for these "process plants."

Figure 10.1 shows a typical chemical plant process. At the figure's center is a production process that is taking place in a production facility called Unit A. It is fed by flows of material *from* other production facilities—specifically, Unit D, Tank 52, and Tank 71. The results of the process are flows *to* other production facilities—specifically, Unit L and Tank 21. In the center, a process transforms the input flows to output flows.

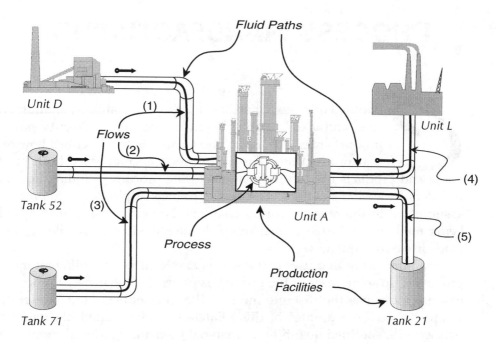

Figure 10.1: Processes.

MORE ABOUT ASSETS

We begin the discussion of a process plant by reviewing what we know about its hardware.

Figure 10.2 summarizes what we know so far about ASSETS and ASSET TYPES. In particular, an ASSET may be one of two kinds of INVENTORY (PRODUCT INVENTORY or PART INVENTORY), or it may be a DISCRETE ITEM. A DISCRETE ITEM may be either a PIECE OF EQUIPMENT (used in the plant) or an OTHER DISCRETE ITEM (such as a manufactured product for sale).

In Chapter Eight, we saw that an INSTRUMENT was an important subtype of PIECE OF EQUIPMENT. Another subtype of PIECE OF EQUIPMENT is PRODUCTION FACILITY—the equipment directly involved in producing the company's products. In Figure 10.1, the units, tanks, and pipes are all examples of PRODUCTION FACILITIES, as is the plant as a whole. Specifically, Figure 10.2 shows that a PRODUCTION FACILITY may be a storage TANK, a PRODUCTION UNIT, a piece of PIPE, or some OTHER PRODUCTION FACILITY.

Note that, in Figure 10.2, we have removed the supertype INVENTORY. In the following discussions, PART INVENTORY and PRODUCT INVENTORY will be treated quite differently from each other, so our lives will be simpler if we do not group them together. PART INVENTORY, for example, is shown as being *currently at* a SITE, like all ASSETS. In a process plant, however, where products are liquids and powders, PRODUCT INVENTORY is more likely to be *stored in* a TANK, PIPE, PRODUCTION UNIT, or some OTHER PRODUCTION FACILITY.

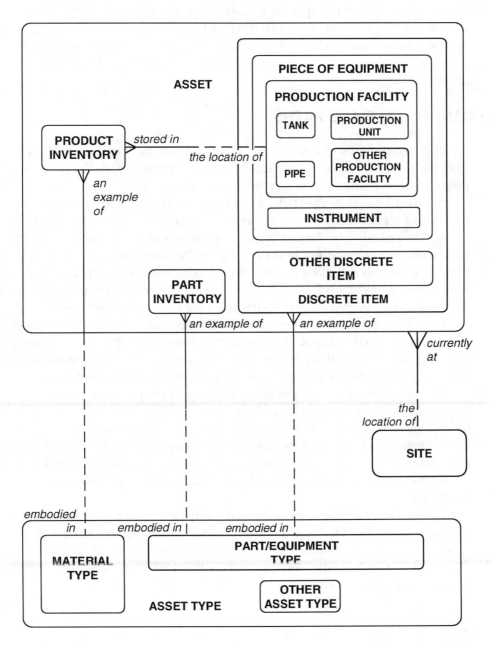

Figure 10.2: Assets and the Process Plant.

The PRODUCTION FACILITY, like all ASSETS, is of course at a SITE, but when it comes to keeping track of PRODUCT INVENTORY, we want to know more specifically exactly which PRODUCTION FACILITY it is *stored in.*

In Figure 10.2, the single relationship between ASSET and ASSET TYPE has been broken down into three specific relationships: between PRODUCT INVENTORY and MATERIAL TYPE; between DISCRETE ITEM and PART/EQUIPMENT TYPE; and between PART INVENTORY and PART/EQUIPMENT TYPE. The more general relationship is also true, but the more specific relationships are helpful in the discussion of process manufacturing.

STRUCTURE AND FLUID PATHS

Of all the company's ASSETS, the most important is the plant itself. It, a PRODUC-TION FACILITY, is composed of smaller PIECES OF EQUIPMENT, each of which is composed of even smaller PIECES OF EQUIPMENT, and so forth.

Figure 10.3 shows the PHYSICAL STRUCTURE ELEMENTS of the plant's PIECES OF EQUIPMENT (PRODUCTION FACILITIES and INSTRUMENTS). Each PHYSICAL STRUCTURE ELEMENT *either* must be *the use of* another particular ASSET (such as the PIECES OF EQUIPMENT just referred to), *or* it must be *the (generic) use of* an ASSET TYPE, which may be *embodied in* a PIECE OF EQUIPMENT. The relationship points to the outer boundaries of ASSET and ASSET TYPE, to allow for the use of lubricants or other MATERIAL TYPES, as well as spare parts from the PART INVENTORY.*

Note that, here, we are not concerned with OTHER DISCRETE ITEMS, so for the sake of clarity that entity and the DISCRETE ITEM supertype (both shown in Figure 10.2) have been left off Figure 10.3. Also, we are here assuming that we are not concerned with the physical structure of PART INVENTORY items.

The structure of the products made in a process plant, however, is different from that of discrete products: In a process plant, the structure of PRODUCT INVENTORY is described in terms of its CONSTITUENTS, although some PRODUCT INVENTORIES are *of* only one MATERIAL TYPE. Specifically, each PRODUCT INVENTORY must be either *an example of* a single MATERIAL TYPE or *composed of* one or more CONSTITUENTS, each of which must be *the presence of* a MATERIAL TYPE. (See Figure 10.4.)

Structure is not the only way that parts of a processing plant are linked together, however. Of equal importance is the network of paths materials can take in their trip from one end of the plant to the other. This network can be represented in exactly the same way as the network of structures is represented, albeit with a different entity.

---

* Astute readers will recognize PHYSICAL STRUCTURE ELEMENT as a variation on ASSET STRUCTURE ELEMENT. Your situation will dictate how you mix and match these terms.

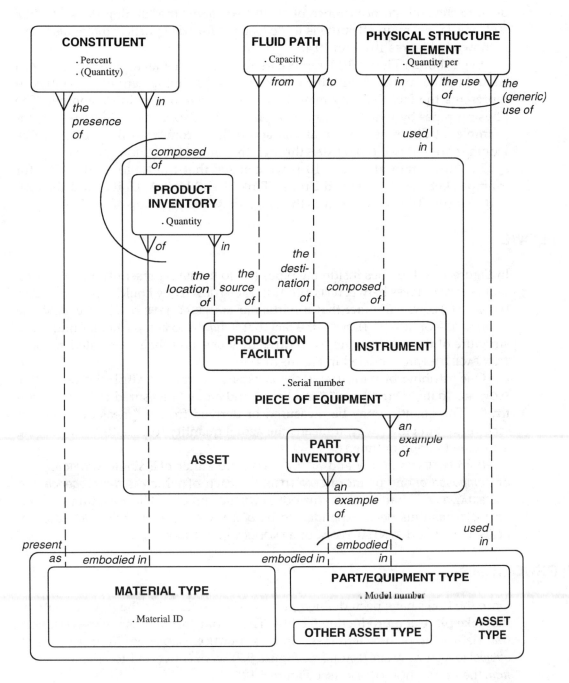

Figure 10.3: Structure and Fluid Paths.

The FLUID PATH represents the route (presumably through a pipe) *from* one PRO-DUCTION FACILITY *to* another. If it is possible to pump crude oil from the loading dock to the still, an occurrence of FLUID PATH *from* "the loading dock" *to* "the still" exists. Its main attribute is its "capacity" for transporting materials. This is shown in Figures 10.3 and 10.4.

Even though Figure 10.1 represents the FLUID PATH as a pipe, a FLUID PATH should not be confused with the pipe or pipes that implement it. A FLUID PATH represents the fact that any material can flow *from* one point *to* another. The physical pipes by which this is accomplished are PRODUCTION FACILITIES. If, for example, at different times material could flow from A to B, or B to A, this would represent two FLUID PATHS through the same PRODUCTION FACILITY.

Looking again at Figure 10.1, we can see that the FLUID PATHS exist, for example, between Unit D and Unit A, Tank 71 and Unit A, Unit A and Tank 21, and so forth. The arrows next to the pipes show the direction of the flow.

FLOWS

In Figure 10.1, the lines inside the pipes (FLUID PATHS) represent FLOWS of partic-ular MATERIAL TYPES between PRODUCTION FACILITIES. They could represent either POTENTIAL FLOWS—the fact that a particular MATERIAL TYPE *could* be *through* the FLUID PATH—or ACTUAL FLOWS—the fact that it *did* do so at a particular time. The structure of these FLOWS, the FLUID PATHS they use, and their associated PRODUC-TION FACILITIES are modeled in Figure 10.4.

One attribute of POTENTIAL FLOW is "standard rate." Attributes of ACTUAL FLOW are "date," "start time," "end time," and either "measured rate" or "quan-tity." (The quantity may be measured or derived from a "measured rate" or vice versa, but either way, it means the actual quantity to pass this way during a specified period of time.)

Both POTENTIAL FLOW and ACTUAL FLOW are either *of* a single MATERIAL TYPE or *composed of* one or more CONSTITUENTS, each of which is *the presence of* a MATERIAL TYPE (that is, a mixture of MATERIAL TYPES). The meaning of CON-STITUENT has thus been expanded to be *of* a MATERIAL TYPE that is *in* either an ACTUAL FLOW, a POTENTIAL FLOW, or a PRODUCT INVENTORY.

PROCESSES

Once the flows have been defined, it is possible to describe the transformations that take place at a production facility. These transformations are the PROCESSES that define the plant's activities. In a PRODUCTION ORDER environment, ASSETS *subject to* ACTUAL ASSET USAGE (see Figure 5.7) were converted to ASSETS *received from* the PRODUCTION ORDER* (see Figure 5.10).

---

* That is, the ASSETS were *received from* the PRODUCTION DELIVERY *from* the PRO-DUCTION ORDER . . .

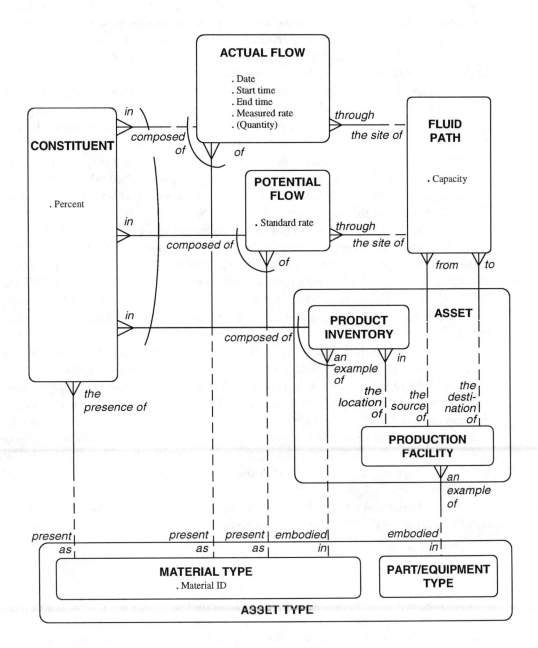

Figure 10.4: Flows.

In a continuous process plant, however, the model is simpler: Here, in Figure 10.5, a PROCESS is simply specified as being *fed by* one or more (input) FLOWS and is *the source of* one or more (output) FLOWS. That is, each FLOW (which must be *through* a FLUID PATH) may be *input to* one PROCESS and may be *output from* one

PROCESS. One complication, however, is the fact that there may not be a single quantity of each input and output flow. A flow may, for example, progress at a particular rate for twelve minutes, be increased by ten percent for six minutes, and then be reduced by fifteen percent for another thirty minutes.

Since the flows are independent of each other, the set of rates for all flows together is required to describe the process.

In Figure 10.1, the engineers set up the PRODUCTION FACILITY Unit A to be the site where a particular kind of PROCESS takes place. The PROCESS uses the FLOWS 1, 2, and 3, and converts them into FLOWS 4 and 5. Each PROCESS must be *performed at* one or more PRODUCTION FACILITIES. Since a PRODUCTION FACILITY may also be *the site of* one or more PROCESSES, the entity PROCESS LOCATION is introduced to record the fact that a PROCESS may be performed at a PRODUCTION FACILITY. That is, each PROCESS LOCATION is *of* a PROCESS *in* a PRODUCTION FACILITY. The data model for this is shown in Figure 10.5.

The PROCESS is defined in terms of the temperature, pressure, and other settings that are to be in effect when it takes place. That is, it may be *conducted under* one or more CONDITIONS, where each CONDITION must be *of* a particular VARIABLE. If, for example, the process were to take place at between 150°C and 200°C, there would be two CONDITIONS of VARIABLE "temperature." One sets the lower boundary, and one sets the upper boundary. This is elaborated upon further, below.

As with ASSETS and ASSET TYPES, the distinction between the real and the ideal also applies to processes: Each PROCESS EXECUTION must be *based on* one PROCESS. Where the PROCESS was *expected to be performed at* one or more PRODUCTION FACILITIES, a PROCESS EXECUTION can only *be at* one PRODUCTION FACILITY. Engineers initially define PROCESSES in terms of POTENTIAL FLOWS: Each PROCESS must be *fed by* one or more POTENTIAL FLOWS and must be *the source of* one or more POTENTIAL FLOWS. Each PROCESS EXECUTION, on the other hand, must be *fed by* one or more ACTUAL FLOWS and must be *the source of* one or more ACTUAL FLOWS.*

Figure 10.6 shows the relationships among PROCESS EXECUTIONS, PROCESSES, and the ACTUAL and POTENTIAL FLOWS into and out of them.[†]

---

* To be consistent with the terminology used in the rest of the book, PROCESS EXECUTION should probably be called PROCESS, while the definition of the process should be called PROCESS TYPE. Because people in the industry, however, typically refer to the standard definition of process when they use the term, the departure from the convention in this chapter seems appropriate.

[†] Note that, to keep the diagram manageable, ASSET has been removed, as has PROCESS LOCATION. The latter entity has been collapsed into the many-to-many relationship shown between PROCESS and PRODUCTION FACILITY.

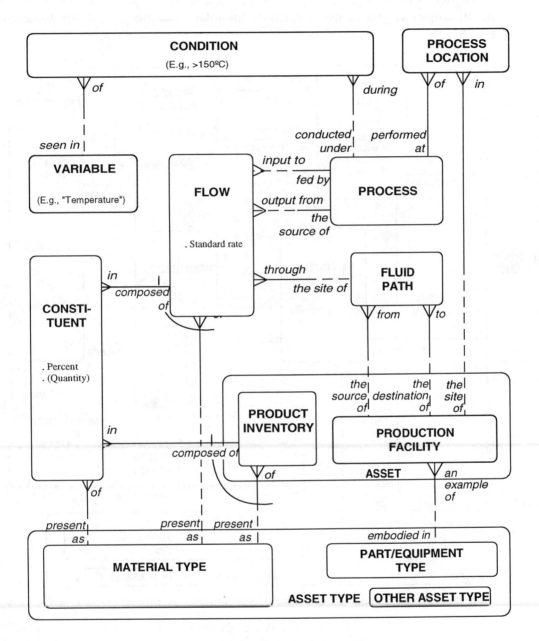

Figure 10.5: Process Entities.

An important measure of the productivity of the plant is *yield*. For any given period of time, the yield is normally calculated as the total "quantity" of all output ACTUAL FLOWS divided by the total "quantity" of all input ACTUAL FLOWS. Sometimes, not all outputs are desirable—some are by-products that must be disposed of at some cost. In this case, yield could be calculated as the total "quantity" of all *useful* (where "useful" is defined by the economics of the plant) output ACTUAL FLOWS divided by the total "quantity" of all input ACTUAL FLOWS.

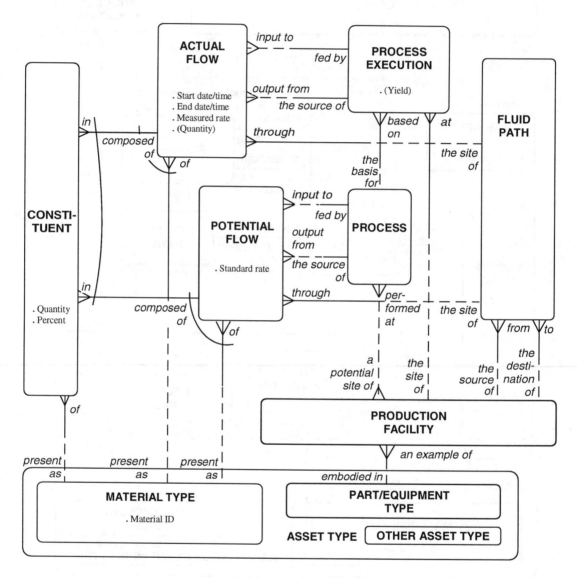

Figure 10.6: Actual Processes.

MONITORING PROCESSES

Because process manufacturing is continuous, monitoring it must be continuous as well. To the extent possible, INSTRUMENTS are usually installed throughout a plant, to indicate how the processes are going, with controllers attached to them to drive automated regulatory devices. In this section, we discuss the data involved in monitoring a process plant.

Previously (see Figure 10.5), we noted that a PROCESS is defined by the CONDITIONS under which it is carried out. When PROCESS is distinguished from PROCESS EXECUTION, the same distinction must be made for CONDITIONS. In Figure 10.7, the entity has been given two subtypes, STANDARD CONDITION and ACTUAL CONDITION, to designate the CONDITIONS that are *for* PROCESSES and PROCESS EXECUTIONS, respectively.

Process plants are controlled by setting pairs of thresholds, or "set points," for certain variables, and then observing the actual values of these variables. Figure 10.8 shows that each SET POINT must be *on* one TAG, *to control* a PROCESS. That is, each PROCESS may be *defined in terms of* one or more SET POINTS *on* TAGS. The attributes of SET POINT are "high value" and "low value." If the "value" of a MEASUREMENT goes above the SET POINT'S "high value" or below its "low value," the equipment is adjusted in some way—a valve is opened or closed, a pump is started, or some other action is taken. These values are *in terms of* a specified VARIABLE, and are *expressed in* one UNIT OF MEASURE.

Tags and Measuring Points

Each point where measurements are taken is identified by what is typically called a "tag number," so we will call the entity that represents these measurement points a TAG. (See Figure 10.8.) Each TAG is *to monitor* either a PRODUCTION FACILITY or a FLUID PATH. In the former case, it might be measuring a level in a storage tank, and in the latter, it might be measuring the quantity of a flow. Each TAG must be *implemented by* an INSTRUMENT that physically takes the measurements.

A TAG has as its primary attribute "tag number," and each TAG is *to measure* a single VARIABLE *expressed in* a given UNIT OF MEASURE.

Each TAG may be *the source of* one or more DIRECT MEASUREMENTS (usually, a *lot more*). These MEASUREMENTS turn out to be logically equivalent to the OBSERVATIONS in the laboratory that we discussed in Chapter Eight. As with those OBSERVATIONS, we have not only DIRECT MEASUREMENTS (comparable to TEST OBSERVATIONS) but also DERIVED MEASUREMENTS (comparable to DERIVED OBSERVATIONS). As with DERIVED OBSERVATION, each DERIVED MEASUREMENT must be *calculated from* one or more SUMMARIZATIONS, each of which is *the use of* another MEASUREMENT. And while it is not shown in Figure 10.8, the derivation logic previously described in Figure 8.3 for DERIVED VARIABLES (using SUMMARY RULES) also applies here.

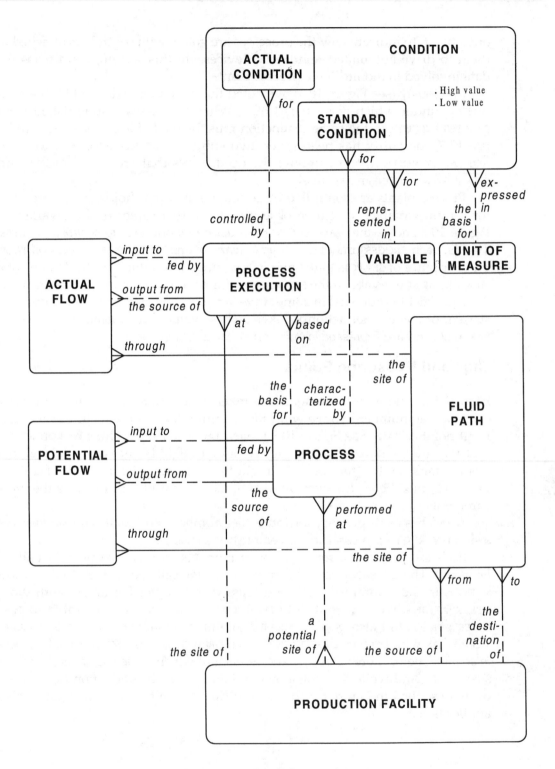

Figure 10.7: Conditions and Settings.

The VARIABLE and UNIT OF MEASURE for each DIRECT MEASUREMENT is determined by the TAG from which they are taken. DERIVED MEASUREMENTS, on the other hand, must be defined explicitly as being *in terms of* one VARIABLE and may be *expressed in* one UNIT OF MEASURE. The primary attribute of MEASUREMENT is "value," which is also the primary attribute of our old friend the laboratory OBSERVATION. The INSTRUMENTS in a typical plant are of various kinds, measuring pressures, temperatures, flows, and so forth. In many cases, each "value" of a MEASUREMENT obtained is fed back directly to process controllers—devices that compare this information with the "high value" and "low value" of a corresponding SET POINT. If the value is outside the range, the controller manipulates the servo-motors that open and close valves and throw switches as necessary to get the measurement value back in line.*

Each MEASUREMENT "value" and the corresponding SET POINT "high value" and "low value" are briefly available to plant operators. These in fact constitute the basic data that could be consolidated and summarized for management, to reveal what and how much has been produced in a given period, and at a cost of what and how much raw material. In the past, however, the sheer quantity of data has made it prohibitively expensive to store and massage for management purposes. Database technology is now making such storage and manipulation more practical, which will mean that in the future, plant managers will have a much more accurate picture of what is going on in their plants than has been possible in the past.

The Laboratory

As noted above, both OBSERVATIONS in the laboratory and MEASUREMENTS in the plant are gathering "values" of key VARIABLES in the production process. The difference is that in the plant, the MEASUREMENTS/OBSERVATIONS are being taken directly from the production process. Not everything can be measured directly, however. Some measurements require the sampling of material from various points in the process and submitting them to the laboratory for later analysis.

The laboratory model we saw in Chapter Eight, then, is of direct concern to a process plant. There are, however, two elaborations required to the model we developed in Chapter Eight, which we show in Figure 10.9. In Chapter Eight, we said that each SAMPLE is *taken from* one ASSET. This could be a PIECE OF EQUIPMENT or an INVENTORY. In the context of monitoring a plant, however, we are only concerned with SAMPLES that are *taken from* a particular kind of PIECE OF EQUIPMENT—a PRODUCTION FACILITY. Second, we have introduced the concept of FLUID PATH, and while SAMPLES might be *taken from* storage tanks (PRODUCTION FACILITIES), they might also be *taken from* the places where material flows—the FLUID PATHS.

---

* Note that the comparison activity is a business process (not a chemical process) that is not explicitly represented in the model.

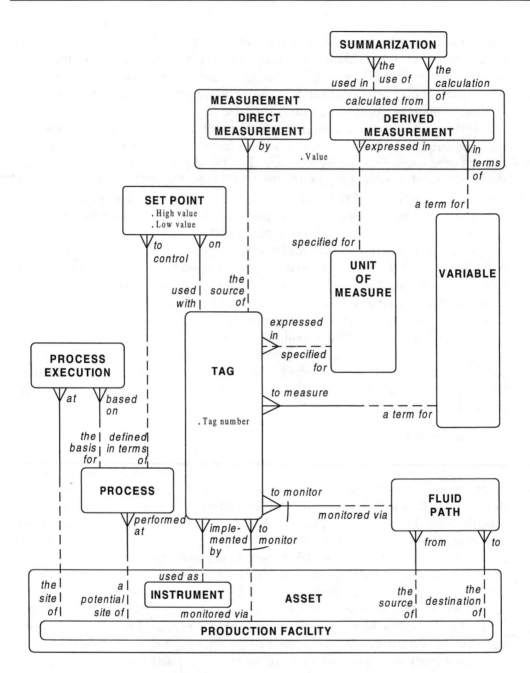

Figure 10.8: Conditions, Tags, and Measurements.

The laboratory is an important element in monitoring the status of the plant. Using the laboratory takes time, however, and when an enterprising inventor appears at the company's doorstep with an instrument that can be installed on the production line to eliminate a laboratory procedure, the plant engineer will be likely to make the swap.

For this reason, it is important to place the laboratory model from Chapter Eight alongside the monitoring model described here, to see how laboratory analysis is completely replaceable with direct monitoring.

In Figure 10.9, a shaded area highlights the portion of the model that describes the laboratory. This shows that, if the laboratory as a whole is treated as a large entity, its role is identical to that of the TAG. Either a SAMPLE or a TAG must be *taken from (to monitor*, if a TAG) either a PRODUCTION FACILITY or a FLUID PATH. Moreover, a TAG, *implemented by* an INSTRUMENT, may be *the source of* one or more DIRECT MEASUREMENTS, while a TEST *implemented by* an INSTRUMENT and *conducted on* a SAMPLE may be *the source of* one or more TEST OBSERVATIONS (which are, after all, a kind of DIRECT MEASUREMENT).

The main difference between the two ways of monitoring the plant is that, while a TEST may involve different VARIABLES and UNITS OF MEASURE for each TEST OBSERVATION, a TAG must be gathering information *in terms of* only one VARIABLE, *expressed in* only one UNIT OF MEASURE. That is, TEST is not directly connected to UNIT OF MEASURE or VARIABLE, while a TAG is.

Translation of Tag Values

As with the relationship between laboratory TESTS and OBSERVATIONS, one of the things a TAG can do is be *the source of* one or more MEASUREMENTS that are *indications of the presence of* one or more MATERIALS. As with the other similarities between TAGS and laboratory TESTS shown in Figure 10.9, this would be modeled the same way it was for laboratory TESTS in Chapter Eight.

In addition, however, these MEASUREMENTS can also determine the values of other attributes of the model. In their raw form, MEASUREMENTS from TAGS are simply a set of labeled numbers. A "tag" file can hold literally millions of records, each of which consists merely of a tag number, a date, a time, and a value. What is needed is a way to translate these lists of numbers into meaningful information. For example, as shown in Figure 10.10, a "value" of a MEASUREMENT *from* TAG BC-107 (*in terms of* the VARIABLE "volume") may in fact be the "quantity" of an ACTUAL FLOW *through* a FLUID PATH (or the "quantity" of a PRODUCT INVENTORY *in* a PRODUCTION FACILITY, as was shown in Figure 10.9).

The problem now is to indicate just which TAG will produce values for another attribute in the model. This requires some meta-modeling, where the elements of the model are themselves objects of the model. What we are seeing here is a kind of phase shift, in which the domain of the data associated with TAGS is different from the domain of the data in the rest of the model, and we are trying to link them together. In Chapter Four, we introduced the idea of an entity named ATTRIBUTE (see Figure 4.16). Here, in Figure 10.10, we have an attribute named "entity" as well as an attribute named "attribute." It is a little strange, but it works.

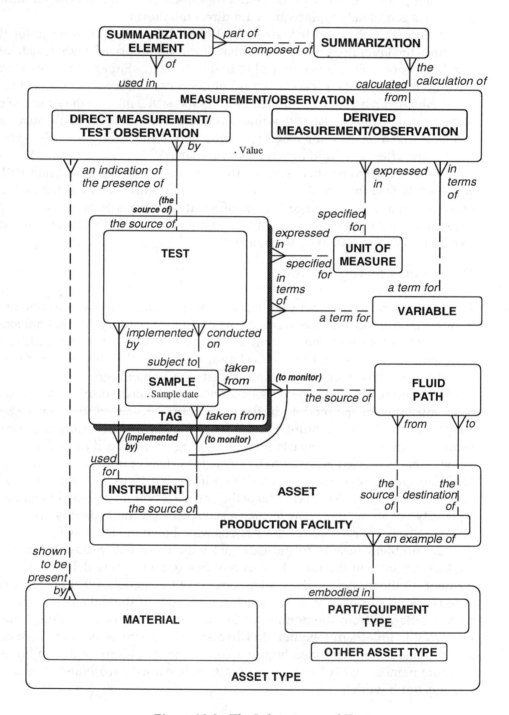

Figure 10.9: The Laboratory and Tags.

In Figure 10.10, the curved arrow shows the path by which the "value" of a MEASUREMENT *by* a TAG (for a particular date and time) becomes the "quantity" of an ACTUAL FLOW *through* a FLUID PATH (for the same date and time) that is *monitored via* that TAG. Capturing the "quantity" of a FLOW is done in two steps: We first have to specify that we are looking for the VARIABLE (for example, "mass") that represents that "quantity."

We do this by setting up a VARIABLE USAGE *of* a VARIABLE *in* the FLUID PATH. This states that a particular attribute of all occurrences of a specified entity related to this FLUID PATH will be expressed in terms of a particular VARIABLE. For our example here, a VARIABLE USAGE is defined to say that the "quantity" of all ACTUAL FLOWS *through* the FLUID PATH from Unit A to Tank 21 (see Figure 10.1) will be expressed in terms of "volume." That is, the FLUID PATH will be *measured via* a VARIABLE USAGE that collects TAG data in the "quantity" attribute of the entity ACTUAL FLOW, and is *of* the VARIABLE "volume."

As mentioned above, Figure 10.10 shows "entity" and "attribute" as attributes of VARIABLE USAGE. This is because it is necessary to say to which entity and attribute the VARIABLE USAGE refers. Other entities besides ACTUAL FLOW could be attached to FLUID PATH, and there could be other attributes in ACTUAL FLOW that are being captured. It may be of value to move TAG data into one or more of these as well. By specifying the entity and attribute involved in VARIABLE USAGE, a VARIABLE could be mapped to any attribute of any entity related to FLUID PATH. For purposes of our example here, however, just assume that the value of "entity" is "ACTUAL FLOW" and the value of "attribute" is "quantity." That is, the VARIABLE USAGE here is defining "volume" as the VARIABLE to be used for the "quantity" attribute in the entity "ACTUAL FLOW."

Now that we know the VARIABLE, the second step is to locate the TAG that is *to monitor* this FLUID PATH and that is *in terms of* that VARIABLE. Once we have done that, the "value" of any MEASUREMENT *by* that TAG, which is at the same "date/time" as an ACTUAL FLOW, becomes the "quantity" of that ACTUAL FLOW. For example, TAG XC-437 happens *to monitor* that FLUID PATH, and happens to be doing so *in terms of* the VARIABLE "volume." This makes it a good choice as a source of data. Thus, the "value" of any MEASUREMENTS *by* TAG XC-437 at 3:00 P.M. on January 24, will provide the "quantity" for the ACTUAL FLOW that is occurring at 3:00 P.M. on January 24.

This is all well and good, but unfortunately, the VARIABLE in which terms an attribute is described, may be a DERIVED VARIABLE, of the sort we discovered in the laboratory model. This would mean that the data for the attribute must be DERIVED MEASUREMENTS, which are normally associated with TAGS only indirectly. The VARIABLE in question might be an average of many readings over a fifteen-minute period, or it might be "volume" derived from "mass" and "density" that are measured by two different TAGS. This will require us to introduce the DERIVED MEASUREMENT and DERIVED VARIABLE entities discussed in Chapter Eight (Figure 8.3) and earlier in this chapter (Figure 10.8). Creative use of these entities, along with SUMMARIZATION and SUMMARY RULE, make it possible to define the link from TAGS to the derived attributes in the model. (We are not going to be that creative here, however.)

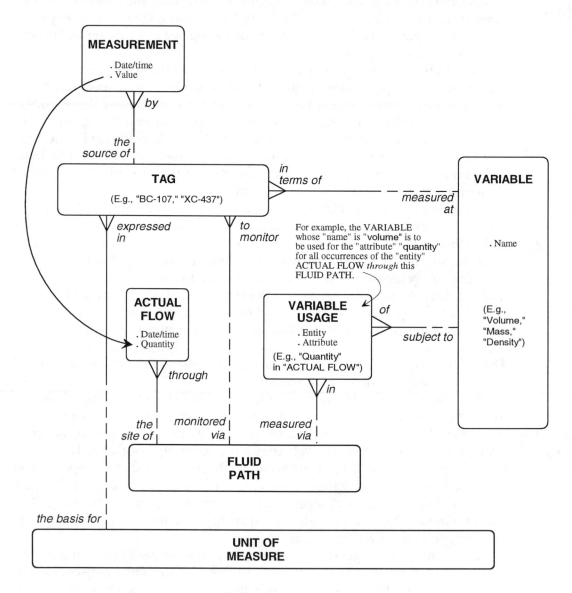

Figure 10.10: Variable Usage.

11

DOCUMENTS

*I*n modern computer-literate usage, the word "document" has come to mean any named package of text. *Webster's Ninth New Collegiate Dictionary* in 1987 defined "document" as "a writing conveying information," or even "a material substance (as a coin or stone) having on it a representation of the thoughts of men by means of some conventional mark or symbol."[1] This could be a letter to Grandma, an electronic mail message, or a contract. As multimedia technology takes over, this definition will probably even include such non-written material as moving pictures and sound recordings. This is a major departure, however, from the word's original meaning, which as recently as 1964 was defined in *Webster's New World Dictionary of the American Language* as "anything printed, written, etc., *relied upon to record or prove something*"[2] (emphasis added).

Most documents defined in the modern sense shouldn't appear on a data model at all. A document according to this meaning is nothing but a manifestation of the data that are already represented by the model. Indeed, a major challenge to systems analysts is to refuse the client's request simply to mimic a current report. The objective of this book has been to see how to get underneath a body of data's current representation in order to understand its inherent structure.

However, many documents that are written records relied upon to prove something (in the original sense) are themselves things of significance that must be prepared, distributed, and otherwise managed.

The research divisions of pharmaceutical companies, for example, are in the business of producing documents called New Drug Applications (NDA's) for drug regulatory agencies, such as the U.S. Food and Drug Administration. An NDA certifies the safety and usefulness of a pharmaceutical proposed for marketing. The NDA document is composed of hundreds of other documents, which are the results of individual studies. (It should be noted that a tractor-trailer is usually required to transport an NDA to a drug regulatory agency. This suggests that NDA's are indeed things of significance to pharmaceutical— and trucking?— companies.)

Other government agencies also must record the fact that required documents have been produced. Indeed, all industries responding to government regulations must certify that they are in compliance by producing the correct documentation.

In a different context, another example of an organization that must keep track of documents is the public library. Libraries were among the first organizations to address the issues of keeping track of where documents (in this case, books) came from, where they went, and how to find the one wanted.

Contributing to the need for better ways to manage documents are the optical disk and hypertext technologies, which, as mentioned above, are redefining the concept of the document itself. The technology itself is turning compact disks and electronic mail files into things of significance. Even though many of these documents are merely representations of other data, their very volume makes it important for us to organize them so we can find them again.

This dual nature of documents, which serve both as representations of other data, and as things of significance in their own right, provides a challenge to data modelers.

THE DOCUMENT

It should not be surprising that the central entity in this discussion is DOCUMENT. For our purposes, a DOCUMENT is defined as any published piece of written or visual or aural material that must be kept track of. While the word "document" in conventional usage ambiguously refers both to the physical piece of paper (or word processing file) and to its contents, for the sake of consistency here, the entity DOCUMENT will refer to the contents only. The physical manifestation of those contents is contained in the entity COPY, where a DOCUMENT may be *published as* one or more COPIES. Traditionally, a COPY has been on paper, but these days a COPY need not be physical. It could be an electronic file or message, whose physical existence as such does not have to be recognized.

Whatever the medium, however, we at least want to know who created each DOCUMENT and when, who authorized it (if that was necessary), and who received it. We also want at least enough information about its content to be able to find it. Thus, our first model looks like Figure 11.1, in which each DOCUMENT may be *published as* one or more COPIES.

As shown in Figure 11.1, attributes of DOCUMENT include "title," "abstract," "author," and so forth. Logically, "content" could be considered an attribute, but until very recently, this was not practical. The entity DOCUMENT is intended to *describe* DOCUMENTS, not *contain* them. (It was enough if computer system databases could keep track of the location and topics of documents, without expecting them to keep the documents themselves.) With the advent of optical storage and other advanced database technology, however, "content" as an attribute may not be far off. The boundary between the card catalogue and the library itself is growing ever more fuzzy.

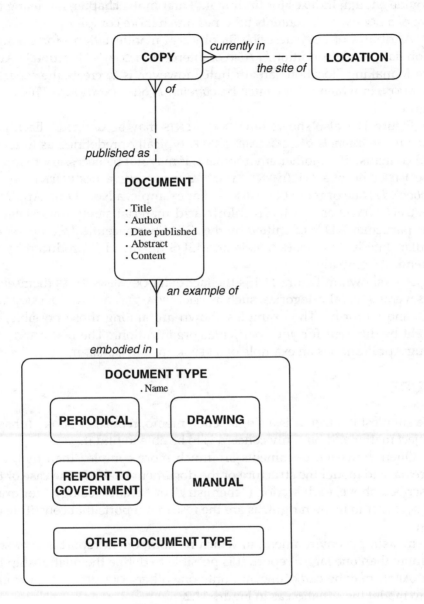

Figure 11.1: Documents and Copies.

At least initially in this discussion, however, we are not concerned with the content of a document, beyond what is needed to represent its structure, and to provide enough indexes for finding it. Later in the chapter, modeling the structure of a DOCUMENT's contents becomes much more complex.

Attributes of COPY describe its physical manifestation—for example, "creation date" and "condition." Also of interest is a COPY's "location." An alternative to making "location" an attribute, however, is to create the separate entity LOCATION, in which a COPY must be *currently in* one LOCATION.* This is shown in Figure 11.1.

Figure 11.1 also shows how DOCUMENTS may be defined. Each DOCUMENT must be *an example of* a DOCUMENT TYPE, typically predefined as to its structure and contents. (In another environment, it may not be necessary to *require* that a DOCUMENT be *of* a DOCUMENT TYPE.) Conversely, a DOCUMENT TYPE may be *embodied in* one or more DOCUMENTS. For example, a New Drug Application is a DOCUMENT TYPE, as is a hydrochloric acid material safety data sheet (MSDS). The particular NDA submitted by the XYZ Pharmaceutical Company on a particular date is a DOCUMENT, as is an MSDS for the HCl produced by the ABC Chemical Company.

Also shown in Figure 11.1 is the fact that DOCUMENT TYPES themselves come in several general categories, such as PERIODICAL, REPORT TO GOVERNMENT, DRAWING, and so forth. The examples shown are among those possible, but they might be different for your particular organization. The DOCUMENT TYPE New Drug Application is an example of a REPORT TO GOVERNMENT.

STRUCTURE

The simplest DOCUMENT is a single letter, memo, report, or book. It has a single subject matter and our only concern is to be able to find it.

Often, however, documents are much more complex than that, making it necessary to model the structure of the document itself. In the case of the NDA described above, each section ("chemistry" or "pharmacology," for example) is a DOCUMENT in its own right, as are the research reports that constitute each section.

In a simple environment, in which no component report is ever seen to be in more than one larger report, it is possible to define the relationship that each DOCUMENT may be *part of* one and only one other DOCUMENT. This would allow us to model the situation as in Figure 11.2.

Unfortunately, in many cases, smaller DOCUMENTS become part of more than one (possibly many) larger DOCUMENTS. For example, some of the pre-clinical studies that are part of a request to do clinical research (an Investigational New Drug application, or IND) also appear in the NDA that follows. This requires

---

* In "cyberspace," location is becoming difficult to define.

that we borrow from the ASSET STRUCTURE ELEMENT example in the manufacturing model, in which components showed up in more than one assembly. The DOCUMENT version of this is shown in Figure 11.3.

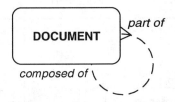

Figure 11.2: Simple Structure.

In Figure 11.3, the entity DOCUMENT STRUCTURE ELEMENT describes *the use of* one DOCUMENT *in* another DOCUMENT. That is, if a DOCUMENT appears in three other, larger DOCUMENTS, three occurrences of DOCUMENT STRUCTURE ELEMENT each link that document to one of the three larger ones.

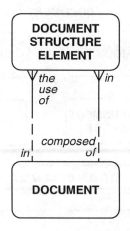

Figure 11.3: A More Complex Structure.

Figure 11.3 shows the case in which the DOCUMENT is created from scratch, with minimal guidance from the DOCUMENT TYPE. A similar structure, however, may also be defined for the DOCUMENT TYPE. That is, an NDA must *always* contain a "chemistry section" and a "pharmacology section," for example. This is better represented in Figure 11.4, in which each DOCUMENT TYPE STRUCTURE ELEMENT is *the use of* one DOCUMENT TYPE *in* another DOCUMENT TYPE. This is as compared with DOCUMENT STRUCTURE ELEMENT, which shows the *actual* structure of a *real* document. The latter shows that one DOCUMENT is used in another DOCUMENT, independent of what its standard structure should be—although the DOCUMENT STRUCTURE ELEMENT may be *based on* a DOCUMENT TYPE STRUCTURE ELEMENT.

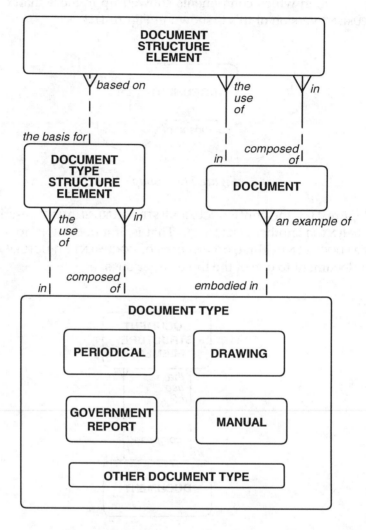

Figure 11.4: Document Type Structure.

ROLES

There are many connections between DOCUMENTS and PARTIES, especially PEOPLE. We want to know who created the DOCUMENT, who got a COPY of it, who authorized it, and so forth.

Authorship

Among the most important initial attributes of a DOCUMENT is "author." There are two problems with making this an attribute, however: First, the author has attributes. You might want to know the author's nationality, address, or whatever. The second problem is that a DOCUMENT may have more than one author, and a PERSON may write more than one DOCUMENT.

For these reasons, we will assume that authors are simply examples of the PEOPLE we discussed in Chapter Three. While in many cases, a DOCUMENT may be *created by* just one PERSON, there are enough examples of two or more PEOPLE sharing AUTHORSHIP of the DOCUMENT that it is appropriate to split this fact out as a separate entity. Here again, we can use the "mostly it's one, but sometimes it's more than one" structure, as shown in Figure 11.5. That is, each DOCUMENT must be either *created by* one PERSON, or *created by* one or more AUTHORSHIPS, in which each AUTHORSHIP is the fact that a particular PERSON participated *in the preparation of* the DOCUMENT.

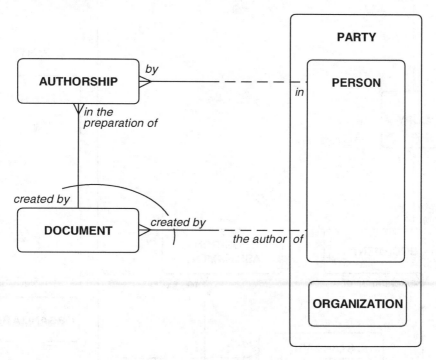

Figure 11.5: Authorship.

It is possible that DOCUMENTS may be recorded simply as having been *created by* a department or other ORGANIZATION (rather than *created by* a PERSON). In these circumstances, a DOCUMENT would be *created by* a PARTY or an AUTHORSHIP would be shown as being *by* a PARTY. This would not limit it just to being *by* a PERSON. If this is true in your organization, simply move the relationships shown to PERSON so that they now point to PARTY.

Receipt of Documents

In many cases (for example, in electronic mail systems), it is important to record where documents were sent. This is a matter of adding another relationship at least to PERSON, if not to PARTY. In simple cases, we need only to assert that each COPY must be *to* one and only one PERSON. In more complex cases, where it is necessary to keep track of the routing of each COPY, the more elaborate version shown in Figure 11.6 is necessary. This shows that a DISTRIBUTION is *of* a particular COPY *of* a DOCUMENT *to* a PARTY.

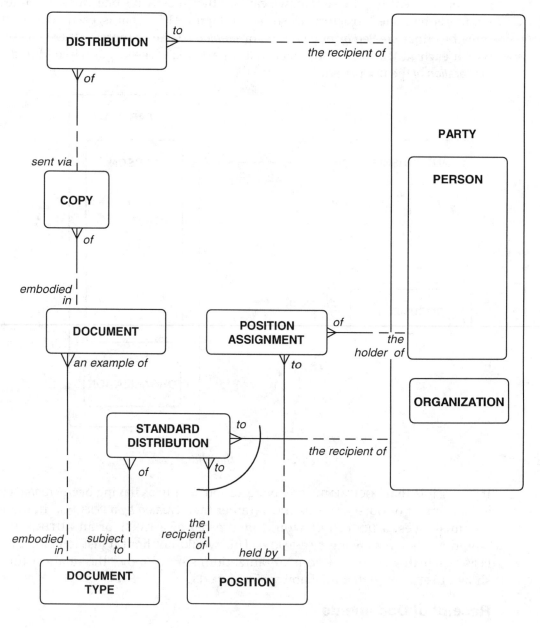

Figure 11.6: Distribution.

Also shown in Figure 11.6 is the fact that a particular DOCUMENT TYPE might be *subject to* one or more STANDARD DISTRIBUTIONS—each *to* a particular POSITION or *to* a particular PARTY. This is useful, in order to describe what is to be done with standard DOCUMENT TYPES. For example, a "Weekly Status Report," may have two STANDARD DISTRIBUTIONS—one to "The President," and one to "Joe Schmoe."

Other Roles

We have seen how AUTHORSHIP records the PEOPLE creating a DOCUMENT, and DISTRIBUTION describes who sees COPIES of it. In some organizations, this can get complex. For example, it may be necessary to know who is subscribing to various PUBLICATIONS. This is represented by the entity SUBSCRIPTION, in which each SUBSCRIPTION must be *by* a PERSON and *to* a PUBLICATION (a kind of DOCUMENT TYPE). This is shown in Figure 11.7. A SUBSCRIPTION is a special kind of distribution, which some might want to model explicitly.

Certain types of documents may have to be authorized by specified individuals. In Figure 11.7, an APPROVAL *of* a DOCUMENT must be *by* a PERSON. The APPROVAL required for a DOCUMENT is defined in terms of the DOCUMENT TYPE *embodied in* the DOCUMENT and the POSITION authorized to approve that DOCUMENT TYPE. Specifically, an APPROVAL REQUIREMENT is defined to be *for* a DOCUMENT TYPE, *by* a POSITION. A business rule requires that the PERSON who is *the giver of* the APPROVAL *of* a DOCUMENT must be in a POSITION that has been authorized to do so. That is, the actual APPROVAL must be *by* a PERSON who is *the holder of* a POSITION ASSIGNMENT *to* an appropriate POSITION. In this case, an "appropriate position" is one that is *the holder of* an APPROVAL REQUIREMENT *for* the DOCUMENT TYPE *embodied in* the DOCUMENT.

Note that the data structure gives us the terms by which to express the business rule about APPROVAL REQUIREMENT, but it does not enforce that rule. Program code must be added to any system implementing this model to ensure that the PERSON who is *the giver of* APPROVAL of a DOCUMENT *is also* authorized to do so, according to the rule stated in the last paragraph.

Access to a document may be explicitly restricted. That is, an ACCESS PERMISSION is defined to be *for* a DOCUMENT, and it must be *given to* either a POSITION or a named PERSON. Optionally, another relationship can be added to state that each ACCESS PERMISSION must be *given by* a PARTY.

SUBJECT AND CONTENTS

Indexing and classifying documents can be addressed at several levels of sophistication. Initially, we'll simply recognize that there are a set of TOPICS that are of interest. An INDEX ENTRY, which is *a reference to* a TOPIC *for* a DOCUMENT, records the fact that the DOCUMENT is about that TOPIC. (See Figure 11.8.) That is, each DOCUMENT may be *referenced by* one or more INDEX ENTRIES, each one of which must be *a reference to* a TOPIC. Looking at it from the other direction, each TOPIC may be *in* one or more INDEX ENTRIES *for* a DOCUMENT.

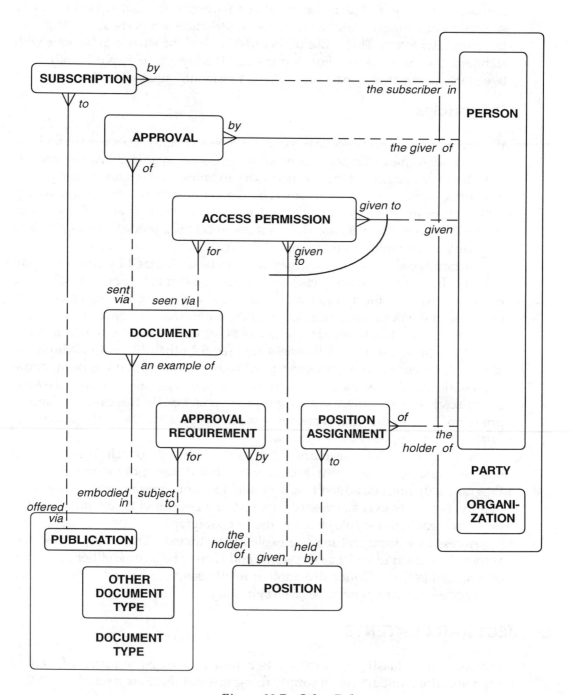

Figure 11.7: Other Roles.

A more sophisticated approach is to establish relationships between DOCUMENT and other parts of the model. For example, as shown in Figure 11.9, if the documents that concern us are maintenance manuals or drawings, we might say that each DOCUMENT must be *about* one or more ASSETS or ASSET TYPES.

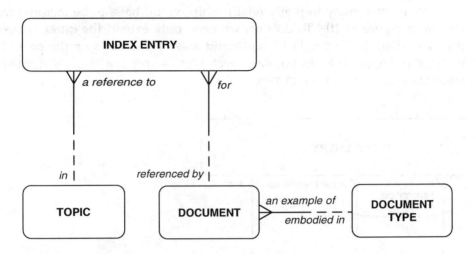

Figure 11.8: Topics and Index Entries.

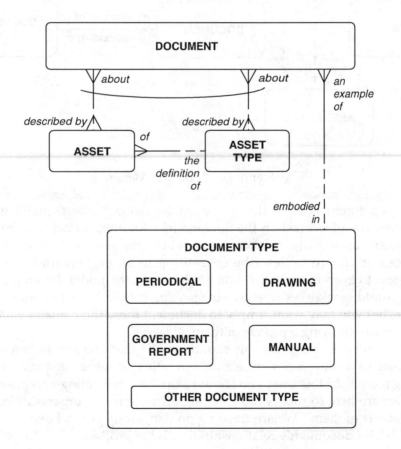

Figure 11.9: Documenting Products.

Assuming that an ASSET or ASSET TYPE might also be *described by* one or more DOCUMENTS, this many-to-many relationship would have to be factored out, as shown in Figure 11.10. To do this, we need only extend the INDEX ENTRY idea shown earlier. In Figure 11.10, ASSET and ASSET TYPE now take the part played by TOPIC in Figure 11.8. In this case, each INDEX ENTRY *in* a DOCUMENT must be *a reference to* one ASSET or ASSET TYPE.

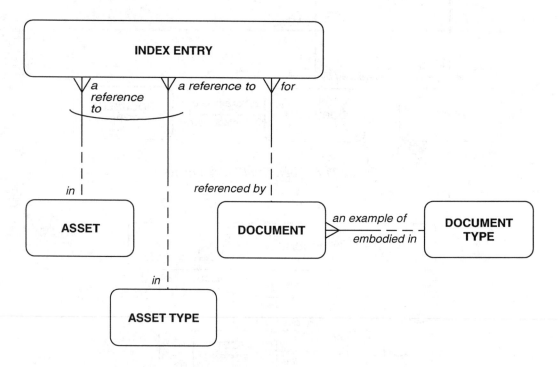

Figure 11.10: Subject Matter.

Things get more complicated as we realize that DOCUMENTS may have as TOPICS *anything else* of interest on the data model. An INDEX ENTRY may be *a reference to* a PARTY, an ACTIVITY, an ACCOUNT, or what have you, as shown in Figure 11.11. If DOCUMENTS are to describe everything in an organization, and are to be indexed to everything in the data model, any data model drawing of this situation would quickly become unmanageable. This isn't to say that it shouldn't be done, but you may want simply to document these topic relationships, without necessarily drawing a picture of them all.

Of course if things get this bad, it may be that you are no longer modeling documents as things of significance, but rather simply as displays of the underlying model. In this case, you should skip the whole thing. As previously stated, we are here to model things of significance to the organization, not representations of them. We are treading on dangerous ground once it is necessary to model a document's relationship to a large proportion of the entities in the model.

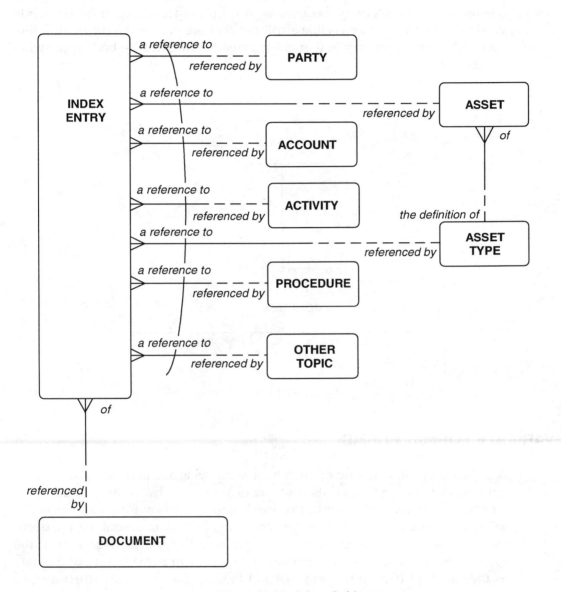

Figure 11.11: More Subjects.

VERSIONS

The fact that DOCUMENTS may be held in multiple versions can be dealt with in two ways: The first simply says that a DOCUMENT may be *an amendment to* another DOCUMENT. This is appropriate when anything in the document may change from version to version. If, on the other hand, the document is basically unchanged, but only specified characteristics change, like language or format, then it may be appropriate to specify that the DOCUMENT may be *changed in* one or more VERSIONS *of* the DOCUMENT. Attributes that change from version to version appear in VERSION, while attributes that are part of the inherent definition of the DOCUMENT stay in that entity. (See Figure 11.12 for both approaches to this problem.)

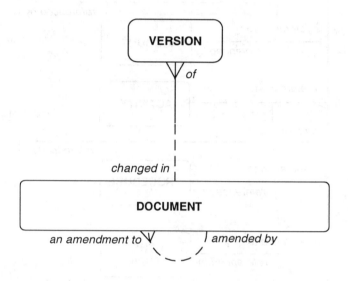

Figure 11.12: Versions.

VARIABLE FORMAT FORMS

A particularly difficult kind of document to model is one that varies in its internal structure, depending on its contents or purpose. Two examples are noteworthy: pharmaceutical clinical research data collection forms and material safety data sheets. In each case, the structure of the data describing the document is not so much derived from the business as from the structure of the form itself. The modeler's assignment is to represent the structure of the data as they are captured on these forms, and then to transform this structure into the business terms of the rest of the model.

In the first example, clinical pharmaceutical research consists of clinical trials (studies) where, in each trial, compounds are administered to subjects, and then the subjects' responses are observed. Some of the participants are given the compound being tested, and some are given a control substance—usually a placebo. Depending on the compound, the purpose of the study, and the point in the study at which observations are being taken, different kinds of information must be captured. The data collection forms, therefore, contain a variable number of blocks (or, in some companies, modules), in which each block may contain from one to a large number of observations. These observations may be single numbers, arrays of numbers, or text. What observations are contained in a block depends on the study and the point during the study when the data are captured.

A similar problem arises with the material safety data sheet, a document required by the U.S. Occupational Safety and Health Administration (OSHA). The MSDS must accompany every container of any material deemed dangerous (which is to say, nearly every material), from the material's creation through its destruction. The form describes the characteristics of the material and is intended to alert anyone handling the material of any hazards that might be encountered and any precautions to be taken. Because of the vast variety in the kinds and forms of materials covered, the form is tailored to the kind of material it describes. The form contains a variable number of sections (not every MSDS requires every section) and, as with the clinical trials case report form, each section might contain simple text, one or more numbers, or a complete matrix of data.

To model the variable structure of these documents is a challenge. We discuss each below.

Clinical Trials Observations

Clinical data for a STUDY are gathered when a SUBJECT visits a study site, when he or she is observed at home, or when laboratory results are gathered.* Each of these events is an OBSERVATION POINT. (See Figure 11.13.) That is, an OBSERVATION POINT *about* a SUBJECT is either a VISIT (at a hospital, a clinic, or at the SUBJECT's home) or a LABORATORY TEST. Each LABORATORY TEST that is conducted must be *derived from* a VISIT. Each LABORATORY TEST or VISIT must take place at an identified "date" and "time."

---

* By the way, since clinical research is usually done on a blind basis, "name" is *not* an attribute of SUBJECT. The physician conducting the study is the only person who knows that SUBJECT "123" is Sally Doe, and this information is not made part of the clinical data. On the other hand, even though the physician does not know if the medication given is the test compound or the control substance, that information *is* part of the study data. While the medications given are not included in the model we are discussing here, the model that would include such information must reflect the fact that *someone* knows exactly what compounds are given to SUBJECT "123." This suggests a modeling situation in which it is important to model correctly a set of data that are not necessarily going to be widely available. In systems design, it is important to carefully design access paths that will only make data available that are appropriate to each user.

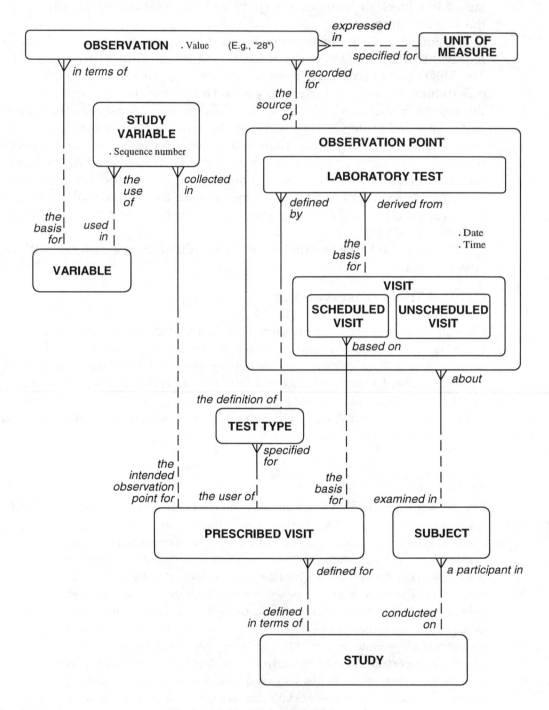

Figure 11.13: Visits and Observations.

A VISIT (at a particular date and time) must be either a SCHEDULED VISIT or an UNSCHEDULED VISIT. A SCHEDULED VISIT must be *based on* a PRESCRIBED VISIT, which is *defined for* the STUDY. In other words, when a STUDY is designed, its structure is *defined in terms of* one or more PRESCRIBED VISITS. For example, a particular STUDY may involve 23 PRESCRIBED VISITS. Each PRESCRIBED VISIT may be *the basis for* one or more actual SCHEDULED VISITS *about* a SUBJECT.*

While a SCHEDULED or UNSCHEDULED VISIT is at a "date" or "time," a PRESCRIBED VISIT is defined only in terms of the number of weeks since a patient entered the study. For example, each patient in a study may have PRESCRIBED VISITS at weeks one, three, five, and so forth.

Each PRESCRIBED VISIT may also be *the intended observation point for* a specified set of STUDY VARIABLES, where each STUDY VARIABLE represents *the use of* a VARIABLE *collected in* a PRESCRIBED VISIT. The first (SCHEDULED) VISIT will collect demographic data, initial readings of blood pressure and temperature, among other things, while the fourth (SCHEDULED) VISIT might be *the basis for* a particular kind of LABORATORY TEST, and so forth.

Thus, each PRESCRIBED VISIT may be *the basis for* one or more of the actual SCHEDULED VISITS. (Of course, a SUBJECT may also be *examined in* one or more UNSCHEDULED VISITS, if circumstances call for them.)

Each OBSERVATION POINT (VISIT or LABORATORY TEST), then, may be *the source of* one or more OBSERVATIONS, each of which must be *in terms of* a VARIABLE. Note the similarity of this structure to the model of TESTS and OBSERVATIONS described in Chapter Eight (Figure 8.4) and to the model of MEASUREMENTS described in Chapter Ten (Figure 10.8). In fact, the LABORATORY TEST and OBSERVATION entities are exactly as described there, complete with an OBSERVATION being *in terms of* a VARIABLE, *expressed in* a UNIT OF MEASURE. The only difference is that, here, VISIT is both playing the role of SAMPLE, and being itself *the source of* OBSERVATIONS.[†] Data are collected in clinical trials via documents called case report forms (CRF's). One case report form describes (is formatted for) one PRESCRIBED VISIT. Figure 11.14 shows that each PRESCRIBED VISIT may be *described in* many CRF PAGES. Logically, a PRESCRIBED VISIT may be considered equivalent to the case report form that describes it.

---

* Since the relationship is in fact from the supertype OBSERVATION POINT, we have to say it is *about* a SUBJECT—even though a VISIT is obviously *by* a SUBJECT.

[†] We could say that the VISIT is *the source of* the PHYSICAL OBSERVATIONS shown in the laboratory model, except that in this context, it is not quite complete. While PHYSICAL OBSERVATIONS may indeed be made (pallor, for example), a VISIT can also be *the source of* OBSERVATIONS on the VARIABLES "temperature," "systolic pressure," and so forth. These are numerical measurements taken during VISITS, while the laboratory can only take numerical measurements from TESTS.

Previously, in Figure 11.13, we defined a STUDY VARIABLE as being *the use of* a VARIABLE *collected in* a PRESCRIBED VISIT. In fact, the definition of a STUDY VARIABLE'S use in a PRESCRIBED VISIT is *via* the CRF PAGE, as shown in Figure 11.14. That is, each STUDY VARIABLE must be *the use of* a VARIABLE *in* a CRF PAGE, which is *for* a PRESCRIBED VISIT. (Each CRF PAGE may be *composed of* one or more STUDY VARIABLES.)

The data to be collected may be grouped into standard BLOCKS. These are standardized so that data may be compared across studies. One block, for example, might encompass the demographic data gathered when a SUBJECT first registers to participate in the STUDY. Other blocks may constitute standard ways of describing hematological data, cardiovascular information, and so forth. In Figure 11.14, each BLOCK must be *composed of* one or more BLOCK VARIABLES, each of which is *the use of* a VARIABLE.

A BLOCK USAGE is *of* a standard BLOCK *on* a CRF PAGE. The BLOCK and its BLOCK VARIABLES provide a candidate list of VARIABLES to be *used as* STUDY VARIABLES *in* the same CRF PAGES. Note, however, that the model in its present form does not *require* the STUDY VARIABLES actually used *in* a particular CRF PAGE to be the same as the BLOCK VARIABLES in a BLOCK appearing on the same page definition. This is true even if the CRF PAGE consists entirely of standard BLOCKS. For example, the standard hematology block might not include calling for an ECG, but in this study, it might be included. A business rule, embodied in program code, could be introduced to enforce that, if it is deemed desirable to do so, but this constraint cannot be represented on the model.

Similarly, it is also possible to record an OBSERVATION *of* a VARIABLE that was not required on that visit (even if it was a SCHEDULED VISIT). This is true even though the OBSERVATION is *of* a VARIABLE that is used somewhere in the study. That is, someone may record an OBSERVATION *of* a VARIABLE *used as* a STUDY VARIABLE *in* a CRF PAGE that is *not for* the same PRESCRIBED VISIT that is *the basis for* the OBSERVATION.* For example, it may be the case that blood pressure (systolic and diastolic—two observations, actually) is normally collected during visits one, three, and five, but for some reason, the investigator also chose to take it (and record it) during visit four.

An alternative model, which is more restrictive, is shown in Figure 11.15. Here, an OBSERVATION must be *of* a STUDY VARIABLE, where a STUDY VARIABLE defines not just that a VARIABLE is being used *in* a CRF PAGE, but specifically that it is *the use of* a BLOCK VARIABLE (which is *the use of* a VARIABLE *in* a BLOCK) *on* a CRF PAGE.† An OBSERVATION *recorded for* an OBSERVATION POINT, then, must be *of* a STUDY VARIABLE—that is, it can only be one *of* the predefined combinations of VARIABLE, BLOCK, and PRESCRIBED VISIT.

---

* That is, the PRESCRIBED VISIT is *the basis for* the SCHEDULED VISIT, which is *the source of* the OBSERVATION.

† That is, the BLOCK VARIABLE is *in* a BLOCK which may be *used in* a BLOCK USAGE *on* a CRF PAGE.

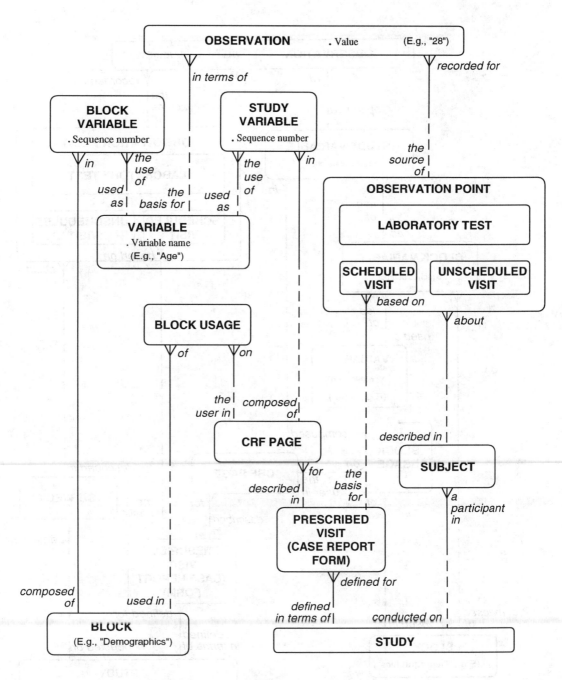

Figure 11.14: Case Report Forms.

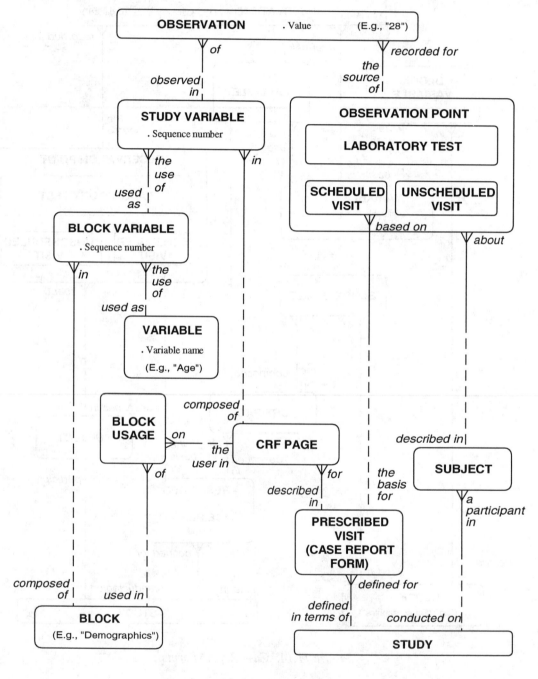

Figure 11.15: A More Restrictive Model.

Figure 11.15 raises the question of what to do about UNSCHEDULED VISITS. We can use this model if we can stipulate that even in UNSCHEDULED VISITS we can take OBSERVATIONS on a STUDY VARIABLE *for* another PRESCRIBED VISIT.* If, on the other hand, an UNSCHEDULED VISIT may be *the source of* an OBSERVATION *of* a VARIABLE that is not *used as* a BLOCK VARIABLE (and hence, not used as a STUDY VARIABLE) anywhere, we will have to return to Figure 11.14.

Note that even with this model, we cannot describe the business rule to verify that when creating an occurrence *of* a STUDY VARIABLE, everything that the occurrence specifies is consistent. We still cannot guarantee (through the model) that the STUDY VARIABLE the OBSERVATION is *of* is *in* a BLOCK, which is *used in* the PRESCRIBED VISIT that the OBSERVATION is *recorded for.*[†]

Material Safety Data Sheets

As noted above, our second example of variable format documents is the material safety data sheet, a form required by law to accompany every container of a hazardous material from its manufacture until its destruction. An MSDS includes, besides the identity and composition of the material, descriptions of hazards, references to procedures for handling it, information on dangerous interactions with other materials, and so forth. The intention is to provide warnings about the material's hazards to the people working with it.

The law provides that certain kinds of information must be included, but so far there is very little consistency in requirements for its format or even some of the specifics of its contents. Still, it would be valuable to be able to store the document on the computer in an organized way, so that it could be retrieved, not only by material, but by the hazards the form describes. The challenge here, then, as in the clinical trials example just discussed, is to find structure in a document for which there are no rules.

The MSDS has all the same problems as the clinical trials case report form: It also is composed of a variable number of sections, in which each section could contain a single number, an array of numbers, or a piece of text.[‡] In

---

* That is, we can take OBSERVATIONS on a STUDY VARIABLE *in* a CRF PAGE *for* another PRESCRIBED VISIT.

[†] For the serious model navigator, the complete sentence is, We still cannot guarantee that the STUDY VARIABLE the OBSERVATION is *of* is *the use of* a BLOCK VARIABLE, which is *in* a BLOCK that is *used in* a BLOCK USAGE *on* a CRF PAGE *for* the PRESCRIBED VISIT, which is *the basis for* a SCHEDULED VISIT that the OBSERVATION is *recorded for.*

[‡] Sometimes, a *lot* of text!

addition, the MSDS suffers from the fact that the data it contains, for the most part, ought to be elsewhere in the model of the material it describes.* The model of the document echoes the underlying business model, but is more convoluted, because it describes the document, not the reality that the document describes. This turns out to be another example of a meta-model, since it describes a structure that itself is describing something else.

Figure 11.16 shows the beginnings of a model for MSDS's. Note that each MATERIAL SAFETY DATA SHEET must be *about* a particular ASSET TYPE, where an ASSET TYPE is either a MATERIAL TYPE or a PART/EQUIPMENT TYPE.[†] It must be *prepared by* a single PARTY, usually the manufacturer.

A MATERIAL SAFETY DATA SHEET must be *composed of* one or more SECTIONS. Each SECTION, in turn, may be *used to record* one or more PARAMETER VALUES, each of which must be *of* a PARAMETER. These PARAMETER VALUES, then, constitute the data contained in the MSDS. The "name" attribute of a PARAMETER, for example, might be "manufacturer," while the "value" of a PARAMETER VALUE could be "Fritz Chemical Company."

A SECTION that is *part of* a MATERIAL SAFETY DATA SHEET must also be *defined by* a SECTION TYPE. SECTION TYPES are defined generically, including, for example, "identification," "chemical properties," and "hazards."

Note that, as with other DOCUMENTS, we are dealing here with an MSDS as an abstraction. As described for DOCUMENTS generally, each MSDS will then be published in one or more COPIES, each of which is *supposed to be*[‡] physically *attached to* every ASSET that is *an example of* the subject ASSET TYPE.

Throughout the world, various regulatory agencies define the requirements for MSDS's differently. An MSDS TYPE is a classification for a MATERIAL SAFETY DATA SHEET, defining whether it is an American National Standards Institute (ANSI) standard, a standard from the European Union, or whatever. (See Figure 11.17.)

---

* Specifically, the MSDS is about the MATERIAL TYPE modeled in Chapter Four.

† Usually, MSDS's are about MATERIAL TYPES—the powders and liquids used in the manufacturing process—but not always. An MSDS is required to accompany aluminum parts, for example, because the dust created when they are machined is hazardous when inhaled.

‡ In addition to "must be" and "may be," we need symbols for "supposed to be." (As modelers, we have to leave this relationship optional, since some assets may not get their MSDS copies, and some copies will wind up in offices, posted on walls, filed somewhere, or the like.)

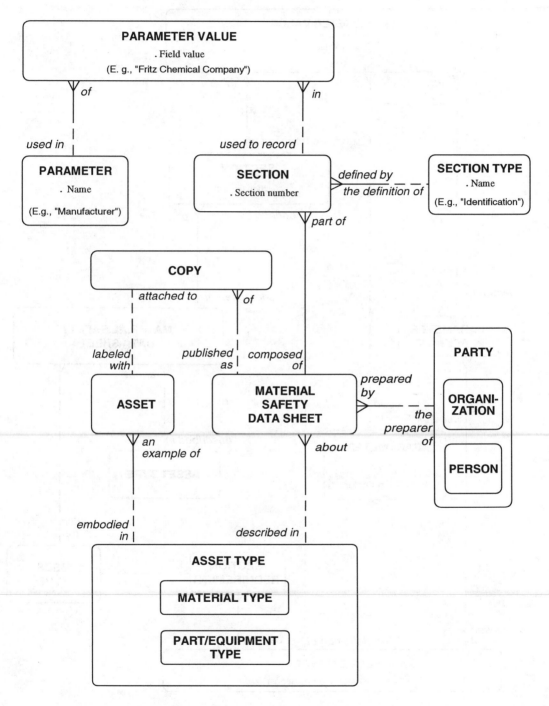

Figure 11.16: Material Safety Data Sheet Definitions.

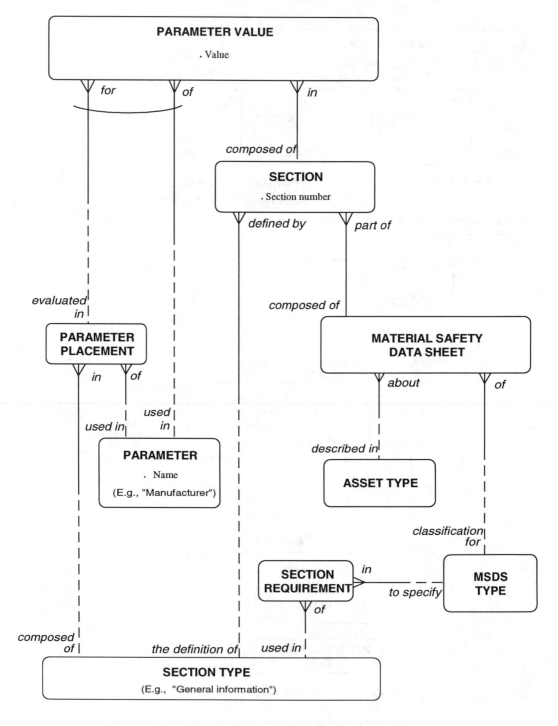

Figure 11.17: MSDS Sections.

An MSDS TYPE defines which SECTION TYPES all MATERIAL SAFETY DATA SHEETS of that MSDS TYPE will be *composed of.* For example, in the United States, the ANSI standard requires sections for "general information," "principal hazardous ingredients," "physical data," and so forth. This is via the SECTION REQUIREMENT entity, each occurrence of which is the requirement *of* a particular SECTION TYPE to appear *in* a particular MSDS TYPE. That is, each MSDS TYPE must be *to specify* one or more SECTION REQUIREMENTS, each of which must be *of* a SECTION TYPE.

Each SECTION TYPE may be *the definition of* one or more SECTIONS that are *part of* actual MATERIAL SAFETY DATA SHEETS. That is, a SECTION is *defined by* one SECTION TYPE. There is no requirement as to the order of the sections or the order of the parameters within each section. For example, the ANSI standard (MSDS TYPE) requires a SECTION TYPE "hazards." On a particular MSDS, a SECTION *defined by* the SECTION TYPE "hazards" may have a "section number" of "3."

Each SECTION TYPE may be *composed of* one or more PARAMETER PLACEMENTS *of* a PARAMETER. That is, a PARAMETER PLACEMENT is *of* a particular PARAMETER, and is *in* a particular SECTION TYPE. If a PARAMETER is *used in* a SECTION TYPE, then that is an occurrence of a PARAMETER PLACEMENT.

PARAMETER PLACEMENT refers to the *standard* use of PARAMETERS in standard SECTION TYPES. For example, "manufacturer" is expected normally to appear in the section "general information." A PARAMETER VALUE, on the other hand, is the *actual* appearance *of* a PARAMETER *in* a SECTION that is *part of* an actual MATERIAL SAFETY DATA SHEET. Remember from above that "Fritz Chemical Company" actually appeared as the "value" for "manufacturer." This might have been in SECTION "1," *part of* a particular MATERIAL SAFETY DATA SHEET.

The arc in Figure 11.17 is for the benefit of data modelers, not end users: In a particular SECTION, you may stipulate that you cannot specify a PARAMETER VALUE *in* a SECTION that is not defined (via a PARAMETER PLACEMENT) *in* the SECTION TYPE that the SECTION is *defined by.* That is, in the first case, the PARAMETER VALUE must be *for* a PARAMETER PLACEMENT, which constrains it *only* to be *of* those PARAMETERS that are *used in* the SECTION TYPE* that is *the definition of* the SECTION that the PARAMETER VALUE is *in.* As an alternative, you could merely say that each PARAMETER VALUE must be *of* a PARAMETER, with nothing to insure that the PARAMETER that appears was previously defined for this SECTION.

In your model, you should use one or the other PARAMETER VALUE relationship shown in Figure 11.17 under the arc, but probably not both.

Because the MATERIAL SAFETY DATA SHEET is fundamentally about an ASSET TYPE, information about the ASSET TYPE will itself be part of the MSDS document. (See Figure 11.18.) An important piece of this information about an

---

* That is, PARAMETERS that are *used in* one or more PARAMETER PLACEMENTS *in* the SECTION TYPE . . .

ASSET TYPE is its composition. In the real-world model, this is the set of ASSET TYPES that are *part of* the ASSET TYPE in question.* We have to put a pointer to this information in an MSDS SECTION.

In Chapter Four (Figure 4.11), the kinds of ASSET TYPE RELATIONSHIPS (ASSET TYPE STRUCTURE ELEMENTS, ELECTRICAL CONNECTIONS, and so forth) were shown as subtypes of that entity. Here, in order to define rules for connecting PARAMETERS to the appropriate relationships (and to leave our options open), we convert the ASSET TYPE RELATIONSHIP subtypes into ASSET TYPE RELATIONSHIP TYPES, as shown in Figure 11.18. That is, "asset type structure element" is now an example of ASSET TYPE RELATIONSHIP TYPE, along with "electrical connection," "incompatibility," and "family structure."

The "incompatibility" of one ASSET TYPE with another, for example, is the fact that the two may not be brought into proximity without causing a fire, explosion, or some other calamity. As another example, "family structure" is a way of grouping materials according to characteristics of interest. A product "family," such as "kerosene-based materials" or "oil-based paints," may be defined as an ASSET TYPE. A FAMILY STRUCTURE, then, is the fact that a particular ASSET TYPE is a member of the family.

In our composition example, to bring the structure of the ASSET TYPE into the MSDS, each PARAMETER VALUE (in the SECTION about composition) may be *about* a component ASSET TYPE. That is, while the MSDS itself is about the compound material, this PARAMETER describes one of its components. The PARAMETER is permitted to refer to the component because it is *a reference to* the ASSET TYPE RELATIONSHIP TYPE "asset type structure." (A business rule, not documented in the data model, should enforce this.) The PARAMETER VALUE, then, is *in* a MATERIAL SAFETY DATA SHEET *about* one material, but it is *about* a component of that material.

Similarly, if a SECTION is to list the ASSET TYPES with which the subject ASSET TYPE is incompatible, a PARAMETER PLACEMENT *in* the SECTION'S SECTION TYPE would be *of* a PARAMETER that was *a reference to* the ASSET TYPE RELATIONSHIP TYPE "incompatibility." PARAMETER VALUES then could be *about* ASSET TYPES that are both *part of* the subject ASSET TYPE,[†] and *defined by* the ASSET TYPE RELATIONSHIP TYPE "incompatibility."

---

* That is, this is the set of ASSET TYPES that are *part of* ASSET TYPE STRUCTURE ELEMENTS (a subtype of ASSET TYPE RELATIONSHIP), which are *in* the ASSET TYPE in question.

[†] That is, PARAMETER VALUES then could be *about* ASSET TYPES that are both *part of* an ASSET TYPE RELATIONSHIP *in* the subject ASSET TYPE.

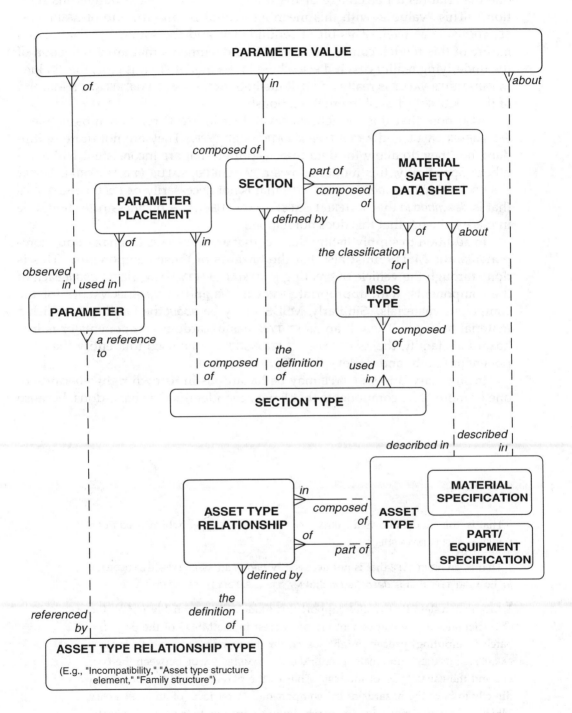

Figure 11.18: The MSDS and Asset Types.

Note that the attribute "value" of PARAMETER VALUE could be "the amount of one material (as a percentage of the other) that will cause a dangerous reaction." This "value"—with this meaning—could be an attribute of ASSET TYPE RELATIONSHIP as well. This bit of redundancy, and the somewhat convoluted nature of this model, comes from modeling documents that are a reflection of the underlying reality covered elsewhere in the model. In this case, the "value" in PARAMETER VALUE is really an attribute both of the ASSET TYPE RELATIONSHIP and of the DOCUMENT describing that relationship.

Also note that this model has several (if indirect) relationships between PARAMETER VALUE and ASSET TYPE RELATIONSHIP TYPE. They are not quite redundant, but they do allow for data to be captured that are inconsistent with each other. Specifically, this model allows a PARAMETER VALUE *in* a MATERIAL SAFETY DATA SHEET,* to be *about* an ASSET TYPE that is not necessarily *part of* the ASSET TYPE that is *described in* that MATERIAL SAFETY DATA SHEET.† A business rule should be in place to insure that this does not happen.

In addition to simply listing the fact that an ASSET TYPE has hazardous components, the MSDS must also list the hazards of those components. This is done through the vehicle of creating MATERIAL SAFETY DATA SHEETS *about* each of the components, with appropriate PARAMETERS and PARAMETER VALUES for the component materials. Similarly, MSDS's may be *about* the families to which a material belongs. Then, if an ASSET TYPE has hazardous components or is in a hazardous family, the ASSET TYPE RELATIONSHIP can be used to identify the component or family, and retrieve the MSDS data for it.‡

In summary, an ASSET TYPE may be hazardous in its own right—because of one or more of its components that have been identified as hazardous, because

---

* That is, this model allows a PARAMETER VALUE *in* a SECTION, which is *part of* a MATERIAL SAFETY DATA SHEET.

† That is, an ASSET TYPE that is not necessarily *part of* an ASSET TYPE RELATIONSHIP *in* the ASSET TYPE that is *described in* that MATERIAL SAFETY DATA SHEET.

‡ In a real system that would support this model, since probably not all the characteristics of the component are of interest in the MSDS of the parent, a batch (computing) process might search for the components and their MSDS PARAMETER USAGES, and create a redundant PARAMETER VALUE between the parent and the PARAMETERS of interest. That is, the parent would be considered directly to have the hazards of the components. A retrieval of an ASSET TYPE'S MSDS then would not have to search down the product structure to get the parameters of the components.

of the family to which it belongs, or because of the ASSET TYPE's incompatibility with one or more other ASSET TYPES. An MSDS for a particular ASSET TYPE, then, may be a composite, consisting of an MSDS for the ASSET TYPE's hazards, an MSDS for the hazards of each of its components, and an MSDS for the hazards of the family to which it belongs. The ASSET TYPE RELATIONSHIP entity allows us to locate all of these MSDS's.

A PARAMETER may be any of several different kinds of things, as shown in Figure 11.19. A PARAMETER may be a simple value or set of values, such as a FIRE/EXPLOSION PARAMETER or a TRANSPORTATION PARAMETER. It may be a REQUIRED PROCEDURE, such as that for an EMERGENCY & FIRST AID PROCEDURE, or a procedure for dealing with a SPILL, LEAK, OR DISPOSAL. If it is a REQUIRED PROCEDURE, it must be *for* a previously defined PROCEDURE or, as it is probably called in this context, a STANDARD OPERATING PROCEDURE. Such a PROCEDURE would be defined as described in Chapter Five.

Figure 11.19 also makes explicit REACTIVITY PARAMETER, TOXICITY PARAMETER, and COMPOSITION PARAMETER. These are all examples of PARAMETERS that are *descriptions of* the ASSET TYPE RELATIONSHIP TYPE entity as just described.

Note that the ASSET TYPE RELATIONSHIP TYPES that are *referenced by* these PARAMETERS (*INCOMPATIBILITY* and *ASSET TYPE STRUCTURE ELEMENT*) are shown in this diagram as pseudo-entities, like those in Chapter Seven. This is to clarify the business rule that *a particular kind of* PARAMETER must be related to *a particular occurrence of* (or set of occurrences of) ASSET TYPE RELATIONSHIP TYPE.

For example, REACTIVITY PARAMETER is *a description of* ASSET TYPE RELATIONSHIPS whose ASSET TYPE RELATIONSHIP TYPE is "incompatibility," shown here by the pseudo-entity *INCOMPATIBILITY*. Similarly, a TOXICITY PARAMETER defines the extent to which the material is poisonous, which may or may not be determined by the amount of a critical component that is present.

The complete models for clinical data collection and material safety data sheets are far more extensive than the fragments shown here. It is, for example, left as an exercise for the reader to model the validation structures for clinical data or the parameter interactions for the MSDS.

You may not have reason to model either clinical data or material safety data sheets. The principles described here, however, apply to any document that has a variable number of sections with different formats, but which must be captured in a structured form.

As you can see, documents are difficult to model because there are few inherent patterns in their structure. You can make general assertions about their authorship, distribution, and so forth, but if they get very complex it is necessary to use meta-models to describe them. At the level where they are normally seen and used, documents can be anything the user wants them to be—forcing us to model the very structure of the user's thought process itself.

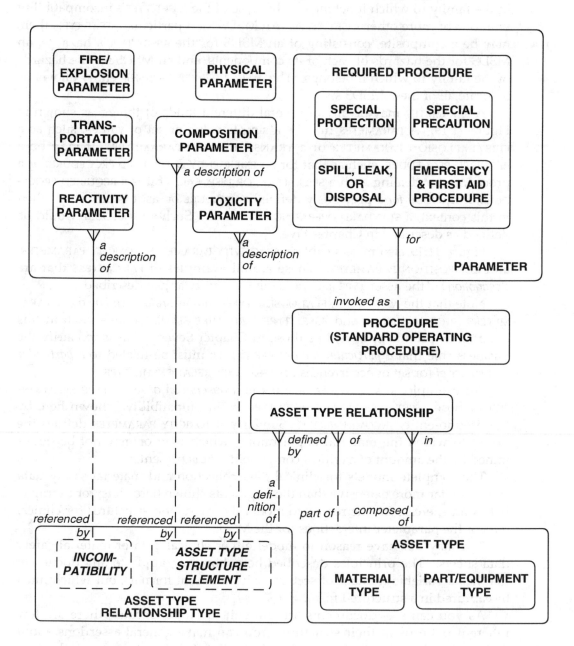

Figure 11.19: Parameters.

REFERENCES

1   *Webster's Ninth New Collegiate Dictionary* (Springfield, Mass.: Merriam-Webster Inc., 1987), p. 371.

2   *Webster's New World Dictionary of the American Language* (New York: The World Publishing Company, 1964), p. 429.

12
LOWER-LEVEL CONVENTIONS

*T*he patterns in this book address the fundamental structures of a business. The idea is that many kinds of business can use some or all components of these models. After the first two chapters of introduction, we saw models for four primary elements that occur in any business or government agency:

- the people and organizations with which the organization deals

- the "stuff" that it manipulates, makes, and uses

- its activities

- its contracts and other relationships with the world at large

The remaining chapters (Chapters Seven through Eleven) addressed more specialized themes that elaborated on the first four groups of patterns. Some were pervasive, like the treatment of accounting or documents. Some were of interest only in specific areas, such as materials planning and process manufacturing. From all of these chapters, however, you should have gotten the sense that contrary to appearance, there is an underlying order to things, and your assignment as a systems analyst is to find it.

Different business situations have been presented throughout the book that apply to a wide variety of organizations. Readers, however, undoubtedly will have observed that even across these models there are common elements. Just as cars are similar to other cars and airplanes are similar to other airplanes (for example, all have fuel lines and steering mechanisms), so too, the models in the various chapters of this book have common elements. This final chapter details some of those common elements.

THINGS, THING TYPES, AND CATEGORIES

The most common structure has been that of the relationship between an instance of a thing and its definition. In this case, the basic structure asserts that each thing must be *an example of* one and only one "thing type," and that each thing type may be *embodied in* one or more things. This concept was first presented in the relationship between ASSET and ASSET TYPE, but also appeared in ACTIVITY and ACTIVITY TYPE, TEST and TEST TYPE, and in many other models, as summarized in Figure 12.1. A less obvious example was PROCESS EXECUTION and PROCESS. In each case, the thing-type entity represented *the definition of* or was *embodied in* the thing itself.

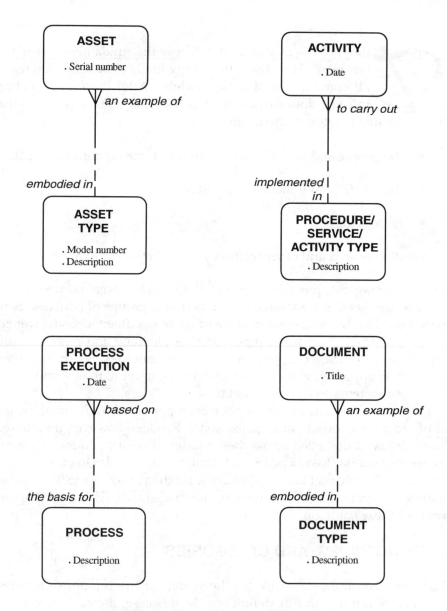

Figure 12.1: Things and Thing Types.

A similar structure, with not quite the same meaning, is thing and "thing category." Examples of this include ASSET and ASSET CATEGORY, ACCOUNT and ACCOUNT CATEGORY, and so forth. Unlike the thing-type entity, the thing category is *not* the *definition* of the instance entity, but is merely a *classification* for it. In this case, the thing-category entity represents groups of things only. That means that it is usually *not* the case that the thing is *of* only one of them. A thing may be *classified into* more than one thing category. It is appropriate, therefore, to insert the entity "thing classification" into the model, where each thing classification must be *of* one thing *into* one thing category. (See Figure 12.2.)

Invariably, CATEGORIES and their memberships differ from department to department in a typical organization. Each CLASSIFICATION, then, may be (or must be, depending on your circumstances) *by* a PARTY—either a PERSON or an ORGANIZATION.

The concepts in this book have wide applicability, even beyond business and government. For example, imagine a theatrical production company. It has available in its repertoire any number of PLAYS of various kinds. What pays the bills, however, is the actual PRODUCTION of a particular PLAY in one or more PERFORMANCES. Here again, the thing type (the PLAY) will be *embodied in* (*presented in*) one or more things (PRODUCTIONS). Figure 12.3 shows the PRODUCTION as a concrete (well, sort of) thing, which is an embodiment of a PLAY. The PRODUCTION, in turn, is the definition of one or more PERFORMANCES, so a similar relationship exists between them. Each PRODUCTION may be (one would hope it is "must be") *given in* one or more PERFORMANCES.

PLAYS may be classified, of course, into comedies, tragedies, musicals, and so forth. Modern PLAYS often fall into more than one category. Figure 12.3 shows this DRAMATIC CLASSIFICATION *of* each PLAY *into* a DRAMATIC CATEGORY. In this example, two thousand years of tradition have sorted out the classification scheme pretty well. It isn't really necessary, therefore, to assert who is doing the classifying. On the other hand, if you want to satisfy our *avant garde* friends, who insist on strange combinations of categories in their plays, you can see how easily this classification responsibility could be added to the model. (A relationship to PARTY could be added to say that each DRAMATIC CLASSIFICATION must be *by* a PARTY.)

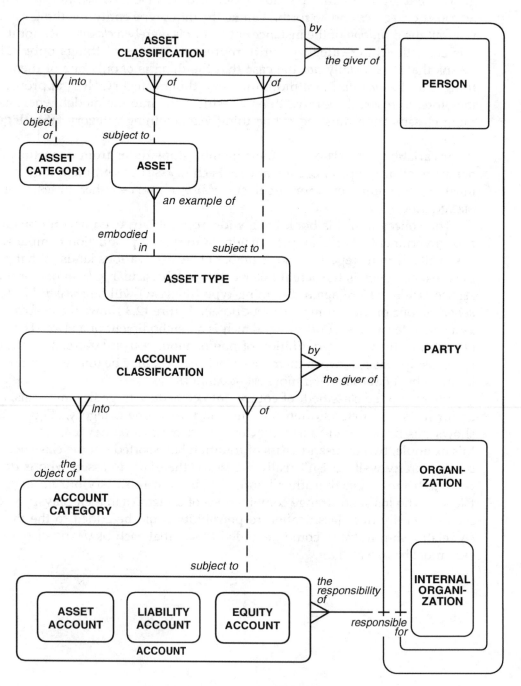

Figure 12.2: Things and Thing Categories.

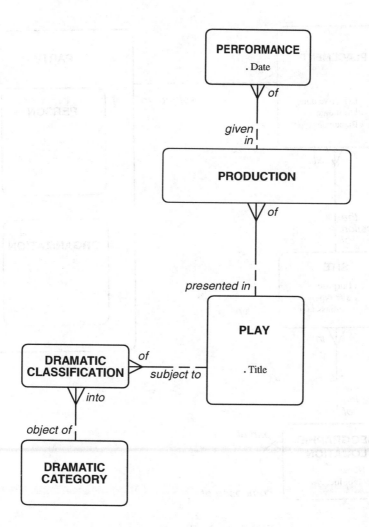

Figure 12.3: Plays, Performances, and Dramatic Categories.

ADDRESSES

Chapter Three included an extensive discussion of the ADDRESS and SITE entities. As borne out by the length of the discussion in that chapter, this turns out to be a subtle problem, without a single answer. In general, though, we asserted that each PARTY may be *subject to* PLACEMENT *in* a SITE. (See Figure 3.11, reproduced here as Figure 12.4.) Typically, "address text" is an attribute of SITE. Each SITE, in turn, must be *in* a GEOGRAPHIC LOCATION, where a GEOGRAPHIC LOCATION may be *composed of* other GEOGRAPHIC LOCATIONS.

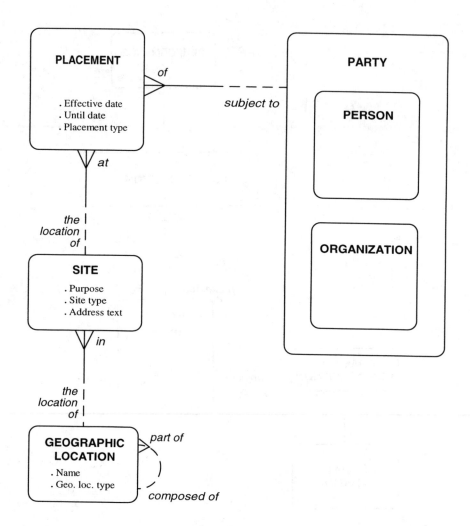

Figure 12.4: Placements and Sites.

There are variations on this, of course. Some are more complex, and some are simpler. In our theatrical example, it is only necessary to say that each PRODUCTION must be *at* a particular VENUE (another word for SITE), as shown in Figure 12.5. Actors being generally an itinerant lot, it's not always possible to say where they are,* so we normally don't have to worry about a PERSON's or an

---

* The stage manager should know, of course, but we probably don't have to keep that in our database.

ORGANIZATION'S PLACEMENT at a SITE. Not that we can rule that out as a future requirement, mind you.

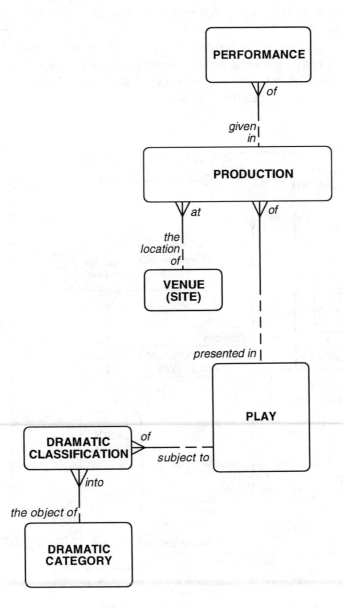

Figure 12.5: Dramatic Venue.

ROLES

In Chapter Five, we saw that various PARTIES could play different roles in work orders and activities. That idea was also used in Chapter Six, when we covered CONTRACTS.

Figure 12.6 shows a version of Figure 5.5 in which a WORK ORDER ROLE is *played by* a PARTY (either a PERSON or an ORGANIZATION) *in* a WORK ORDER. As a different kind of role, an ACTIVITY ASSIGNMENT may be *of* a PARTY *to* either an ACTIVITY, or an ACTIVITY STEP.

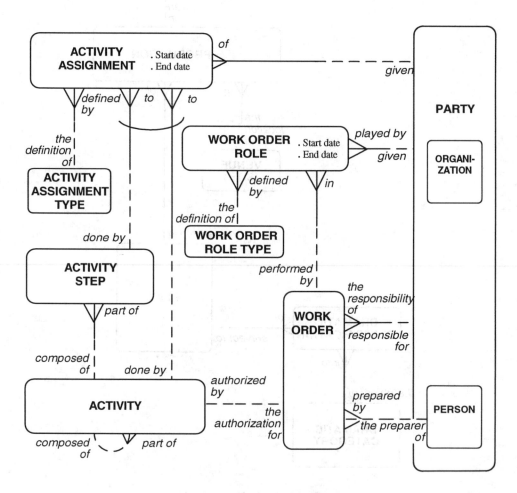

Figure 12.6: Roles and Assignments.

Following the pattern described at the beginning of this chapter, each ACTIVITY ASSIGNMENT must be *defined by* an ACTIVITY ASSIGNMENT TYPE (such as "recorder"), and each WORK ORDER ROLE must be *defined by* a WORK ORDER ROLE TYPE (such as "project manager"). A WORK ORDER ROLE, then, is the fact that a PARTY plays the role defined by a WORK ORDER TYPE. Similarly, an ACTIVITY ASSIGNMENT is the fact that a PARTY is assigned an ACTIVITY ASSIGNMENT TYPE.

The ROLE entity, of course, was tailor-made for our dramatic example. Figure 12.7 shows this, where each DRAMATIC ROLE must be *played by* a PERSON *in* a PRODUCTION. In fact, since understudies sometimes appear in place of the regular actors, we must say that each DRAMATIC ROLE must be *either in* a PRODUCTION overall *or in* a particular PERFORMANCE.

A primary attribute of DRAMATIC ROLE could be "character." Values here would be "Julius Caesar," "Henry Higgins," and so on. In fact, however, since CHARACTERS are defined by the PLAY for all productions of it, instead of an attribute, a separate entity for CHARACTER is needed. Each PLAY may be *about* one or more CHARACTERS,[*] and each DRAMATIC ROLE is *the portrayal of* one CHARACTER. That is, each CHARACTER must be *in* one PLAY,[†] and it may be *portrayed by* one or more DRAMATIC ROLES.

RESOURCES

Chapter Five described activities and their consumption of resources. In manufacturing and maintenance environments, as in many others, these resources are primarily labor and materials. (In Chapter Five, labor usage—called TIME SHEET ENTRIES—was shown in Figure 5.6, and ACTUAL ASSET USAGE was shown in Figure 5.7.) Figure 12.8 shows a simplified version of this, showing the ACTUAL ASSET USAGE *of* an ASSET, and the TIME SHEET ENTRY *by* a PERSON.

---

[*] Here we must distinguish between a real-life requirement (it is difficult to imagine a play without characters) and an information system constraint. (We should be allowed to define a new play without having immediately to list the characters.) This is probably another use for our to-be-invented notation for the relationship that "initially may be but eventually must be."

[†] Yes, it is true that Hamlet appears both in *Hamlet* and in *Rosencranz and Guildenstern Are Dead.* It is left as an exercise for the reader to correct the model accordingly.

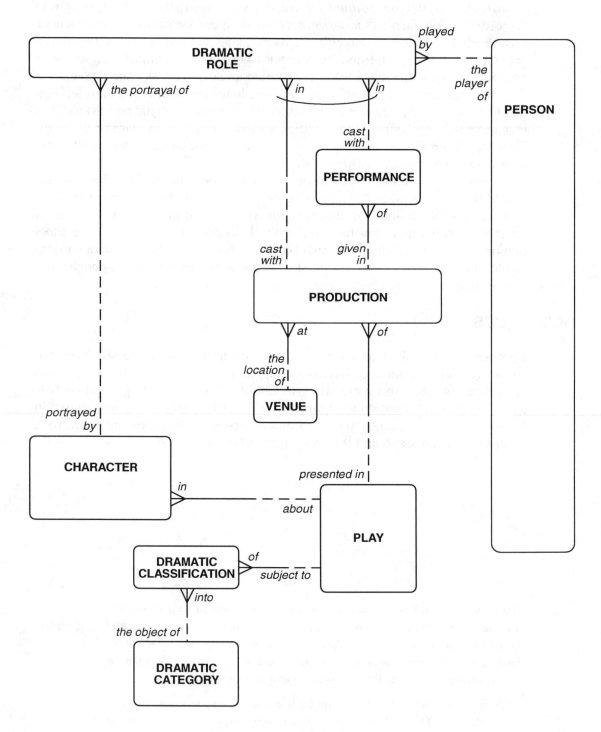

Figure 12.7: Dramatic Roles.

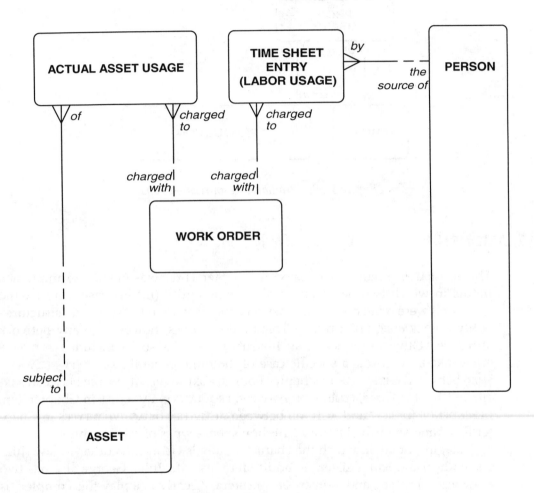

Figure 12.8: Resource Usage.

Other resources may be shown with the same structure, however. A dramatic example of this is shown in Figure 12.9, using stage props. Each PROP USAGE must be *of* one PROP *in* one PRODUCTION.

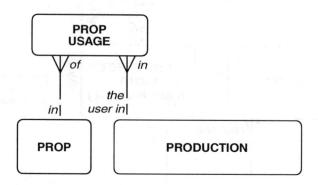

Figure 12.9: Dramatic Resources—Props.

RELATIONSHIPS

The GEOGRAPHIC STRUCTURE ELEMENT in Chapter Three was the first example of a model in which two occurrences of a single entity (in this case, GEOGRAPHIC LOCATION) were related to each other on a many-to-many basis via a "structure" entity (GEOGRAPHIC STRUCTURE). This model applies, however, to any network structure. Other examples of such structure entities so far include ASSET TYPE STRUCTURE ELEMENT (as a specific case of the more general ASSET TYPE RELATION-SHIP) between ASSET TYPES in Chapter Four, REPORTING RELATIONSHIP between PAR-TIES in Chapter Three, FLUID PATH between PRODUCTION FACILITIES in Chapter Ten, DEPENDENCE (DESIGN and ACTUAL) between ACTIVITIES or ACTIVITY TYPES in Chap-ter Five, and so forth. Figure 12.10 shows these types of relationships.

Imagine a play in which the character Sally is George's mother-in-law (Juli-a's mother) and Sam's sister. In addition to his wife, Julia, George also has two ex-wives, a brother, and a mistress. Et cetera. Clearly in a play this complex (is it Russian or is it simply derived from a soap opera?), it would be useful to add the entity CHARACTER RELATIONSHIP *from* one CHARACTER *to* another, in order to keep them all straight. (See Figure 12.11.)

VARIABLE LENGTH RECORDS

In Chapter Four, we discussed the problem of describing different ASSET TYPES, when different kinds of ASSET TYPES had different attributes. This was solved by the model in Figure 4.16, modified here as Figure 12.12. Where in Chapter Four (Figure 4.2) we showed that both ASSETS and ASSET TYPES (well, PRODUCTS and PRODUCT TYPES) could be *subject to* one or more CLASSIFICATIONS, here, the catego-ry of interest is the one that defines the *format* of the ASSET TYPE. We call this particular category ASSET TYPE CLASS, and we assert that each ASSET TYPE may be *of* only *one* ASSET TYPE CLASS. Conversely, each ASSET TYPE CLASS may be *the structural definition for* one or more ASSET TYPES. The IBM ThinkPad® Model 755CE, for example, will get its attributes from the fact that it is in the ASSET TYPE CLASS "laptop computers."

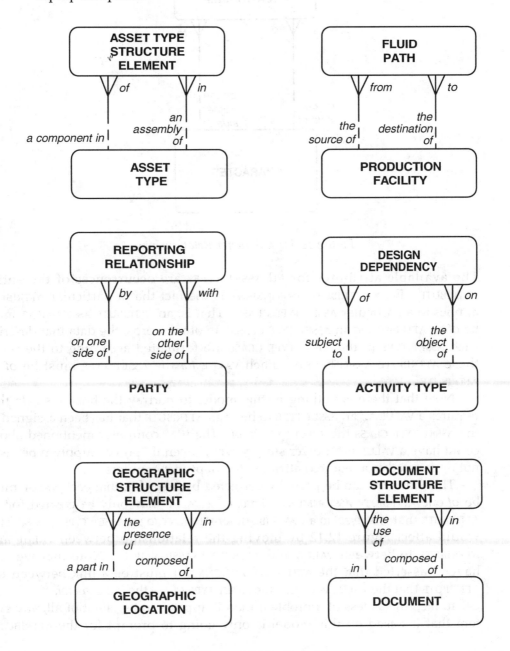

Figure 12.10: Structure.

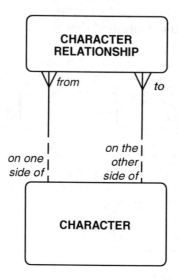

Figure 12.11: Character Relationships.

The available attributes for all ASSET TYPES are occurrences of the entity ATTRIBUTE. Each ATTRIBUTE ASSIGNMENT is the fact that a particular ATTRIBUTE applies to a particular ASSET TYPE CLASS. That is, an ATTRIBUTE ASSIGNMENT must be *of* an ATTRIBUTE *to* an ASSET TYPE CLASS. In other words, the data that describe each ASSET TYPE in the ASSET TYPE CLASS are formatted according to the set of these ATTRIBUTE ASSIGNMENTS. Each VALUE *for* the ASSET TYPE must be *of* an ATTRIBUTE.

Note that there is nothing in this model to portray the business rule that requires a VALUE *for* an ASSET TYPE to be *of* an ATTRIBUTE that has been assigned to the ASSET TYPE CLASS the ASSET TYPE is *of*. The IBM computer mentioned above could have a VALUE *for* "power supply type," even if "power supply type" was not designated as a required attribute for "laptop computers."

This situation can be partially corrected by asserting that each VALUE must be *of* one ATTRIBUTE ASSIGNMENT. That is, a VALUE may only be created for an ATTRIBUTE that is *subject to* an ATTRIBUTE ASSIGNMENT *to* an ASSET TYPE CLASS. This would affect Figure 12.12 by moving the relationship between VALUE and ATTRIBUTE to between VALUE and ATTRIBUTE ASSIGNMENT. Note that we still haven't asserted that the ATTRIBUTE ASSIGNMENT must be a link between the ATTRIBUTE that the VALUE is *of* and the ASSET TYPE CLASS the VALUE is *for*.

In fact, this is less of a problem than it appears to be. First of all, any system that is based on this model is only going to prompt for the ATTRIBUTES assigned to this ASSET TYPE CLASS anyway.* Moreover, it is conceivable that over time, certain ATTRIBUTES will cease to be of interest. If they were not permitted to be kept, great effort would be required to clear the corresponding VALUES out of the database. Better to leave them be, even if they are *of* ATTRIBUTES that are no longer used.

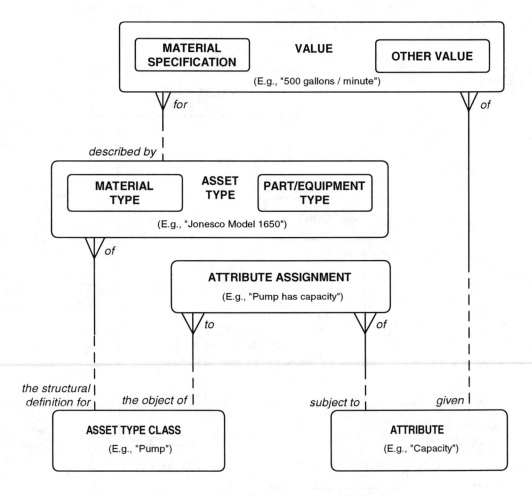

Figure 12.12: Asset Types and Attributes.

* For those who are interested, this structure can be implemented in a system with two data-entry screens. The first is for specifying ASSET TYPE, ATTRIBUTE, and ATTRIBUTE ASSIGNMENT. An administrator uses this to specify the kinds of things about which data are to be collected and their characteristics. The second screen is for entering the data themselves. It first prompts for the name of the ASSET and its ASSET CLASS. Based on the ASSET CLASS, it displays the names of the ATTRIBUTES appropriate to that ASSET CLASS, and prompts for the "value" of the VALUE *of* each ATTRIBUTE *for* that ATTRIBUTE TYPE.

This technique turns out to have wide applicability. We saw in Chapter Four, for example, that a bank, whose "products" are bank accounts, uses the same model (see Figure 4.17, reproduced here as Figure 12.13). The bank has the same problem with different product types (ACCOUNT TYPE) having different attributes (PARAMETERS). It must deal with interest rates, minimum balances, time periods, and so forth. Not only is that basic structure of ACCOUNT and ACCOUNT TYPE similar to that for ASSET TYPE and ASSET TYPE CLASS, but the problem of variable attributes also applies.

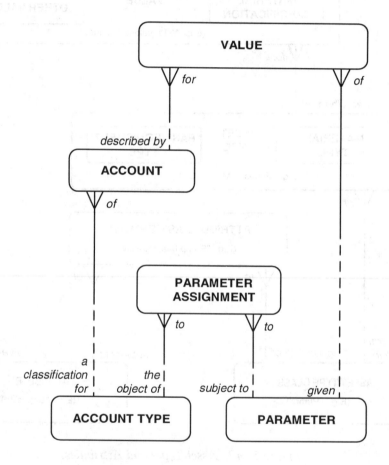

Figure 12.13: The Bank Version.

In Chapter Eight, a similar structure accommodated laboratory TESTS where the VARIABLES measured differed, depending on the TEST TYPE. Figure 8.4 showed how EXPECTED OBSERVATIONS associated VARIABLES to TEST TYPES, just as ATTRIBUTE ASSIGNMENTS here link ATTRIBUTES to ASSET TYPE CLASSES. Similarly, an OBSERVA-

TION *in terms of* a VARIABLE *on* a TEST TYPE* is directly analogous to a VALUE *of* an ATTRIBUTE *for* an ASSET TYPE. Much more complex examples were the clinical research data collection sheets and the material safety data sheets presented in Chapter Eleven.

In our production company example, we could assert that different kinds of plays have different attributes and apply the Figure 12.12 model to them—but that probably would be excessive.

USUALLY ONE, SOMETIMES MANY

Most of the time, a PLAY must be *written by* one PERSON. This is shown as the many-to-one relationship line at the bottom of Figure 12.14, and is very straightforward. The problem is that sometimes you'll get a play that is *written by* more than one person. Rats! Now we have to add the intersect entity AUTHORSHIP. In Figure 12.14, each AUTHORSHIP is *of* a PLAY and *by* a PERSON, so that we can say that each PLAY may be *written by* one or more AUTHORSHIPS, each of which is *by* one PERSON.

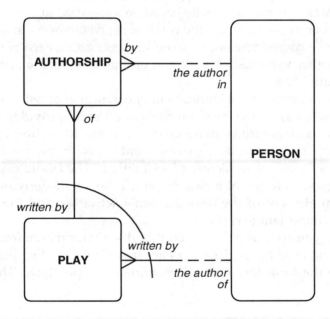

Figure 12.14: Usually One, Sometimes Many.

---

* Well, actually, it is *on* a TEST, which is *an example of* a TEST TYPE.

Strictly speaking, this intersect entity now makes the many-to-one relationship we started with redundant. After all, if the AUTHORSHIP entity makes it possible to say that any number of people could have written a play, that certainly includes the case in which only one person wrote one. We don't really want to eliminate the simpler relationship, however, when *most of the time* there is only one author.

The solution to this problem is to keep both elements in the slightly redundant notation shown in Figure 12.14. In this, we see that each PLAY must be *either written by* one and only one PERSON *or written by* one or more AUTHORSHIPS, each of which must be *by* one PERSON. Examples of this appear in Chapters Eight (INSTRUMENT USAGE—Figure 8.7), Ten (FLOWS—Figure 10.6), and Eleven (DOCUMENTS and AUTHORSHIPS—Figure 11.5).

MATHEMATICAL EXPRESSIONS IN THE DATA MODEL

In Chapter Eight, we saw that a DERIVED OBSERVATION may be calculated from one or more SUMMARIZATIONS, each of which is *the use of* another OBSERVATION. This was originally shown in Figure 8.3, and is reproduced here as Figure 12.15. This SUMMARIZATION is indirectly based on a SUMMARY RULE to derive the DERIVED VARIABLE that is the basis for the original DERIVED OBSERVATION. A DERIVED VARIABLE may be *derived from* one or more SUMMARY RULES, each of which must be *the use of* another VARIABLE. A variation on the same theme appeared in Chapter Ten as Figure 10.9.

This is an example of storing a mathematical expression in the data model. UNIT OF MEASURE CONVERSION on the same model provides another example, although its structure is somewhat different. Modeling expressions is not something you want to do very often, but occasionally, it is necessary in order to represent a complete picture of a situation. The laboratory where this came up is a good example of a case in which the act of deriving data is itself an important element of the organization's activities, and the structure of that process is important to capture.

When you are compelled to do this, draw your model from the reverse Polish notation used by the Hewlett-Packard calculator: Expressions in this notation take the form {argument 1, argument 2, operator}. Thus, 2+2 becomes {2,2,+}.*

---

* Try to limit the operators that you use to plus and minus. If multiplication and division are required, the model gets very complex.

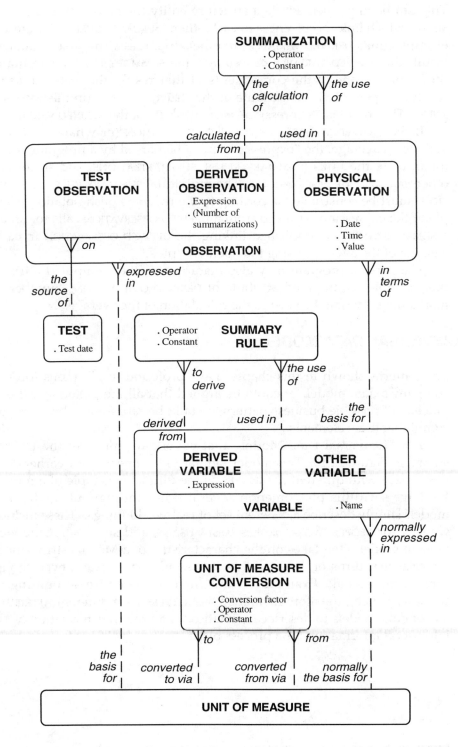

Figure 12.15: Expressions in the Data Model.

This can be implemented via a structure entity (like ASSET TYPE STRUCTURE ELE-MENT), which links occurrences to each other. SUMMARY RULE in Figure 12.15, for example, links DERIVED VARIABLES to other VARIABLES. The first argument is the result (the DERIVED VARIABLE *derived from* the SUMMARY RULE, for example), and the second is one of the components of that result (the VARIABLE *used in* the result). "Operator" is an attribute of the structure entity (in this case, SUMMARY RULE). The complete "expression" is an attribute of the DERIVED VARIABLE.

If the DERIVED VARIABLE or DERIVED OBSERVATION (or whatever) is complex, such as an average, the "expression" must be parsed by a program and used to manipulate the links (SUMMARY RULES, SUMMARIZATIONS, and so forth) to the other VARIABLES or OBSERVATIONS. The individual SUMMARY RULES or SUMMARIZA-TIONS must be constructed according to the reverse Polish notation. For exam-ple, if the expression retrieved from a DERIVED OBSERVATION calls for an average, a SUMMARIZATION is established linking the DERIVED OBSERVATION to each other element of the average, using the operator "plus."

The parsing program may also manipulate other computed attributes. In this example, a computed attribute of DERIVED OBSERVATION, "number of sum-marizations," would be used in the calculation of the average.

THE UNIVERSAL DATA MODEL

The patterns shown in this chapter have profound implications throughout a company's data model. It could be argued that all the patterns in this book—indeed, all possible business patterns—could be represented by a single model combining these elements.

The "Universal Data Model" that covers all things in the Universe* is shown in Figure 12.16. This model, similar to the one we saw earlier describing ASSET TYPES with different ATTRIBUTES, is the ultimate example of a meta-model. We have seen this phenomenon several times throughout the book. Some models simply describe a coherent set of real-world things. These include what we saw for PEOPLE, WORK ORDERS, ASSET USAGE, and so on. But the world we have to model often takes on the characteristics of a Möbius strip—the loop of material that turns on itself so that it has only one surface, even though it is three dimensional. Examples of this include the entire accounting chapter (Chapter Seven), the aforementioned ASSET TYPES with different ATTRIBUTES, the use of data models to describe calculations, and the transformation of TAG data into useful information for a process plant.

---

* Well, all right, perhaps not *all* things . . .

Gödel's theorem in mathematics asserts that every logical system has an underlying inconsistency—something that can be expressed in the system, but that cannot be proven [1]. As we get closer to the edges of data modeling, we begin to catch glimpses of its reckoning with that theorem. Even so, there is a lot we can do to describe the world around us, if we are willing to free our minds from the concrete and come to grips with the abstract concepts we have been dealing with here.

For example, in the Universal Data Model, the world is composed of THINGS, each of which is *of* a THING CLASS. The THING CLASS is *the structural definition of* the THING. Each THING CLASS may be *the object of* one or more ATTRIBUTE ASSIGNMENTS, each of which must be *of* an ATTRIBUTE. Each THING may be *described by* one or more VALUES, each of which is also *of* an ATTRIBUTE.

And, of course, each THING is likely to be related to one or more other THINGS. Specifically, a THING may be *on one side of* one or more RELATIONSHIPS *to* other THINGS. Each RELATIONSHIP must be *an example of* a RELATIONSHIP TYPE, which constitutes *the definition of* it.

This model can be elaborated upon in a couple of interesting ways not shown here: First of all, it is possible to cite domains (sets of legal values) at each of two levels. An entity can be added, called LEGAL VALUE (or, by theoreticians, DOMAIN ELEMENT), in which each LEGAL VALUE is *either for* an ATTRIBUTE *or for* an ATTRIBUTE ASSIGNMENT. That is, each ATTRIBUTE could be *defined to accept* one or more LEGAL VALUES, and each ATTRIBUTE ASSIGNMENT *to* a THING CLASS could be *given* one-or-more (actually, two-or-more) LEGAL VALUES that applied to the ATTRIBUTE only in the context of the THING CLASS.

In addition, this model can contain the formats for the VALUES. This is tricky to portray in a data model beyond a simplistic assertion that "format" is an attribute of ATTRIBUTE. The implementation of formats depends entirely on the facilities of the database management system on which the system is ultimately implemented. The format issue introduces the object-oriented concept of behavior, since, when you assert that "format" is an attribute of ATTRIBUTE, you are effectively defining the behavior of the ATTRIBUTE (an example of an "object") when it is finally implemented.

It is tempting also to expand the model to incorporate some of the other structures we have discussed. For example, we could insert THING TYPE between THING and THING CLASS. This would make it look more like the model in Figure 4.16 of Chapter Four. This is unnecessary at this meta-level, however, since THING CLASS, THING TYPE, and THING from that point of view are simply examples of THING from the point of view of the meta-model shown here, with relationships among them.

If it seems unreasonable that such a large number of phenomena can be described by so few entities, just remember that our whole industry is predicated on the notion that we can describe the world with a sequence of 0's and 1's.

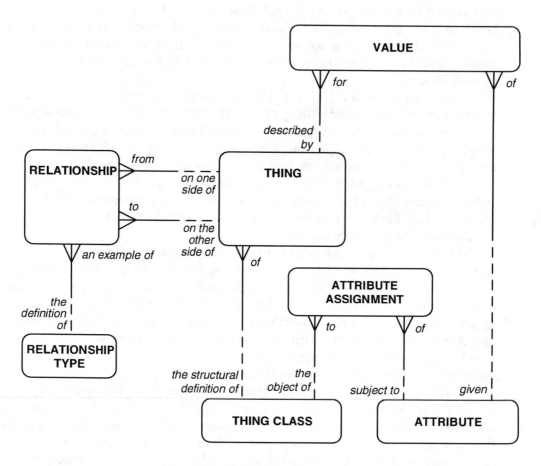

Figure 12.16: The Universal Data Model.

A FINAL EXAMPLE

Figure 12.17 shows our complete model for the theatrical production company. It seems that all the world's a stage, after all!

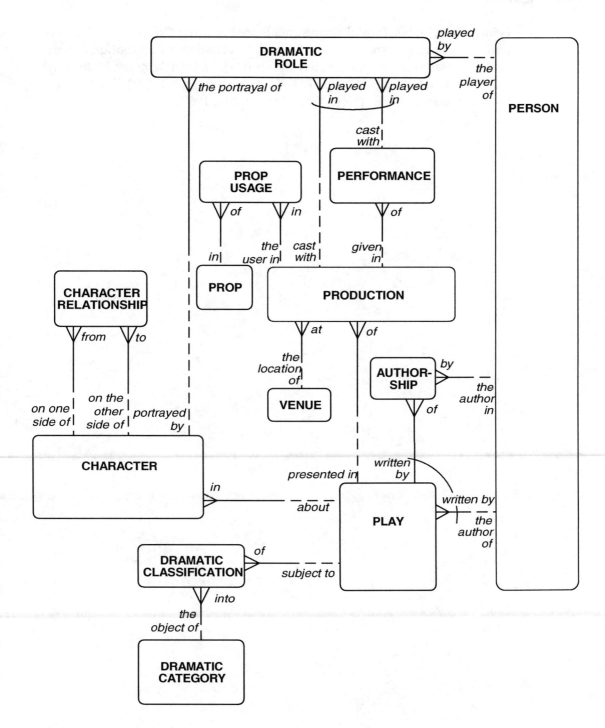

Figure 12.17: The Theatrical Production Company.

REFERENCES

1   Gödel, Kurt, "Über formal unentscheidbare Sätze der *Principia Mathematica und verwandter Systeme I* [On Formal, Undecidable Propositions of the *Principia Mathematica* and Related Systems, I]," *Monatshefte für Mathematik und Physik*, Vol. 38 (1931), pp. 173-98. See also: Kurt Gödel, *On Formally Undecidable Propositions* (New York: Basic Books, 1962).

BIBLIOGRAPHY

The primary source for information on modeling using the techniques described in this book is

Barker, Richard. *CASE*Method™: Entity Relationship Modelling.* Wokingham, England: Addison-Wesley Publishing Co., 1989.

In addition, modeling guidance using this approach is in

Rodgers, Ulka. *ORACLE: A Database Developer's Guide.* Englewood Cliffs, N.J.: Prentice-Hall, 1991.

Philosophical approaches to modeling data and organizations may be found in

Beer, Stafford. *The Heart of Enterprise.* Chichester, England: John Wiley & Sons, 1979.

Sowa, John. *Conceptual Structures: Information Processing in Mind and Machine.* Reading, Mass.: Addison-Wesley Publishing Co., 1984.

The following describes an approach to viewing data models from different perspectives:

Hay, David C. "Visualizing Database Structures." *Database Programming and Design*, Vol. 7, No. 6 (June 1994), pp. 39-45.

For a presentation of business rules in conjunction with data models, read

Ross, Ronald G. *The Business Rule Book: Classifying, Defining and Modeling Rules.* Boston: Database Research Group, 1994.

Other books on various data modeling techniques include

Bruce, Thomas A. *Designing Quality Databases with IDEF1X Information Models.* New York: Dorset House Publishing, 1992.

Embley, David W., Barry D. Kurtz, and Scott Woodfield. *Object-Oriented Systems Analysis: A Model-Driven Approach.* Englewood Cliffs, N.J.: Prentice-Hall, 1992.

Flavin, Matt. *Fundamental Concepts of Information Modeling.* New York: Yourdon Press, 1981.

Halpin, T.A. *Conceptual Schema and Relational Database Design,* 2nd ed. Sydney: Prentice-Hall Australia, 1995.

Martin, James. *Recommended Diagramming Standards for Analysts and Programmers.* Englewood Cliffs, N.J.: Prentice-Hall, 1987.

_____, and Carma McClure. *Diagramming Techniques for Analysts and Programmers.* Englewood Cliffs, N.J.: Prentice-Hall, 1985.

Rumbaugh, James, Michael Blaha, William Premerlani, Frederick Eddy, and William Lorensen. *Object-Oriented Modeling and Design.* Englewood Cliffs, N.J.: Prentice-Hall, 1991.

Shlaer, Sally, and Stephen J. Mellor. *Object-Oriented Systems Analysis: Modeling the World in Data.* Englewood Cliffs, N.J.: Prentice-Hall, 1988.

_____. *Object Lifecycles: Modeling the World in States.* Englewood Cliffs, N.J.: Prentice-Hall, 1992.

The seminal books on systems analysis in general are

DeMarco, Tom. *Structured Analysis and System Specification.* Englewood Cliffs, N.J.: Prentice-Hall, 1978.

Gane, Chris, and Trish Sarson. *Structured Systems Analysis: Tools and Techniques.* Englewood Cliffs, N.J.: Prentice-Hall, 1979.

McMenamin, Stephen M., and John F. Palmer. *Essential Systems Analysis.* Englewood Cliffs, N.J.: Prentice-Hall, 1984.

Yourdon, Edward, and Larry L. Constantine. *Structured Design: Fundamentals of a Discipline of Computer Program and Systems Design,* 2nd ed. Englewood Cliffs, N.J.: Prentice-Hall, 1979.

For good basic descriptions of material requirements planning theory and software design, see

Landvater, Darryl V., and Christopher D. Gray. *MRP II Standard System: A Handbook for Manufacturing Software Survival.* Essex Junction, Vt.: Oliver Wight Publications, 1989.

Wight, Oliver W. *Production and Inventory Management in the Computer Age.* Boston: Cahners Books International, 1974.

Finally, just to see that computer systems analysts are not the first people to try to understand what is really going on, read

Descartes, René. *Discourse on the Method of Rightly Conducting the Reason and Seeking Truth in the Field of Science,* trans. Laurence J. Lafleur. Indianapolis: Bobbs-Merrill Co., 1960.

Kant, Immanuel. *Critique of Pure Reason,* trans. Norman Kemp Smith. New York: St. Martin's Press, 1929.

Nagel, Ernest, and James R. Newman. *Gödel's Proof.* New York: New York University Press, 1958.

Plato. *The Republic,* trans. B. Jowett. New York: The Modern Library.

INDEX

NOTE: Page references to entity names are prefaced by *Enty.* References to attribute names are prefaced by *Attr.* References to pseudo-entities are prefaced by *Psu.* References to a main entry are indicated by a ~ symbol.